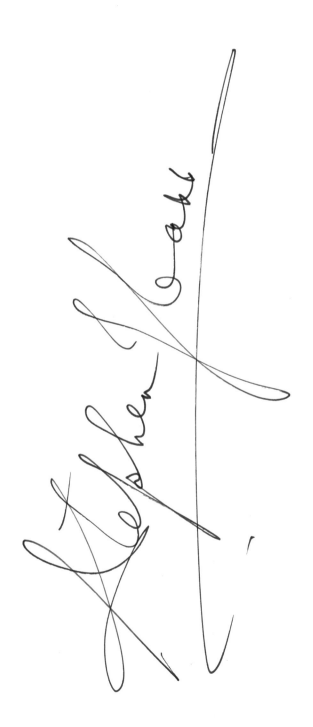

MW00679530

# SURPRISED BY LAUGHTER

# Surprised by Laughter
## Some Good News Out of Africa

*by*

STEPHEN CARR

The Memoir Club

© Stephen Carr 2004

First published in 2004 by
The Memoir Club
Arya House
Langley Park
Durham
DH7 9XE
Tel: 0191 373 5660
Email: memoirclub@msn.com

British Library Cataloguing in
Publication Data.
A catalogue record for this book
is available from the
British Library

ISBN: 978 1 84104 100 9

Typeset by George Wishart & Associates, Whitley Bay
Printed by J F Print, Sparkford, Somerset

*To my wife Anne without whose courage and company I would have heard much less laughter.*

# Contents

# Illustrations

# Foreword
## The Lord Plumb of Coleshill

THOSE WHO have been wrestling with the development dilemma in Africa, not fully appreciating the difference between travelling to see countries and travelling to see people, will enjoy reading this book.

It is obviously the humanitarian spirit that has inspired Stephen and Anne Carr to respond to the needs of people whose way of life is mostly primitive and of poor material quality.

Many would question the tale of the rainmaker but admire the stories of the dam building, creating a lake to hold fish, and of Anne's dairy herd. Stephen successfully proved that the assumption of the extreme conservatism of African farmers did not hold when they were presented with examples of practices which really worked in ways which they saw as advantageous. Whether it is new crops, new varieties, the use of fertilizer or more productive animals, this book provides numerous examples of acceptance and change when the lead that farmers have been given fits in with their own needs and constraints.

Having listened to many of Stephen's stories over the years of our friendship and hearing many success stories together with a few failures, I well understand his criticism of some advice given by agricultural departments across Africa. A few more hands-on operators like Stephen would be a good investment.

He admits to being economical with the truth on one occasion when challenged by a policeman at a road block while transporting strawberries, the only time he claims that he bribed an official in Africa. I am sure that the strawberries worked wonders for the officer!

Encouraging tea growers to market a quality product by only picking 'two leaves and a bud' must have required strong leadership and skilled discipline, but again it proves that farmers will respond positively if they have confidence in practical advice. Stephen was obviously proud of his tea growing.

However, Stephen's sudden enforced departure from Uganda under Amin's regime brought development to a halt. The tea estates were shut down. To be able to help get them started again and then return later to celebrate the fortieth anniversary of the founding of the scheme must have given tremendous satisfaction and confirmation of the need for good government as well as good management.

These reflections also emphasize the importance of growing cash crops. 'Why grow tea or coffee for foreigners to drink or strawberries to be savoured by the elite instead of concentrating on local food supply?' is a question critics may ask. Stephen Carr has proved that it provides a strong cash buffer to serious hunger.

Our first contact with Stephen and Anne was through CMS when they were adopted as missionaries by our church in Coleshill. I admit to being somewhat sceptical of missionaries until I heard some of their stories of struggle and progress in the parts of Africa where they worked. It was understandable therefore that their first church in Uganda, designed with the help of an architect, was built by the people themselves, who have seen it stand the test of time and enjoyed worshipping in it together over many years.

The story of life in Sudan, Uganda and Kenya demonstrates a commitment and an experience which we can only share as the story unfolds.

With that experience, during a decade of village work in Uganda, Stephen claims he possibly put a quarter of a million dollars into farmers' pockets. He suggests that when recruited to work for two weeks on an IMF mission to get the Ugandan government to increase the prices paid to farmers he put tens of millions of dollars into the pockets of hundreds of thousands of farmers by stimulating work and increasing production. This proves beyond doubt the increased powers of persuasion of someone who understands both the producer and the product.

Anne and Stephen have been a team together from their early days at Wye College and throughout the whole of their continuing career as missionaries. Stephen rightly has included a chapter on the tremendous service Anne has given through the work of her Trust among street children and deprived families. Again this was a 'hands-on' charity with a minimum of resources, the benefits of which still continue, as does their work among small scale farmers in Malawi.

Amid the doom and gloom in today's uncertain world full of strife, it is a pleasure to read a story of two people who have tried to achieve the impossible and of the courage and resilience of the families among whom they have lived.

The story starts with the noise of laughter almost fifty years ago, even though a civil war was simmering. Having just shared in the celebration of their Golden Wedding I enjoyed reading *Surprised by Laughter* and am delighted to have the pleasure of writing this foreword.

# Introduction

*'The greater part of our happiness or misery is caused by our disposition and not by our circumstances.'*
Martha Washington, wife of George Washington

IT WAS A sweltering hot afternoon in the forest area of the Southern Sudan. I had been cutting timber for our new home all the morning and was now exhausted. I went and lay on my sleeping mat on the beaten earth floor of the friend's hut in which I was staying. My neighbours in the small village gathered in groups under trees to chat away the hottest hours of the day. As I lay, half asleep, I realized that laughter was the dominant sound coming to me from these groups. As the laughter died down in one group it started up in another, and I found it difficult to identify any interval in which there was no sound of laughter drifting into my hut.

The border of the Sudan and Congo was not an easy place in which to live in the mid-1950s. The hot, wet forest favoured an extraordinary array of diseases. There was no child vaccination and no rural medical services, so that life for most people was short and often painful. There was virtually no cash economy outside the small towns, and in rural areas the population relied on the produce of the farms that they hacked out of the forest. A year's farming effort could be wiped out in a few hours by a herd of elephants or a large troop of baboons, leaving a family to face hunger and real hardship until another crop could be raised. Added to this, a civil war was simmering and the security situation was deteriorating. Yet the sound that drifted through the villages was of laughter.

Almost fifty years later I sit writing at my desk in our home in a village in Malawi, one of the poorest countries in the world. Our house is situated on the side of a steep hill, and behind it is a wooded area which provides the fuel for the population on the almost treeless plains below. Every morning a stream of women and young girls climb up the steep, rough path beside our house. Later in the day they return with huge loads of firewood on their heads, edging their way down a path which I find difficult to negotiate with no load at all. Yet as they pass they fill the air with their banter and their laughter.

I have no desire to glorify a harsh, precarious and often painful way of life, nor to romanticize poverty. What I hope to do in this book is to pay tribute to the amazing fortitude and resilience of millions of rural African families as they face hardship and bereavement, and in particular to the village neighbours who for much of my adult life have surprised me by their laughter.

# CHAPTER 1

# Little Cause for Laughter

THE DAWN OF 18 August 1955 seemed much like any other at the Village Teachers Training Centre situated a couple of miles from the small administrative headquarters of Yei, set in the midst of the seemingly endless forest of the Sudan-Congo border. The Centre's group of mud block buildings with thatched roofs housed a hundred or so young men and women who were training to be teachers in the primary schools scattered across this vast, thinly populated region commonly described as 'the most primitive area in the British Empire'. Dawn saw the male students go for their daily work on their farm plots where I joined them, while my wife, Anne, went with the young women to their vegetable gardens. None of us had any idea that the events of this day would precipitate a conflict which would change the lives of thousands of people for half a century and change also the whole direction of our own work.

The practical period over, we all went to breakfast and an hour later we started our normal round of teaching. The staff of four expatriates and two Sudanese was headed by John Parry. He was an ordained Welshman with a somewhat portly figure, relaxed manner and slow speech, which disguised a man of great ability. I had soon found out that he was able to be so relaxed because he was so efficient, and he made an excellent principal. His wife, Helena, had come to the Sudan as a single missionary and had been involved with girls' education for many years both before and after her marriage. This was a couple with a deep love of the Southern Sudan and its people and a maturity born of many years of experience. Matayo and Cornelio, the Sudanese members of staff, were also men with years of teaching experience behind them. Anne and I were in a very different situation. We were young and, although I had spent a couple of years teaching in Nigeria, we had been less than a year in the Sudan in August 1955 and were still firmly wearing our 'L plates'. But in John we had a good leader, and we enjoyed living and working in a community which had a united purpose and suffered little friction.

Just before the end of morning classes the only saloon car in Yei drove up to the Centre and parked at the Parry's house. The Mitilias family, the most prosperous of our small trading community, were going to have lunch with the principal. This was a rare event and attracted considerable interest among the students, who only slowly dispersed to their dining building for lunch. The car was still there when we re-assembled for afternoon classes at two o'clock. These were always the most testing of our teaching skills as we faced a group of well fed students on a hot, oppressive afternoon when sleep was so much more attractive than learning. A half an hour later, however, sleep was the last thing on anybody's mind as a volley of shots rang out from Yei. No Southern Sudanese civilian was allowed to own a gun, so that the rare sound of rifle fire had to mean trouble of some sort.

We dashed out of the classrooms and a few minutes later a great pall of flames and smoke rose up over the site of the government offices, all of which were thatched. Then we knew for certain that there was serious trouble. We did not have long to wait to learn the nature of that trouble. Two students had gone to the local dispensary for treatment and now, despite whatever sickness they were suffering, they came running up the hill, to be immediately mobbed by their fellows.

'What's going on, what's happening, who is shooting, what is the fire?'

The questions came thick and fast.

'A group of Southern soldiers have come from the army barracks at Torit (200 miles away). They have shot every Northern Sudanese they could find. They have killed all the officials and burned down the government offices. There are dead bodies of men, women and children lying in the street and we had to pick our way between them to get back here.'

So started the hostilities which, with varying levels of intensity, have racked the Sudan to this day.

The Parrys and the Mitilias family soon joined us and quickly grasped the seriousness of the situation. The shooting was now more sporadic but new pillars of flame were going up as other offices were torched. The senior Mitilias made a quick decision.

'I am not going down into that lot,' he said. 'Come on, into the car and we go straight down to the safety of the Congo. Is there some way out of here that avoids the centre of Yei?' I was detailed off to show him a small track that led directly on to the main road to the border, and the Mitilias family left to stay with their Greek friends in the nearest Congolese town. Little did I realize the impact that their departure would have on us as I waved them on their way.

There was no possibility of resuming classes, and Matayo suggested a football match to take people's minds of the news. Nobody responded to his suggestion so there was little we could do but let the students cluster in their tribal groups to wonder, somewhat fearfully, what these events could mean. The staff agreed that it was too dangerous to attempt to investigate the situation on the ground that evening, and so we had to spend the remaining hours of the day with a semblance of normality which belied our worries as to what these events would mean for ourselves, our work and the country to which we were all so attached.

Farm work was forgotten the next morning and the students were assembled and then set some study to keep them from too much speculation and worry. John Parry appeared at our door soon after breakfast.

'I think that it would be safe for us to go down to Yei now, Stephen. There was no shooting in the night and the British do not seem to be their target anyway. I will go down to what's left of the government offices and see what news I can pick up. Would you go and check up on the Mitilias' house and see if you can find any news at that end of town?'

We set out on our bicycles and parted at the edge of the small town. I soon came across dead bodies scattered across the road and found it difficult to continue. I had not been involved in the war and the sight of these slaughtered people was deeply disturbing. I persisted to the Mitilias' compound and started by checking on the large corrugated iron stores which they used for fuel and produce. The doors seemed untouched and I was about to move away when I heard a distinct knocking on the wall of the nearest store. I went to inspect what it was and a whispered voice said

'Please help us. This is Abdulla and I am here with Ahmed and our families. We got warning from one of our children's Southern Sudanese playmates just before the shooting began and came to the Mitilias for help, but found that they were not here so we hid in this store. We are eleven of us with seven children. We have had no food or water since mid-day yesterday. Please, please save us.'

Anne and I had both done well at the Arabic school in Omdurman and so I had a reasonable grasp of the language.

'I cannot possibly help you now,' I said, 'but I will really try and get you out of here tonight. Have you got a watch?'

'Yes,' came the reply.

'Then be ready to move at nine o'clock to-night, but do not try to get out now, however thirsty you are, or you will certainly be killed.'

'What are you doing here?' came a sharp voice behind me. Swinging round I was faced with a policeman in uniform a few yards away. I did not know what he had heard and, trying to keep my voice steady, I replied 'I am a friend of the Mitilias and they have gone to the Congo, so I was just checking that nobody was trying to loot their things. I am so glad that you have come, would you please help me to check the house?'

I received a suspicious stare but I hurriedly went past him and invited him to follow me into the house. This was a spacious brick building, a mansion by Yei standards, and furnished accordingly. It bore witness to thirty years of judicious trading (some would use less polite adjectives) in the Southern Sudan. None of us locked our doors in those days and so we simply walked into the house. Nothing had been touched and I looked to see if I could find any keys with which to lock the main door, but I was unsuccessful. My companion remained aloof and sullen until we reached the kitchen, where I suggested that as all the food there would be spoilt before the family returned, it would be sensible if he packed it into one of the large baskets and took it with him. This cheered him up no end and a few minutes later I was able to walk with him along the road and well away from the families in the store.

John joined me a few minutes later. 'All the soldiers have gone,' he said.

'They have pushed on to Maridi (150 miles away) to do the same thing there. The police are in charge here. They were perfectly friendly to me but are proud of what they helped to do and determined that no Northern Sudanese shall survive.' I told him what I had found, and he became very grave.

'Let's get out of here,' he said, 'and talk this over at home.' As we started to cycle back a few Southern Sudanese, presumably old established family servants, had come to try and take some of the bodies for burial. They were pushed away by a couple of policeman who said that the bodies should rot where they were.

Once home Helena, John, Anne and I sat down to discuss the situation. None of us had any illusions as to just how dangerous a rescue operation would be. If we were stopped in the town by police then both the Northerners and John and I would certainly be killed. Likewise the same thing would happen if barriers had been set up on the road to the Congolese border to prevent any Northerners from escaping. Once we were recognized then revenge could be taken on our wives and even on the students. It was Helena who cleared the air. 'We just cannot leave those poor people to die in that store or be butchered by the police. We have got to help, whatever the risks.' Anne and I agreed, so then we had to develop a plan. John and I went down to the mission education office to find that the Sudanese in charge had already left, in common with most of the local population. Luckily he had not taken the small truck he used for delivering educational materials. We broke open his petrol store and took out a couple of four-gallon cans to fill the tank. The starting handle was in the cab and I gave the engine a couple of sharp turns and it started. We decided not to move it then so as not to raise suspicions or questions and went back home for lunch.

The following hours were not easy. This was a very different kind of danger to an accidental meeting with a leopard on a footpath, even less like a near miss in a car, when the danger had passed almost before one was aware of it. This was a danger into which we were entering fully conscious of the possible consequences. Worse still it was one about which we had nine hours of anticipation before we could start acting. Time dragged by. Anne and I tried not to talk about what the night might bring but we had been married for just over a year and the thought that this might be the end of that relationship was not easy to bear. At last it was half past eight and John came round to our house to collect me. We kissed each other goodbye and I cycled off with him to collect the truck. Fortunately it was a moonlit night and so we could manage without torches, which could have attracted attention. Once again a good swing on the starting handle got the truck running and we set out for the Mitilias compound. We did not use headlights and met no one on the way, which was a relief as we had been at a loss to think of a plausible reason for driving round Yei at such a time as this. I jumped out and guided John back to the store, where I whispered to the waiting families that it was safe to come out. 'Get straight into the truck as quickly as you can, bang on the cab when you are ready, and then keep absolutely quiet.' I got back into the cab and a minute later there was a tap to let us know that they were ready. With no lights we carefully weaved our way through the bodies and were almost to the edge of the town when one of the women in the back started screaming. John slapped his foot on the accelerator and burst onto the open road. We dare not stop. As long as we were moving local people with spears and arrows could do little to hinder us, but stationary we would be helpless.

It was twenty miles to the border, but the dirt road was rough and the truck was old so it took us an hour to get to the safety of the border post, and all the way the wailing in the back of the truck continued. 'What on earth do you think that you are doing?' was my first comment, 'did you want us all to get killed?' Then the truth came out. One seven year old boy had been fast asleep and in the pitch dark of the store and in the panic of the moment he had been left behind. We handed over the families to the

Belgian officials and set out once more for Yei. We started at the store, without much hope, but it was empty. We went to the child's family home but it was deserted. By this time there were a number of hyenas working on the bodies in the street, and we found it difficult to imagine the horror facing a small boy who found himself abandoned in the midst of this scene. As one last hope John said 'Let's try the Roman Catholic mission. It's nearer to town than ours'. Amazingly, the little boy was there. He had walked a mile in the dark in the midst of the dead bodies of his friends and neighbours and with a real threat from the wild animals. The priest was delighted to see us, we put the boy in between us in the cab and soon after midnight we set out once more for the border, now reasonably confident that there were no road blocks on the way. The scenes of rejoicing which greeted our arrival were more than compensation for all the fear and worry of the day, and once again we headed back to Yei. We left the truck at the education office and cycled up to John's house to find two extremely upset wives. We had estimated that we would be back before midnight and now it was nearly three in the morning and they were convinced that something had gone badly wrong. Bed did not bring sleep as the tension would not die down, but dawn came at last and we started to think about what our next steps should be.

Twelve years later I was giving a lecture at Nottingham University and when it was over a Northern Sudanese student came up to me. 'Were you in Yei in 1955?' he asked. When I replied that I had been he continued 'Did you have anything to do with taking Abdulla's family to the Congo?' Once again I confirmed that I had. 'That was the greatest disgrace that ever overtook our family,' he said. 'Far better that they had been killed than that they had been saved by English infidels.' I could only reply that in 1955 the families involved had not shared his view and that I had no regrets at all for what John and I had accomplished that night. But the events of those two days had given nobody any cause for laughter.

CHAPTER 2

# A Gleam of Light

THE NEXT TWO DAYS were spent in a kind of limbo. Yei had no post office or telephone system and there was no local radio station so we had no idea what was going to happen. We tried to give the students some interesting projects to keep them occupied, but nobody's mind was really on their work. At last John came to our house at six thirty in the evening to say that through the crackle of his ancient radio he had heard on the six o'clock news from the BBC that the British Governor-general in Khartoum, the capital over a thousand miles away, was sending Northern Sudanese troops to restore order in the South. There was no mention of British officials accompanying them to limit revenge on civilians.

'We need to move away from here,' John said. 'All the local people have fled and if troops come to Yei our students and schoolchildren will be the only civilians that they find. Let's meet with the others first thing to-morrow morning.'

The others were the three heads of the boarding schools on the mission compound, two for girls and one for boys, so that we had over seven hundred young people for whom we were responsible. We met at seven o'clock the next morning and quickly agreed that we must move everybody to a less obvious place. It was decided that the nearest village primary school some seven miles away and well off the road would make a good site. As the youngest member of the group I was detailed to go and see what the situation was at the school and warn anybody whom I might find there of our plan. It did not take me long on my bicycle to reach the school and I found that, unlike in Yei, people had not fled and the teachers and their families were still there. I gave them what news I had and asked if we might use their school as a camping place for a few days until we saw how the situation developed. They fully supported our plan and straight away agreed that local women would collect firewood in advance of our coming so that the children could cook a meal as soon as they arrived.

I returned to the mission where it had been assumed that there would be no objection to our plan and preparations were underway to move everybody out the next day. Loads of cooking utensils and all the sickles that

7

we could find were put together and rations drawn out for every child, ready for a dawn departure the next morning. So as the sun rose a long straggling procession of young people set out, ranging in age from nine to twenty. Most of the Sudanese teachers had already sought safety elsewhere but a few of the most senior staff were still present to help organize the exodus. The children were subdued for a short while and then they saw the opportunity that this offered for an enjoyable adventure. It started with increasing chatter, then laughter and finally singing so that soon we had a walking concert half a mile long. The expatriates took their bicycles so that they, who were least at risk, could move backwards and forwards to monitor the situation. John had his 'saucepan' radio firmly attached to his cycle carrier as our only means of contact with the outside world.

It took almost three hours to reach the school where, as promised, firewood was awaiting us and some older girls were detailed off to start cooking. The school consisted of just one large room and this was allocated to the smallest children. The rest of us went off with our shared sickles to cut the seven-foot-tall grass to make small huts for our shelter. All the children knew what to do and by early evening there were a couple of hundred tiny beehive huts scattered around the school compound. Anne and I duly constructed our own little shelter and then joined the communal meal. The children were by now in great form and thoroughly enjoying this exciting break from school. As soon as the meal was finished they gathered round several large fires and started singing. The staff eventually had to intervene and get them to their little huts. Anne and I were young enough and tired enough to fall asleep quite easily on the heap of grass that we had cut for a mattress, but were not hardened enough to sleep through the steady drips of water falling on our faces once the rain started in the middle of the night. Luckily it only lasted a couple of hours, but it was quite enough to convince us that we were going to do some serious thatching the next day.

The next morning quickly demonstrated that what we had thought might be a frightening experience for these young people was being turned by them into a most enjoyable holiday camp with singing and laughter being the dominant sounds. We were not the only ones whose hut had leaked and so a lot more grass was cut and some serious building work carried out. Chores were all finished by the afternoon and so we organized games and sports, and in the evening the youngsters embarked on their own mini-concerts with singing and dancing. Unfortunately the Southern Sudan had dropped out of the BBC news and so we had no way of knowing what was happening. The next morning John came over to me and said 'I think that you and I better go into Yei this morning and see if we can pick up any news, if we cannot get any from the radio'.

We cycled on a completely empty road into a shopping area which was also deserted. The hyenas were now so bold that they were finishing off their work in broad daylight, but there were also dead bodies in some of the houses which the hyenas could not reach, and the smell was sickening. We moved on to the police station and found it was also deserted. The policemen had obviously got the message that Northern troops were on their way, had abandoned their uniforms and disappeared into the bush. There just was nobody to give us any news at all and so we went up to the mission to check that all was well there. It was also deserted and there was no sign of any theft, and we cycled back to the camp. We repeated the exercise the next day with the same result, and so that evening John called a staff meeting to decide what we should do. We had anticipated the rapid arrival of soldiers, and had hoped that we could negotiate with them for the safety of the children, who had nothing to do with the killing, and then return the children to the schools and get them back to work once more. It was now obvious that this was not going to happen. 'We can't keep seven hundred of us in a camp in the bush for weeks on end,' said John, 'and we cannot have the children in the schools unprotected when the soldiers first arrive and see for themselves the atrocities which were carried out. I think that we are going to have to send them home.' The other staff were horrified. In normal times the education department provided lorry transport for the children at the beginning and end of each term. Now John was suggesting that they should walk. 'Do you realize, John, that I have nine year olds who come from over 300 miles away. I am responsible for them and I just cannot send them off to walk to home,' said Philippa, the headmistress of the girls primary school.

'What do you suggest?' said John, 'take them back to Yei and risk the consequences of a raid by infuriated soldiers? Camp here for weeks on end with no reliable food supplies for so many children?' The arguments went back and forth for a long time but it was finally agreed that we would have to send the children home. They would be setting out with only a snack and a blanket to walk through country still full of wild animals and depending for food and shelter on the good will and generosity of villagers who belonged to different tribes.

Once the decision had been made some substantial planning had to be done. Each head gathered together their own young people and first sorted them out by their district of origin, then by their sub-district, and finally by their village. Lists were made and groups were formed, distances were assessed and ages checked. In every group there had to be at least two young men of over sixteen to take responsibility for the others, and so boys had to be moved from one group to another, which often meant that they would have to make substantial detours from their own homes. It was evening before everything was finished. A group of girls was detailed off to get up well before dawn and cook a last meal so that the children would at least start with some food in their stomachs. Luckily we had a dry night, so everyone woke refreshed.

The children were assembled in their groups and sent to get some breakfast. By eight o'clock all was ready and we gathered for a last song together, a prayer for their safe journey and off they set. They burst into song as soon as they started walking, and any visitors would never have imagined what a journey lay before them. The nearest homes were less than 50 miles away but many of the children had to cover 200 and four of the groups had to go for more than 300 miles. The only miserable faces around seemed to be those of the staff, worried as to whether they had made the right decision, how the children would survive among people of a different language on their way and how many of them would finally reach their parents. Our worries were baseless. When the schools re-assembled a year later we found that not a single child had been lost, that families on the way had helped and fed them and that the young leaders had been outstanding in shouldering their responsibilities. One sixteen year old boy had walked 140 extra miles to deliver a small girl to her home. Here indeed was a cause for rejoicing and for laughter but unfortunately we did not know that outcome as we dismantled our camp. The Sudanese staff who were still with us asked to be allowed to seek safety elsewhere and the half dozen missionaries moved back to their own homes.

Although the Centre's farm and gardens could not have fed 700 children they were producing far more than we could eat. 'I cannot bear to see this going to waste,' Anne would say as she staggered in with yet another basket of produce, her Scots blood getting the better of her housekeeping skills. Everybody had more food than they could possibly use and we were soon to have a further bounty added.

With no students and little that we could do to be of help to anyone John came over a couple of days after our return and said 'Why don't you give yourselves a break and do a good turn at the same time? The Mitilias took nothing with them and I am sure that they would appreciate it if you took some essentials to them. Their pick-up truck is in their yard and I expect that you will be able to get it going. Have a day out in the Congo and you might pick up some news.'

We cycled down to the deserted town and started with the pick-up. Breaking open the petrol store made me feel unreasonably guilty, but after all it was for the owners' benefit. Anne found a funnel and we poured two jerry cans of fuel into the tank. I rooted around a bit before I found the starting handle, but then with a couple of sharp swings the engine was running. Then we started on the house, trying to work out which clothes belonged to who and which might be their most precious objects of sentimental value. It took an hour to pack up three cases, load them on the pick-up and set out on our way. We travelled along the road to the border in a very different frame of mind to that which I had with John and the Northern Sudanese just a week before. At the border the Belgian officials were eager for news but there was little that we could give them and they likewise could offer us little information. They let us through without any trouble and we drove on for another twenty miles enjoying the superior quality of the Congolese road. The Greek community in Aba the nearest town was small and we soon located the Mitilias. Warmly welcomed, we enjoyed the best lunch that we had tasted for a long time. Other Greeks came round to ask about the Sudan and finally in mid-afternoon we said that we really must get back. With a profusion of thanks ringing in our ears we got back to the pick-up to find a large wooden crate in the back. We said there must be a mistake but 'it's just a small token of the Greek community's appreciation' we were told. Now it was our turn to offer thanks, and we set off on an uneventful journey right back to John's house where our 'hamper' could be inspected. Christmas wasn't in it! Olives, tinned salmon, white flour, a gallon of wine – an array of luxuries such as we had not seen for many a long day. We divided the spoils evenly between us so that Anne now had a luxury store to add to her mountain of home-grown food. We felt relaxed after a happy day away from the stresses of the previous week.

'It can't be,' I said. 'It is,' said Anne, 'and I can see it'. We had heard a drone in the sky and run out to see what it was. There had never before been a plane over Yei but now we could see two circling over the town. 'They are coming this way, I am sure,' said Anne as she ran into the house to get a pillowcase to make a white flag. The planes swooped low over the mission, turned and came down even lower. They were RAF planes and we could see the pilots easily. No need for a white flag but every reason to wave wildly. They did a third run and then flew off to the West, presumably to check out Maridi the next town along the border. The sequel to this excitement was not long in coming. John, Helena, Anne and I were all straining to listen to the BBC six o'clock news and heard 'An RAF reconnaissance mission to-day flew over Equatoria in the Southern Sudan and established that there are still at least twelve British people living outside of the capital, Juba. The British government is particularly concerned about their welfare because unless emergency food supplies can be dropped to them, then hunger will drive them out.' So were the first seeds of doubt about official communications sown in my mind as we got ready for the delicious, but far too ample, dinner that Anne had prepared.

I remember very little of the following days. I developed a very serious bout of typhus which none of the drugs that Anne had available would touch. I just raved on with a raging temperature day after day and Anne wore herself down to a shadow with worry and constant nursing. Finally the Northern troops did arrive. There was some unpleasantness but on the whole they behaved with restraint and it was an army doctor who finally came up with the drug which dealt with my illness, and I am quite sure saved my life. I was just a skeleton, and it was decided that I must be taken to the nearest good hospital 600 miles away in Kampala, Uganda. There was an elderly Humber car that had been left by a British official in Juba, the capital of Equatoria, which he had asked to be driven to Kampala if ever anybody wanted to go there. The mission decided that this was just what we needed, the car was delivered to Yei and Anne embarked on the most skilful driving of her life as she took this ancient vehicle, which had no brakes at all, on a 600 mile journey on dirt roads at the height of the wet season. The journey was not without its hazards, but eventually we reached Kampala and I started on the process of returning to someone who looked a bit more like a human being, while Anne got some sleep, some rest and some freedom from worry, which soon worked marvels on her resilient young body. We were starting to look like our original selves, but in fact the crisis of the previous weeks was to change the pattern of our lives for many years to come.

# CHAPTER 3

# How Did We Get Here?

THERE ARE SOME dates which stick in the minds of even those who are quite uninterested in history. For an older generation the third of September 1939 is one such. This is the day on which England declared war on Germany, and the events which followed that day impinged in ways great and small on the lives of millions of people, among whom I was one. We had spent the summer of 1939 on a South American cruise, which included a two week stay in Buenos Aires. The Argentine had a strong hold on my parents' emotions. My mother, a singer, had been offered an attractive contract with the Colon Opera House in Buenos Aires in 1913 and had moved there in that year from La Scala in Milan. Within a year she had attracted the attention of a prince of the Coburg family, and numerous family photographs bear witness to the lavish lifestyle that she enjoyed in his company. In 1916 he proposed to her, she accepted and the official engagement was announced. The wedding bells never rang however because it was at that point that a dashing young English officer visited Buenos Aires, swept my mother off her feet in a whirlwind romance and induced her to cancel her engagement to her prince and join forces with an impecunious young Englishman. The prince allowed her to keep his magnificent engagement ring and the beautiful diamond brooch that he had given her and she wore these to the end of her days. I never discovered whether my father saw her wearing of his rival's jewels as a symbol of his victory over a far wealthier man or that my strong willed mother had simply informed him that he had no option in the matter. He wangled a passage for her to England and they were married in 1917, all of which is part of the reason why we found ourselves in Buenos Aires in 1939.

Our ship was due to sail on the evening of 3 September and the news of the outbreak of war reached us at mid-day. Some snap decisions followed, with my father going off to fight for the second time and my mother and I being left in the safety of Buenos Aires. Within a week friends helped my mother to rent a house in the suburbs and I found myself in St Alban's College, a fairly small and friendly English language school, into which I settled easily enough. Two happenings of my school years shaped my

future. In 1940 when I was twelve I damaged my lungs in an accident and
before the days of antibiotics this soon turned into a life threatening event. I
spent some weeks in hospital and on my discharge my mother was told to
get me into the mountains to allow clean air to continue the healing.
Friends identified a ranch in the south of Cordoba Province belonging to
the Bridger family who were prepared to welcome me, and I was exposed
to farming for the first time. This became my home for the holidays for the
rest of my stay in the Argentine and provided one of the pillars of my
future life. My illness prevented me from playing any games at school and
earned me a C3 classification when I had my British army medical, but
years spent in the outdoors worked their healing power and by my twenties
I was able to enjoy a fully active life.

The second happening which had a profound influence on me was the
friendship of the history master at school, Charles Cohen. My father's ship
was sunk on South Atlantic convoy by a German battleship in early 1940
and he was taken prisoner, so that I did not see him for almost six years and
Cohen became a father figure for me. He was neither handsome nor
athletic and yet his remarkable Christian faith had a profound influence on
many of my contemporaries. Sunday afternoons at his house brought my
vague beliefs to life in a way in which school attendance at the local
Anglican church had not achieved. Those meetings laid the foundations of
the driving force which has determined the pattern of my life ever since. It
was hardly surprising that I became an avid historian and, because Cohen
had gone to Cambridge, that I would want to follow in his footsteps. So my
application to enter the University in October 1945 went on the now much
safer convoys to England as the war drew to its close. Because most young
men were still in the forces I obtained an easy admission and I looked
forward to the possibility of becoming a university lecturer in history and
fantasized about the mark that I might make on the subject.

As soon as the war in Europe was over my mother and I sailed for
England on a cargo boat which took three weeks to reach Southampton. To
my mother's intense disappointment my father was not there to meet us,
because as soon as he was released from POW camp he had been given
command of a ship and was back at sea. He returned about six weeks later
and we found that we were strangers. He still envisaged me as a cherubic
twelve year old choirboy and what he found was an assertive eighteen year
old with an outlook and attitude quite different to his own. Our
relationship settled down but it was then my turn to be away from home
and we saw too little of each other ever again to establish a really close

rapport. I was an only child on whom he had doted, and I think that the loss of contact with me for six crucial years was one of the bitterest aspects of his imprisonment.

'Mountain top' experiences certainly do not always take place on glorious hillsides nor even, like Paul, on romantic sounding roads. Mine came in an ugly hall in the local grammar school which had not been painted for the six war years, whose chairs were in desperate need of attention and which reflected the worn out look of much of Britain after six years of punishment. The hall was being used by the congregation of the church of St Mark which had been bombed during the war. It was the church in which I had been a choirboy for four years before we went to the Argentine and to which I naturally returned when we arrived at our old home, which had fortunately escaped enemy damage. On the third Sunday after we came back I was sitting at the rear of the crowded hall and discovered that the preacher was not ordained but represented an organization called the Church Missionary Society of which I had never heard. He rose to speak dressed in a wartime 'utility' suit, which was what most of the men in the congregation were wearing. He spoke of the damage done to missionary work by six years of war, the loss of staff and the desperate need for more young people to offer for service in the church overseas. I do not remember that he was particularly eloquent and all I do know is that I experienced an overwhelming sense that this is what I should be doing. Charles Cohen had always insisted that we understood that our lives were not just to be used to do what we felt like doing, but should fulfil a particular purpose in the world. I had opted for history because of his influence, and was looking to teaching because that is what he did. I had simply grown into this ambition but without any conviction that this decision was linked to my Christian faith. I was not sure that I understood Cohen's concept of one's faith being the dominant determinant of what we did with our lives. But in that dingy school hall I did understand, and believed that the call of the speaker had been directed at me. I stayed behind after the congregation dispersed, found the speaker and obtained the address of the CMS. I sat down that afternoon and wrote my letter of application and caught the three o'clock Sunday post.

The answer was not long in coming and I was invited to go to London to meet the Candidate's Secretary a couple of days later. My father was at sea and my mother thought that I was going to some religious meeting so I encountered no problems. I do not know what I thought a missionary would look like. The Sunday preacher had been the first that I had met and

I had been too absorbed by what he was saying to take much notice of his appearance, and my only other source of information had come from somewhat unflattering descriptions in books. Whatever my preconceptions, Geofrey Rogers came as quite a surprise. A young forty year old with a mop of black curly hair, he was not only good looking but had one of the most delightful smiles that I had seen, and a manner which immediately put me at my ease. He looked more like a popular sportsman than the dull missionary image of some literature. Having established what had brought me to him he asked of my immediate plans. 'I am due to be going to Cambridge in two weeks to read history' I replied. 'Do you have any other interests?' he asked. 'Well yes, I have spent a lot of time on farms and I really enjoy working with animals.' His face lit up with that wonderful smile. 'Are you serious enough to switch studies at this late stage and read agriculture instead of history? We desperately need good agriculturalists.' I did not hesitate. 'Yes,' I said, and changed the whole course of my life.

Charles Cohen had helped with my applications for Cambridge but I had no-one to whom I could turn for advice on reading agriculture. Geofrey gave me a name, rang the person straight away and got his agreement that he would meet me in a couple of days' time. When we met I still hoped that I might go to Cambridge and simply change my studies. I soon found out that while Cambridge possessed many admirable qualities its degree in agriculture was not one of them. I was therefore going to have to cancel my place there. My mentor put London University's Wye College at the top of his suggested list with Reading as a runner up. I had heard of London University and felt that I was taking a substantial drop down the academic ladder by making this change, but my mind was set and I just wanted to get the best training that I could to fulfil my new ambition. I applied to Wye, went for an interview, was offered a place but was told that the College was being refurbished after having been an army headquarters during the war and that I would have to wait at least two years before I could be admitted. Apart from which I had to work for at least a year on an English farm before I could be considered for admission. I was devastated. I had anticipated being overseas in three years time and now I was being given a timetable which seemed to an eager young man to be stretching into the far distant future. There appeared to be no options, I had been attracted to the whole setting of Wye at the foot of the Downs in a most beautiful part of England, and so I swallowed my disappointment and faced the double challenge of telling my father of my new plans and finding a farm on which I could work.

Father returned from a long voyage to Australia a week later and I had to explain the situation to him immediately as he had expected to find me at Cambridge. He was not pleased. He was deeply disappointed that I showed no intention of following in the family footsteps and going to sea. Both of his brothers were naval officers and his eldest nephew was already preparing for a seafaring life. He had realized that I had no interest at all in such a career, but at least reading history at Cambridge was a socially acceptable activity. Being a missionary was something quite different and he made his opposition perfectly clear. I had to have his support as I had no chance of being offered a means tested scholarship and with farm wages at £3.10s per week, of which half went for board and lodging, I had no hope of saving the couple of thousand pounds that it would cost me to go to university. I did have one trump card up my sleeve.

'When I was young,' my father had told me, 'my father was determined that I would become a lawyer, but all that I wanted to do was go to sea. When I was sixteen I ran away to sea, an adventure which lasted six hours, after the captain had reported me to the police who delivered me back to my father. He thought he had the answer and so he signed me up on a 700-ton sailing ship for a two and a half year voyage, in the certainty that I would be cured for good and all and then come back and do as he wished. As you know it did not work, but I promised then that I would never try to force any son of mine to adopt a career that he did not want to follow.' As kindly as I could I reminded him of that promise, which he ruefully admitted that he had made, so at least he did not try and force me back to Cambridge. I would have to wait for another day to see if he would fund my fees at Wye.

My next challenge was to find a farm on which to fulfil the demands of the college. At this point my mother came to my rescue. Like most good mothers she was more concerned about my health than the kind of degree for which I was going to study, and was delighted at the prospect that I would be working out in the open air again, which she was sure was the best treatment for my lungs. She contacted her network of friends and soon found one who knew a family in Gloucestershire with a large farm who might help. Using her name as an introduction I wrote to the Lowsley-Williams who owned Chavenage, a 2,000-acre estate, near Tetbury. To my delight they said that they would give me a trial to see how I got on in their household. There followed two delightful years. They owned a large Elizabethan manor house and I entered a different pattern of life to that which I was accustomed. Throughout the winter there were frequent large formal dinner parties with a range of eminent and interesting people and week-end house parties including members of the royal family, senior service officers, Oxford dons and leading industrialists. I was soon treated as a young member of the family and enjoyed a fascinating insight into a particular stratum of English society. But like every other member of the family most of our time was spent trying to extract as much food as possible from the land to help maintain the meagre rations of the urban population. We worked ferociously long hours, particularly in summer when milking started at five a.m. and double summer time allowed us to go on harvesting until ten o'clock at night. It is almost impossible to imagine the difference that exists in Britain between the attitude to farmers in 1945, when they were the heroes of the hour whose sweat was all that kept hunger from most people's doors, and the antipathy between town and country people to-day.

By the end of my first year at Chavenage my father had realized that I had developed a passion for farming and so he generously agreed that he would pay my fees for Wye. I am sure that he believed that in another four years I would have forgotten about missionary work and would settle down to farm in England. As I was working he said that I would have to provide for all my other expenses. He had no idea of the pittance that farm workers were paid at that time and even with the most stringent economies I was finding it difficult to save one pound per week. But I was glad enough to have the university fees paid for and was sure that I would be able to scrape together enough to cover my other expenses, even if rather frugally. In mid 1947 I received the shattering news that I would not be admitted to Wye until October 1948. I had, by this time carried out nearly every operation on the farm and acquired a wide range of skills. The Lowsley-Williams felt that it would be a good thing to spend the next year on a quite different kind of farm. And different it turned out to be. I moved on to a hill sheep farm on the Clee Hills in Shropshire. No member of the family was literate, there was no running water, electricity or indoor toilet, the nearest road was four miles away and to reach the nearest town involved a ten mile walk. There was no tractor or modern farming equipment and hand labour provided most of the power on the farm. All this I accepted, but it was the food which nearly drove me away. Fat pork, eggs, bread and potatoes were the basis of the diet three times a day and seven days a week. No vegetables ever darkened the kitchen door. It was only the fear of being thought too feeble to cope with a bit of hardship which kept me there through my first weeks. Slowly I got used to this totally different pattern life, came to appreciate the warmth and honesty of the family with which I was living and realized that I was not only acquiring a range of fresh farming skills but was learning to enjoy living in a community of people of a very different background from my own. In the end I was actually sad to leave the Clee Hills when the time came to go to Wye, and I went back there for a month or two each year to help the family out during my summer vacation.

Wye provided me with three delightful years. I was one of only two of the male students who had not fought in the war and was the youngest man in the college, but I had no shortage of friends, and after living at close quarters with others in the forces most of the students had developed the skills needed to limit friction in a tight-knit community. Only one student in the college had a car. He was the master of the hunt and so drew a special petrol ration. For everybody else the ration was so small that it was not worth the expense of owning a car. As a result all our social life was centred on the college. There were a dozen different societies, a good orchestra, our choirmaster came over from Canterbury Cathedral to drill us and I found that I had debating skills which carried the college into the finals of the university debating competition for two years running, at a time when debating was important enough for the finals to be broadcast live on the BBC. As in any college the students soon formed groups of close friends. I found this a delight after the isolated situation of the Clee Hills. I also revelled in my studies. The only entrance requirement into any university at that time was a minimum of five credits in School Certificate. I was therefore able to enter a course leading to a Bachelor of Science degree without ever having studied any science at school. The first year was devoted entirely to pure science with no mention of agriculture and I embarked on this without even knowing the formula of water. Everybody else in my year had done at least four years of pure science at school and were simply building on that knowledge, many in a disgruntled manner because they wanted to get on to the farming, but if one failed the first year then there were no second chances to ever get on to the agriculture, so they had to grin and bear it. I was in a totally different situation and every day brought new miracles of knowledge about plants, animals, rocks and the nature of the world. I was fascinated. My mind went into overdrive and at the end of the year I sailed through my Intermediate BSc.

Friendships were beginning to develop into something more serious within our group and by my second year I discovered that Anne Grant was becoming as attracted to me as I was to her. By the end of the second term she felt that the relationship was solid enough for me to be introduced to her parents and invited me to spend the first two days of the Easter vacation at her home before I went to Chavenage. On the last night of term I packed my widely assorted clothes into the battered suitcase that I had found in the attic at home. There was evening dress, still regularly worn to dinner in those days, accompanied by hob nailed boots, thick corduroy trousers and the heavy jackets worn on the farm. I managed to close the first lock but as I gave the final push on the second the top of the case split under the strain. I had no other case, could not buy one in Wye and had to find some way of getting my clothes to my destination. At dawn I cycled up to the college cowshed, begged an empty cow-cake bag and a piece of binder twine from the dairy man and hurried back to bundle my clothes into the sack.

I was unaware that there was a road into Charing Cross station at the time which permitted distinguished people to bring their cars almost to the platforms and so was surprised to find Anne waving to her father's chauffeur as our train drew in to the station. He was soon at our carriage door ready to take our luggage. I handed down Anne's expensive pig-skin case and said that I would carry my own. He insisted that it was his responsibility and so my sack appeared. His face made it abundantly clear that his offer was being withdrawn and so I slung the sack over my shoulder and put it in the boot of the Daimler under his disapproving eye.

I was warmly welcomed into Anne's family. They owned a beautiful Queen Anne house with nine acres of garden, and my interest was quickly awakened by the well populated trout stream that ran through the length of their grounds. This was my first visit so I was quietly scrutinized and not subjected to any serious probing. That started on later visits when it became clear that we were serious about marriage.

Anne was quite apparently the apple of her father's eye and he had anticipated using his wealth to provide her with the style of life to which she was accustomed. He had hoped that she would meet a nice young man at Wye whom he could help to buy whatever farm Anne chose, where she could have her horses, hunt regularly, indulge her interest in farm animals and provide a pleasant week-end retreat for her parents. I was found to be socially acceptable, had obviously acquired a good practical knowledge of farming and her father had heard from Anne that I was doing well at Wye. I told of my intention to be a missionary but even this was accepted as a healthy sign of the altruism which all students should possess and which would be shed with 'puppy socialism' when the time came to marry and develop a career. Finally our official engagement was announced in the national press and then the situation became a lot more difficult. Far from accepting my prospective father-in-law's offer of a farm I had actually gone into the CMS missionary training college and under the Society's rules Anne had gone to the women's college. She did her training at the same time as me but all men had to serve a single tour of duty before being allowed to marry, so when I went off to Nigeria for almost two years she returned to her parents' home. Their only hope now was that I would be completely disillusioned with what I found in Nigeria and would return to farm sensibly in England. My letters soon proved that this was not the case and so Anne's father changed his tactics and told Anne that she could not marry me. She was sorry to hurt her father but was equally unwilling to break off her engagement and she made this clear. 'Alright then, if you insist on marrying this man I will cut you out of my inheritance' he said. Anne's response must have cut him to the quick. 'Well that will be one less thing to worry about!' she said. He kept to his word for about fifteen years until he finally realized that Anne was actually fulfilled in what she was doing. The situation at home became too tense after that and Anne went to live with friends until I returned from Nigeria.

Her father disapproved of what his daughter was doing but certainly did not want to lose her and so he came with her to the airport to meet me and three weeks later provided us with a wonderful and memorable wedding on a glorious May afternoon. We had a two week honeymoon looking after a friends' farm while they went on holiday, and then I had to put in a couple of months of speaking engagements for the Society before we left for the Sudan and the Village Teachers Training Centre at Yei.

# CHAPTER 4

# A Change of Direction

'I WILL NOT BE spoken to like this and I will not tolerate a foreigner criticizing me or my staff. I know where your sympathies lie and I do not want you in this district any longer.' An angry military commander, Major Hassan al Bashir, glared at John Parry across the table in his makeshift headquarters. 'I will issue orders tomorrow that all British missionaries shall be out of Yei within a week.' John had got himself into a difficult situation. For almost twenty years he had dealt with British officials and made his complaints known if he thought that some government action was harming local people. There was still a British Governor-general in Khartoum supported by his British staff, but it was absolutely clear that the new military commander in Yei was quite certain that it was he who was in charge and that he was unwilling to accept critical comment from a 'foreigner'. He stood by his word and a week later all the missionaries had gone. Little work had been done in the short time since order had been restored in the district and, at the height of the rainy season, two months of neglect was allowing the bush to start a highly successful invasion of the mission compound.

In Juba the head of the mission, Brian de Saram was worried. Yei was not only a centre of education but of a large network of schools and churches stretching across tens of thousands of square miles. To have it left without supervision for months on end was not an attractive prospect. Brian was not only a most gracious person but also a good diplomat. He let the situation cool down for a couple of weeks and then he asked for an interview with the new governor of Equatoria, Ali Baldo. He did have one strong card in his hand. The British were soon to pull out of the Anglo-Egyptian Sudan and the Egyptians were hoping that the country would then be re-united with Egypt. They had established a party to vote for such an outcome and Egyptians had come to the Southern Sudan to win support for that party. Ali Baldo and many of his friends in the administration did not want such a union and so had to win the 'hearts and minds' of Southerners despite the atrocities carried out by the soldiers and police. He was astute enough to realize that the loss of the three best schools in the Province and the only

22

teacher training centre for village school teachers would be very unpopular indeed. Brian was not therefore in too weak a position when he went to see the Governor.

'Our concern, sir, is fire. All the buildings belonging to the four institutions are thatched. The dry season is only a few weeks away and if the bush is not cleared and firebreaks cut then all of these schools could be lost.' Ali Baldo was not showing any antagonism so Brian continued 'I am very sorry about what happened with John Parry but I expect that you realize that it takes a little while to adapt to fresh circumstances. We have a young couple, currently in Uganda, who have only recently come to the Sudan and who therefore do not have that colonial background. They were not in Yei when the confrontation between Major al Bashir and John Parry took place and so were not involved in any way. They also speak Arabic, which would be helpful at this sensitive time. I am therefore asking, sir, that you allow me to recall them and post them to take charge of the compound at Yei.'

Ali Baldo thought for a bit and said 'It would not be at all popular with Bashir in Yei. He is still upset and has made his feelings quite clear to me. At the same time I fully accept the logic of your argument and it would benefit nobody if all those buildings were burnt. We have enough reconstruction to do without adding another major task to the list. Give me a few days and I will find the right moment to make the point to Bashir. I don't want simply to make an order, I would like to win his co-operation. I will be in touch with you within a week.'

I have no idea what Ali Baldo said to Major Bashir but a few days later we received a message in Kampala that if the doctors would give me the 'all clear' then we should return to the Sudan. Once again there was a vehicle to be delivered, this time from Uganda to the Sudan. It was a Landrover and, although by no means new, it had been overhauled and the brakes worked. The doctors pronounced me fit, and we set off on a much less traumatic 600-mile journey to Juba than the one that had brought me to hospital a couple of months earlier. We reported to Brian, were most warmly welcomed and the next day, as was the mission custom, I was given written orders relating to my new position. The first one was a bit of a surprise. 'You are to give top priority to playing tennis. This must be given precedence over all other activities.' I looked at Brian. 'What on earth is this about?'

He laughed. 'I have discovered that Bashir is a really keen tennis player and there is nobody else in Yei who can play. It is absolutely essential that you win his trust and I think that it is just possible that tennis might provide the key. He has given in to Ali Baldo but is certainly still opposed to your returning to Yei and will try to find a reason to expel you. You have really got to be very careful what you say and make sure that you do not tread on any toes.' The rest of the instructions were fairly straightforward. Rally the old staff on the mission, take on a hundred extras for a few weeks and get twenty-yard-wide firebreaks round the whole 150 acres. After that clear the bush within the schools and carry out any thatching repairs that were needed.

I had no tennis racquet nor balls so Brian set me up and we set out on the back breaking hundred miles to Yei. The small town had regained some semblance of normality. The market was functioning, albeit with fewer people than usual. Nobody had taken over the Northern merchants' shops but the four Greek traders had returned from the Congo and opened their stores. We found our home smelling of fungus from having been shut up in the hot wet season, but none of our property had been stolen. We received a warm welcome from the people who had returned to the mission and cycled round the different institutions to spot the most serious fire hazards. On the following morning I went down to the Mitilias shop to greet the family and buy some basic stores. The old man was sitting, as always, at the green baize covered table at one end of the shop from where he kept a sharp eye on his son and daughter-in-law who did the actual work. I was invited to sit opposite him, was brought a cup of sweet strong coffee and we exchanged news. A few minutes later Bashir walked in. He saw me, realized who I was, and pointedly ignored me as he moved along the counter to make some purchases. In a gap in the conversation I said to Costis Mitilias 'What a shame it is to see the tennis court having been completely overgrown'. The old man had no idea why I was making this remark but replied, 'yes it is sad, I spent many happy afternoons there when I was younger'.

Bashir came to the table. 'Did I hear you talking about a tennis court?'

'Yes' replied Mitilias, 'we had a good tennis court in Yei but now it is lost in the bush.'

'Where is it?' said Bashir.

'Mr Carr would show you I am sure,' came the innocent reply.

Bashir acknowledged my presence for the first time. Unsmiling he said 'Come with me now in my truck and show me where it is'.

I joined him in his army vehicle and we drove up the road to the District Commissioner's house which he was occupying. 'It's just here on the opposite side of the road to your house'. We got down from the truck and pushed our way for twenty yards through seven-foot-tall grass and there it was. The hard ironstone gravel surface of the actual court had been rolled for so many years that little plant life could grow on it and it looked quite reasonable, but the surround was completely overgrown. Bashir looked around. 'I will have some soldiers here to-morrow to clear this up and repair the net. Do you play tennis?' I replied that I did. 'What's today? Wednesday. Right, I will meet you here at four o'clock on Saturday afternoon.'

We returned in silence to the Mitilias shop, but I reckoned that we had least started to insert Brian's key into the door. I obeyed his order, and on Saturday afternoon donned my white shirt and shorts and cycled the mile to the court. The place had been transformed. The grass and bush had been cleared for twenty yards around, the court itself had been weeded and swept, chalk lines had been redrawn and the net mended. Bashir was already there dressed in the same way as myself and had brought two soldiers as 'ball boys'. Goodness knows how many soldier hours had been spent on this exercise, but I could comfort myself with thinking that there were a lot more damaging things that they could have been doing. The major gave me a curt nod and we started to play. As luck would have it we were very equally matched. It would have been too obvious and insulting if I had deliberately let him win and so we played a highly competitive game. He was scrupulously fair and I really enjoyed myself. After three quarters of an hour we called it a day and in a more relaxed tone he invited, rather than ordered, me to join him at the same time on Monday.

So started a regular ritual. On four evenings a week we would play for about forty-five minutes, and the atmosphere between us became increasingly cordial. Brian's key did not just fit the lock, it was beginning to open the door. I was thoroughly enjoying our games and was delighted that my pleasure was being counted as work. After three weeks Bashir invited Anne and me to have tea at his house and then Anne was also able to link work and pleasure. The previous District Commissioner, who had been murdered, had owned a horse which disappeared on the day of the killing. It had not been seen for months and was assumed to have been killed by lions, when it had suddenly turned up on the football field in the middle of the town. It was in a dreadful condition, emaciated and with a number of septic wounds. Bashir was embarrassed by this reminder of his predecessor and by the fact that it was in such a sorry state. On the off-chance that we might be able to help he asked Anne if she knew anything about horses. She replied in the affirmative and so he asked her help to remove the horse from the town and look after it. Anne jumped at the possibility and Bashir promptly said that she could call on the army for any medicines that she might need. The poor horse offered no resistance to being caught and led up to the mission, although Anne was upset by its terrible condition. It was, however, a strong Sudanese animal which had already proved its durability and the combination of tender loving care and antibiotics soon brought about a complete transformation. Saddlery was found in an outhouse of the DC's residence and Anne started on gentle rides. We invited Bashir to come and see the horse and so he came up to the mission for the first time. He was both amazed and profusely grateful for the transformation that Anne had achieved and so both of us were now enjoying a well liked recreation and at the same time fulfilling our most important function at that moment in time. We kept the horse until we left Yei some months later, by which time there were sufficient officers in the town to include a good horseman who took over responsibility for the animal.

I was doing some other work as well! I had a hundred workers organized into gangs under a foreman, who were clearing the vital firebreaks before the ferocious grass fires started in January as the country dried out. I had done enough manual labour myself to have a shrewd idea of how much a man ought to be able to achieve in a day and so set piece work for all the main jobs, which relieved me of a lot of detailed supervision. Bashir had put movement restrictions on me when I first arrived which precluded me from leaving the area of the town and mission. With our new relationship I asked if this might now be removed so that I could get out into the countryside and see what was happening in the village schools. He readily agreed and so day by day I set off on my bicycle and became really exposed to village life for the first time. I visited schools, found that most teachers were again living in their homes and encouraged them to start classes straight away with a promise that I would record their efforts and have them rewarded once the education officer returned. Being free of teaching and institutional responsibilities was also giving me the opportunity of studying local farms and exposing me to farmers. I could not avoid noticing the huge gap that there was between our nice model farm and the reality of farming in Equatoria. Anne joined me from time to time and we started to think through the implications of what we were seeing. Who was getting it right? Us with our intensively farmed, neat looking plots with their high yields or the local farmers with their untidy looking fields with half a dozen crops planted together, none of which were producing anything like the output that we were achieving from our land. Slowly it began to dawn on us that it was us who had got it wrong, and not just us, but the people who had trained me in Nigeria and a string of British agricultural officers who had served for years in Equatoria. All of us had been brought up and educated in a country in which one tried to extract as much as possible from a limited area of land. High yields are what brought farmers both profit and respect in England. What had this to do with Equatoria, where a population of less than three million occupied an area a third of the size of India. Why would anyone want to care about yield per acre when there were millions of acres lying empty and available free of charge to anybody who wanted them. It was not land that was in short supply, it was labour. It was production per man day that mattered not yield per acre. We were barking up the wrong tree and would face being as ineffectual as many earlier agricultural initiatives unless we changed our ways. But how could we find out how to approach farming in this quite different way? No textbooks on tropical agriculture approached the subject in this way. The only people who really knew were the local farmers who had survived in this hostile environment for generations. How could we tap their knowledge and really grasp what they were doing? We slowly agreed that there seemed to be only one truly effective way and that was to join them. So were the events of 18 August 1955 to shape our lives for years to come.

CHAPTER 5

# We Make the Move

BRIAN DE SARAM came up from Juba to visit us a couple of weeks later. In a country with no telephones or regular postal service, personal visits were about the only means of effective communication. He had come to see how we were getting on by ourselves and to cast his eye over the large educational complex at Yei. As he sat having a drink of fresh lime juice after the hot, bone shaking journey from Juba he said 'I think that I have good news for you. We have an excellent Northern Sudanese provincial education secretary called Sayed al Khatim al Khalifa and he is really keen to get the schools going and is putting pressure on the governor to allow missionaries to return. He realizes that there are so few senior Southern Sudanese trained teachers that, unless he can get outside help, he will not be able to get the Yei group of schools going again. Ali Baldo is very pleased with the improvement in relations between you and Major al Bashir, but he feels it is still too soon to broach the issue of the return of John Parry and all the other teachers. But I am sure we are making progress and that it will not be too long before you will be teaching once again.'

Anne and I looked at each other 'Actually Brian we were going to tell you that we want to leave the teacher training centre.'

'Why on earth?' Brian replied. 'I thought that you liked working with the Parrys, and people have spoken very highly of all that you have done with the farm and agricultural teaching. You have survived all the traumas of the past months very well, why do you want to leave just when it looks as though we should be settling into a period of stability?'

'We have no problem at all with John and Helena and they have been wonderfully supportive of us as we settled in. We also enjoyed the teaching, but we have become convinced that much of that teaching has actually been irrelevant. We are endlessly providing answers to questions that Sudanese farmers are not asking, and that is a pretty good formula for being ineffectual. We think that we have been barking up the wrong tree.'

'But you were sent to Nigeria to prepare you for this work, and you consulted some of the government agricultural staff when you first came to

28

Equatoria. Are you suggesting that they have all been barking up the wrong tree, as you put it?'

'You put us in an awkward position, Brian, and make us look presumptuous, but the basic answer to you question is, yes we do.'

Brian gave us a quizzical look and so I continued. 'The British agricultural staff have been trying to change Southern Sudanese farming for the past forty years, and yet we find that they have made virtually no impression at all on the vast majority of smallholders. Quite frankly we do not want to follow in their footsteps. We have all been demonstrating how to make the best use of land because that is how we were all trained. Anne and I are beginning to see that in a region where land has virtually no value, because it so abundant, the idea of maximizing its use makes no sense. That is why all these years of effort and teaching to try and raise farmers' yields have had so little impact.'

'So what do these farmers want?' asked Brian.

'We are seeing that they are aiming to get as much production as they can from each bit of labour that they invest in their farm, because it is labour that is in short supply. We are also beginning to realize that security of food supply is more important to them than achieving high yields of one particular crop or variety, and so they are hedging their bets in all sorts of clever ways. If the pattern of rainfall changes in a season they have such a range of crops growing that something will do well. If insects devastate one crop there will be another which will survive.'

Brian thought for a bit and then said 'Alright, there seems to be some sense in what you are saying, but why is this just coming out now?'

'In our own case it is because for the first time since we came to the Sudan we have had the time to actually go out and meet farmers and see what they are doing. I think that the agriculturalists working in institutions were, like us, so tied up in the institution that they just did not get enough opportunity to really talk to farmers and find out what were their main objectives.'

'I will accept that,' said Brian. 'I know what it was like when I had to run a school. But what about the few officers that there were in the field?'

'I think that their whole training and background made it virtually impossible for them to accept that the untidy jumble of half a dozen crops of a whole mixture of varieties growing in one field was actually better farming than their neat demonstration farms with single crops and pure stands of single varieties growing in each plot. It just went completely against all that they had ever learned. I think also we have to admit that there was a bit of an attitude that a naked, illiterate Sudanese peasant could not possibly know more about farming than an English agricultural graduate.'

'Alright, then it strikes me that you will just have to change the layout of your demonstration farm and the content of your lessons,' came the reply.

'But the whole point is that we just really do not know what farmers are doing and it is not the kind of detailed information that can be picked up in a half hour chat. This involves a complete transformation of our thinking and understanding of smallholder tropical agriculture.'

'So what do you suggest you do?' asked Brian.

'We want to leave Yei and move out into a village and settle there as members of the local community. We would not draw our mission allowance, would live in the same kind of hut as everybody else and have a small farm like other people and would ask our neighbours to teach us how to farm it so that we would feed ourselves. We think that it will take a couple of years to really get to the root of what and why certain practices are followed and then we believe that we might be able to apply our different knowledge and skills to increase production from people's labour and increase their security of food supply.'

'Phew' said Brian. 'You really are planning to sail out into uncharted waters. No missionary that I have ever heard of has simply gone off into a village and become a peasant farmer. There are certainly going to be obstacles that will have to be overcome. The first is undoubtedly John Parry. If he is allowed back he is not going to welcome the loss of two energetic staff members. Then there are mission rules regarding food and housing. After years of experience CMS has developed standards which it believes are necessary to maintain an expatriate's health in this very difficult climate. Now you are suggesting that you will live in a small mud hut with a cow dung floor and survive solely on native food. I admire your keenness but there is going to have to be an awful lot of talking before you start making any plans. Right, I feel cooler and less thirsty, let's go and inspect what you have been doing round here in the past few weeks.'

Unlike Roman Catholic missionaries we had had not taken an oath of obedience to CMS, but that made little difference. Obedience was expected and required so that 'the work' could best be served. Individuals had little say in where they would be posted or even in the work that they would do. A sudden illness or death in one area could mean that somebody else was uprooted from a home and work in which they had been happily settled for a number of years. At times it could even mean moving to a new language area with all the struggle of mastering another difficult tongue. As mentioned earlier recruits were not allowed to marry until they had served one tour overseas and normally they would also be required to pass their advanced language exam before obtaining permission to marry. I had been excused this because my posting to Nigeria was only for two years, but Anne and I still had a five year engagement. Some of this sounds harsh to modern ears but colonial servants faced a similar situation and it was an accepted part of an overseas posting. One of the hardest conditions of tropical service fifty years ago was that neither government servants nor missionaries were permitted to keep children in the hot, wet tropics beyond the age of seven because of the risks to their health. Thousands of couples faced years of separation when wives went to Britain with the children and the husband stayed in the tropics. Most missionaries in Eastern Nigeria, where I had worked, and in the Southern Sudan opted to either remain single or have no children to avoid such separations. We knew therefore that we could not simply dictate what we were going to do, and had been well aware of the factors against our proposed move which Brian had raised. We were not without hope however. CMS was led at that time by a quite remarkable thinker and visionary, Max Warren. We had met on a number of occasions when I had been in missionary training, he had found that I had some unconventional ideas, had befriended me and, diplomatically, let me know that he would offer his support if I chose to step out of the established pattern of work in a way which he saw would be beneficial to developing a more flexible and innovative Society. During my convalescence in Uganda he had paid a visit to East Africa and had again assured us of his interest and support. Now was not the time to invoke the use of heavy guns, but at least we knew that they existed and could be called into play if necessary.

Brian was a good friend and the rest of his visit went off pleasantly enough and no more was said about our plans. We now had sufficient freedom and time to start quietly looking around for a suitable village in which to settle should we win the battle for a move. Although Yei was only a small town of around 800 people in normal times it still had an influence for several miles around and we wanted to be outside the range of any such urban bias however modest. We started our search about ten miles out of town, using our contact with the village school teachers as sources of information about the character of different small rural communities without giving any hint of our real intentions. We also wanted proximity to water so that we had the potential to do some irrigation if that was appropriate in the future. Slowly we built up information on people, soils and water sources until we narrowed our search down to a small community sixteen miles out of Yei on the Kaya river. There was nothing more that we could do, but at least we would have saved a lot of time if permission to change the direction of our work was granted. Meanwhile I played my regular tennis with Bashir, supervised the maintenance of all the buildings and farmed a small area of land to produce food and try out some new ideas.

Finally the day came when Bashir very reluctantly bowed to pressure from the education department and the governor to permit the other missionaries to return to Yei. I had put our own plans into writing and submitted them to Brian and I was called to Juba some weeks later to face a meeting of the mission's small administrative committee. I put my case as well as I could, stressing the fact that such a move would not just supply the mission with an insight into the real basis of people's farming but also provide a window to the attitudes and beliefs which influenced their perceptions of Christianity. For some years all the CMS missionaries in the Southern Sudan had been tied to institutions of one kind or another with nobody having the freedom to delve deeply into what rural people were thinking and feeling. I received a sympathetic hearing and was told that I would be given a response after further deliberation and consultation with John Parry, who was still in England. Before I left Juba I took advantage of its post office to send a letter to Max Warren, to let him know what was afoot and ask for his support should it prove necessary. I hitched a lift on an old truck back to Anne in Yei and waited for the outcome. I have no idea what went on behind the scenes but we were eventually told that the move had been approved, with three provisos. The first was that we would sign a document to exempt CMS from any responsibility for a breakdown in our health because we would be moving outside their guidelines. The second was that for a year I would spend a full day each week at the Teacher Training Centre organizing the farm, teaching the students agriculture and preparing Cornelio, one of the existing staff, to take over these responsibilities. Finally it would be up to me to get Major Bashir's permission to settle in a village.

We readily agreed to the first two conditions and I set about dealing with the third. By this time our relationship with Bashir was really friendly. Independence had come to the Sudan on 1 January 1956, and although there had been little celebration in Yei when the Union Jack came down, there was at least no ambiguity in our position as being foreign visitors in a country in which Bashir was a senior official. By now he had showed us all the medals that he had earned when serving under Montgomery in the North African war and of which he was very proud. Anne was permitted to visit his wife, who was kept in strict purdah, and we were welcome visitors at his house. Anne sometimes came down to the tennis court to watch us play and then we would go to his house for tea. It was in this relaxed atmosphere that I raised the subject of our moving out into the countryside. He was certainly taken aback, not so much by any security concerns but by the fact that we should actually want to go and live in the midst of people whom he openly considered as savages and to leave the modest comforts of Yei for an inhospitable rural setting. We did our best to help him understand why we wanted to do this but when he finally gave his permission it was, I am sure, on the basis of friendship rather than of comprehension. Then he dropped his bombshell 'I will not have you take Mrs Carr out into the forest unarmed. It is full of wild animals and you are endangering her life. Come to my office to-morrow morning and I will issue you with an order to the armoury to provide you with an army rifle and twenty-five rounds of ammunition'. We were deeply moved. Here was a man who had been profoundly suspicious of all missionaries' motives only a few months before now offering us an army rifle. This was indeed an endorsement of friendship. In the event the firearm was only once used to protect us from a wounded leopard but it was invaluable in our warfare against the large troops of baboons which were the worst scourge of local farmers.

Now I could really go into action. I cycled out to Payawa, the nearest village school to the area in which we wanted to settle. I had got to know Filipo the teacher well and needed his help. 'My wife and I are wanting to move out to Yosepa and Onesimo's area five miles from here, and I would really appreciate it if you could help me in talking to them.' I needed his help for two reasons. The first was that he knew me from attending day courses at the training centre and could vouch for the fact that I belonged to 'CMS' which had a good reputation throughout the district. The second was that I spoke none of the local language, Kakwa, and local people's knowledge of Arabic was very patchy. Most men spoke a broken form of the language but hardly any women spoke it at all. I did not want to prejudice our chances of acceptance because of linguistic misunderstandings. The teacher agreed readily enough and we cycled the five miles to Yosepa's compound together. We were lucky to find both him and Onesimo at home. They were the senior family members of the group which we wanted to join.

The English word village gives a quite wrong impression of the social arrangements in Equatoria. A small extended family group would build huts near to each other which would be surrounded by their farm fields. They had to live right next to their crops to defend them from the constant threat of wild animals. In consequence no group could be very large and there were considerable distances between the members of a community which was then described by outside observers as a village. We were greeted courteously by the two men who were soon joined by a group of inquisitive children. They had seen me as I had been cycling around the countryside in recent months and although I had not spoken to them we were not complete strangers. We circled around the main subject of my visit for some time so as to get a better feel for each other, but finally the reason for my coming had to be broached. I had thought of how best to put it to them and in a mixture of my Arabic and the teacher's Kakwa I made my point. 'I have been teaching farming at the Veeteeseesee'(as the training centre was called) 'but I find that I really do not know enough about farming in this area to be a really good teacher. I am wondering if I could come and live in your community for some time and whether you would be willing to teach me how to farm here'.

This came as a real shock. They had encountered very few white men in their lives but those they had met had always come to tell them what to do. Sometimes it concerned the rules about controlling sleeping sickness, at others to threaten them over the non-payment of their hut tax dues (shades of rates in England, but with far fewer benefits to show for the payment) and occasionally an order to send their children to school. For a white man to come and ask to be taught was a very different matter and the idea was treated with an understandable suspicion as to what my real motives might be. The lengthy conversation in Kakwa which followed went over my head but eventually Filipo said that they had agreed that I could build my hut in their area and that they would help me with my farm. It was now after mid-day and they said that it was too hot to start looking for a site now but that they would wait for me on the following morning.

Dawn had a semblance of coolness as the temperature dropped to thirty degrees for a short while and I took advantage of it to cycle out to Yosepa's. I was welcomed and we set out with his uncle, Aligo, and an older relation Ramadala plus the usual train of children. 'Onesimo and I have thought about what you want and we know a place which has good soil, a clean spring, a small stream and is not too far from the Kaya river. It is a little way from here but is still part of our community.'

We followed an animal track through the dense bush and came to the stream with quite a wide area of marshy land on each side. We walked on a couple of hundred yards and they said, 'this is where we suggest. It is far enough from the swamp to stop you being too pestered by mosquitoes.'

With dense bush on all sides it was not easy to get any real idea of how suitable the area was, but I was now embarking on a course in which I assumed that local people knew better than me, and so I thanked them for the trouble that they had taken and said that it would do very nicely. 'When do you want to start work?' they asked.

'To-morrow,' I replied. They were a bit taken aback and enquired as to who would help me to build. I said that I had nobody else in mind but members of their family and that as I was a stranger I would be happy to reward them for their help. I also asked if there was a hut in which I could sleep in their compound so as to save me cycling thirty-two miles every day from Yei and back and whether I could eat with them. Again there was some surprise but they said that they were sure that something could be arranged. We walked back to where my bicycle had been left and I followed the narrow path for a couple of miles from their home until I reached the small dirt road to Yei.

Anne was anxiously awaiting my news. I could not offer any glowing accounts of fine views or an open grassy field on which we could build, but I could assure her that there would be plenty of water near at hand and that the soil looked good. 'There's quite a bit of clearing to be done before we can even see where the huts will go, but the families say that they will help me. I think that it is too soon for you to come out to see now. Let's get some work started and then you will have a better idea of what your new home is going to be like. I will spend the weekdays out at the site now and come back here for the weekends. You've got the Parrys back so you will be alright by yourself here, and I know that they will keep you busy with teaching now that the students are back.'

I set off the next morning with a heavily loaded bicycle. I had a few clothes, a towel and some basic medicines wrapped in my sleeping mat, a large cross-cut saw, four axes and a panga (the razor sharp two-foot long heavy knife which was the fundamental tool of the Southern Sudan). In my pocket were the water sterilization tablets which were going to be essential if I was to stay healthy.

The journey took a good deal longer than the previous day and the group that was waiting for me were obviously not too happy that we should be starting work when the sun was so high in the sky. In that climate most people managed to do more work in the three hours after dawn than in the whole rest of the day. Once at the site we had to decide which of the larger trees would have to be cut down and we reckoned that we only needed to cut four of them. Three of us started on the trees while the others tackled the tall tangle of grass and shrubby growth that covered the area. They were wonderfully skilled in the use of the pangas and it seemed no time before we had a small clearing. By the end of the morning we had one tree down and cut up into manageable pieces and a thirty-yard square of cleared land. I had not done any sustained heavy manual labour since coming to the Sudan and I was exhausted and hungry. At Yosepa's compound I was shown a small empty hut that I could use and I tentatively enquired where we might be eating lunch. The question was obviously not understood and I tried a variation of Arabic words. At last I got my point across and was duly informed that no such meal existed in the rural areas but that we would be eating when the sun went down. I lay down hungry and tired and realized that I had a lot to learn. As I lay there dozing I found that the dominant sound that was coming to me from my neighbours was laughter. This was the sound that was to fill our days for years to come.

A couple of days later we had cleared an area which Yosepa thought should be big enough for our basic compound. 'How many huts do you want?' he asked.

'Three,' I replied, 'one to sleep in, a bit bigger one to sit and eat in and a smaller one in which to cook. Oh and we will want a small house for our poultry.'

'Chickens don't live in houses' said Yosepa. 'We make a large, strong basket and put it on a tall pole and that's where they sleep, safe from wild animals.'

I agreed that this was an excellent plan. 'But we have ducks as well as chickens and they cannot fly up to a tall roost, so we will have to have a little house for them.'

'We're going to have to put the timbers in the wall touching each other then,' said Yosepa, 'otherwise a leopard will get a paw in and kill them.' He walked over to a nearby bush, cut off a branch with a stroke of his panga and then with his teeth stripped the bark off each side of it. He tied the two pieces together and had a six-foot length of strong 'string'. 'Cut me a couple of pegs please Onesimo,' he said. This was quickly done and Yosepa turned to me. 'Where do you want your sleeping hut?' he asked. I had given some thought to the pattern of our new home so led him to the site. Onesimo drove one of the pegs into the ground, Yosepa looped his string around it

*Hard slog as we cut and carried timbers.*

and with the other sharpened peg drew a circle about twelve feet across. So, in a couple of minutes, was the plan of our bedroom laid out. Aligo and Ramadala went and fetched two very heavy spears that I had seen them carrying in the morning and started to dig holes about a foot apart around the outside of the circle. 'Come on, now the hard work begins, we've got to find straight young trees the size we want with a fork of branches where we want it.' The three of us set off into the surrounding forest, which was dominated by a tree called loso in Kakwa. It was very slow growing and had wood of such density that it was impossible to drive a nail into it without first making a hole with a drill which itself became almost red hot in the process. We located three trees and chopped them down, trimmed off the branches and carried them back to the building site. They were far heavier than I had expected and I had a struggle to keep up with the others. 'Right,' said Yosepa, 'where do you want your door and how high do you want the walls?'

Once again I had given thought to this issue and so could reply straight away. The poles were cut to length and put into the appropriate holes. It was an exciting moment as suddenly the building came to life. The following days were a hard slog as we cut and carried timbers and filled in one hut outline after another. Finally the job was done and we went down

*Reeds tied at nine inch intervals.*

to the Kaya river to cut bundles of reed stems almost an inch thick. These were to be tied at nine-inch intervals around the timbers to provide a solid framework on to which the mud could be thrown. I was told which shrubs had the best bark for making the string that was needed to tie on the reeds and learned how to strip it off the stem. The next stage was the roof, and at least this was not such heavy work as the roof poles were much thinner than the wall timbers. They were fixed on to the wall with bark string and once again reeds were tied around them to make a solid framework on to which to put the thatch. Now they really did look like huts.

The following morning we were joined by a party of young women and girls who had come to cut the grass for thatching the huts. We were surrounded by six- to seven-foot tall grass, the stems of which had ripened and dried at that time of the year, so that it was only a short while before the bundles of grass started to pile up near to the frames of the huts. Yosepa and Onesimo went in search of the strongest and most pliable bark with which to tie the grass in place, and an hour later I started to thatch our bedroom. At least this was a skill that I did not have to learn because I had been taught years before at Chavenage. Ramadala began work on our living room and three days later all our huts were thatched. All that remained was to mud the walls. Once again this involved four young women who came to carry the water from the stream. The mud was to be made from the soil of a termite mound. These tiny creatures built homes between six and eight feet tall and ten feet wide at regular intervals across the countryside. They brought red clay up from deep down in the ground, which made excellent building material. There was such a mound within twenty yards of the hut site and this was attacked by the men, who started to break it up with their hoes. The women poured water on to the lumps of hard clay, until by the end of the morning we had a tall heap of wet clay lumps which were then covered thickly with grass to cut down on evaporation and left to 'mature' until the next day.

The procession which went down to the building site the next morning was much noisier than usual. The men were joined by about eight girls and a gang of small boys so that there was a great deal of banter and laughter along the way. Once we had arrived the grass was removed from the clay and more water was poured on. Then the fun began. We climbed on top of the heap of wet clay and started stamping it with our feet to work out the lumps. The children all dived in and started to sing so that we all stamped in time. The clay had softened overnight and with added water we soon started to develop a thick smooth paste. Every now and again a small boy would sink too deeply into the mix and have to be pulled out before he could start stamping again in a shallower place. After an hour or so Yosepa reckoned that we had enough mud ready for some of the girls to start packing it into the frame of the walls. The bigger boys were detailed off to start forming large balls of mud to carry over to the girls who were working on the huts whilst the older women went on carrying water and the rest of us stamped. The mud was first pressed in between the timbers and when an area of wall had been finished the girl would sit back on her haunches and throw mud at the wall to provide an outer covering. So were our ancestors' wattle and daub houses built a thousand years ago, but I am doubtful as to whether the work was turned into such a noisy or joyous party as I experienced in the Southern Sudan. At the end of the morning everyone went down to the stream to wash. The boys had worked naked and soon had the mud washed off, and the girls were dressed in their normal bunch of leaves fore and aft so they simply had to pull some clean leaves from a bush after they had bathed, tuck them into the strip of bark around their waists and they were clean and changed.

That afternoon I cycled back to Yei and returned the next day with Anne so that she could enjoy watching the fun and also see her new home nearing completion. It was difficult to know what she really thought of

*The girls started packing the mud into the frame.*

these three rather ragged looking huts, with the thatch not yet trimmed and mud still oozing out of the walls. It was a very far cry from the Queen Anne house which she had occupied for most of her life, but she made as many pleasant comments as she could think of under the circumstances. I did my stint of work stamping mud and then accompanied Anne back to Yei. We had dinner with the Parrys and I was able to give them an estimate of how soon we would want to move out to our new home. They were quite obviously disappointed that we were no longer going to be on the staff of the Centre but had realized that this was what we really wanted to do and accepted the situation graciously.

It only required a few more days to plaster the walls with a thin layer of mud to give them a smooth finish, to cut the bottom edge of the thatch to make it even and to smear the floors with a mixture of buffalo dung and black soil gathered from a quite different kind of termite mound and ground up on a normal grinding stone. The huts looked greatly improved. I searched around for six evenly matched stones to put in two groups of three in the kitchen to provide Anne with a place to rest her saucepans over a wood fire. I found a couple of flat stones almost two feet across which I put behind our sleeping hut and then made a grass screen round them to provide our bathroom. For many years to come we stood on the two stones

with a bucket of hot water between us and washed off the sweat of the day.
We soon got into the habit of singing together as we bathed and one of our
very infrequent English visitors was surprised to hear the alto and bass parts
of the madrigal 'The Silver Swan' emanating from behind our hut as the
sun went down over the Sudanese forest. My final job was to cut a few
bundles of grass and lay them out on the sleeping hut floor to dry so as to
provide us with a mattress when we arrived. I am sure that we were
thought to be very soft to require such padding. All the local people lay
their sleeping mats directly on the hard, beaten earth floor of their huts. All
was now ready for the move.

'I've put together a good quantity of dry food from our last harvest,' said
Anne. 'There's a sack of sorghum, some millet, half a sack of green gram
and about the same amount of cowpeas as well as about thirty pounds of
sesame. I have split the sorghum into two bags to make it easier for
carrying. I just hope that we can find some green leaves and fresh fruit in
the village until our own garden starts producing. My main concern is the
poultry. How are we going to move them?'

'I am going to buy some large baskets in the market to-morrow and then
cover them over with sacks and tie them on. The baskets have an open
enough weave. I will get a small one for the cat. My real problem is the
bees.'

I had made myself four bee-hives, burned wax on the outside of them
and put them in the bush near to our house when the wild bees were
swarming. All had been occupied and I now had four strong colonies of
extremely fierce African bees. 'I think that I will have to plug the entrance
up with mud and then put the whole hive into one of those large hessian
sacks that they use for harvested cotton. The first thing that I have to do is
see if I can borrow the education department truck next Wednesday to get
our stuff as near as possible to Yosepa's. That should cut the carrying down
to five miles.'

The truck was borrowed, the poultry and cat had been imprisoned, with
a few stings and the help of one of the students I had been able to enclose
the hives, so our livestock were ready. Our personal luggage was not large.
Two sleeping mats, two folding chairs, two small crates with our clothes in
which then became our cupboards, some cups, plates and cooking utensils
and a carton of food for our immediate consumption, plus the sacks of
grain that Anne had saved. The lorry was not available until eleven in the
morning so that it was almost noon when we met up with Yosepa and a
crowd of his relations waiting to help us carry our goods the five miles to

our home. There was a lot of laughter and pushing and shoving as children tried to get the lightest loads but eventually a long procession started out. There was not only human noise, the cat, the poultry and the bees were all making their displeasure known in no uncertain terms and the only animal that was happy was our 'sort of' Labrador bitch, Lady, who was walking with us and thoroughly enjoying all the new smells. It was three o'clock before we had everything safely delivered and more or less sorted. We took the beehives to the four stands that I had made for them a couple of hundred yards away from our house. The stands were packed around with thorny branches to deter honey badgers, the scourge of local bee-keepers. I planned to slash the hessian away after dark and flick out the mud from the entrances.

A couple of girls had cut bundles of dry firewood as a gift for Anne and so she was able to start cooking our first meal in her new kitchen. The poultry were released into their new house but the cat remained firmly sealed in her basket in which she would spend the night in our sleeping hut to get her used to the sounds and smells of her new home. We stored our few belongings, I bunched up the grass on the floor to make a mattress and put the woven reed sleeping mats on top of it. 'I've got a petrol tin of hot water here, let's get the sweat off before we have our supper.' The bathing facilities proved adequate and we were soon sitting outside eating our first meal. The brilliant stars showing in the gap above us in the forest we were accustomed to, after a couple of years in Africa with no artificial lights to diminish the blackness of the sky. The sounds were less familiar. There was no sound of any human activity, as we were out of ear shot of Yosepa's compound. The multitude of insects we were also used to hearing, but now that we were really in the forest there were other animal sounds which we had not learned to identify: barks, grunts and squeaks, which kept Lady firmly glued to our sides.

After supper I told Anne that I would go and deal with the bees. I took our kerosene lamp and my panga and returned to the stands where the bees were still complaining loudly about their captivity. I slashed the hessian on all four hives and then went to each one to flick out the mud. The bees from the first hive were upon me well before I finished the fourth and grabbed my lamp and ran back to the huts. 'Well,' said Anne as she deftly removed the stings with a sharp knife, 'if the old wives tale is true then you should certainly never suffer from rheumatism from the number of stings you have got this evening'. A bit more of a wash and we turned into our bedroom with dog and cat and were soon fast asleep.

'What's that?' Anne grabbed my arm as we both leapt out of sleep to the sound of the most terrible human screams that either of us had ever heard. Somebody was being tortured in the most horrible fashion in the forest not so far from us. I lit the lamp, picked up my spear, ran outside and was faced with a wall of black forest with dense undergrowth of tall grass, in the face of which my little lamp made no impression. I felt completely helpless as the agonized screams continued. Eventually we returned to our bed wondering whatever we had walked into. Were these seemingly pleasant and friendly people actually practising ritual murder? Who were they torturing and why? Had we been hopelessly naïve to move into the midst of people whom Major al Bashir called savages? The screams eventually stopped but we got little sleep as we lay wondering whether this was in fact the end of our great experiment. At last the dawn came and we dragged ourselves unhappily outside. A bit later a smiling Yosepa and a couple of children came to greet us. We were reserved in our greeting and after a few minutes I enquired as to whether he had heard any screams in the night. He looked genuinely surprised and said he had heard nothing, so I could not press the matter further.

'Have you taken the sacks off your hives?' he asked. 'I am interested to see what they look like, because they are quite different to mine.' I was not in the mood for a social walk but went with him up to where the hives had been set. There was a scene of complete devastation. The hives were on the ground, the roofs had been ripped off and the frames of honeycomb were widely strewn. Angry bees were everywhere and we had to beat a hasty retreat.

'Chimpanzees' said Yosepa. 'They love honey, and you were unlucky that they found your hives so quickly. The thorns would not have stopped them and when you start again you will have to put a lot more protection.'

I was sad at losing my hives but profoundly relieved that it was the screams of chimpanzees inflicting pain on themselves and not a tortured human being which had given us such a dreadful first night in the forest, and that our neighbours were not savages practising human sacrifice, but were in fact the pleasant friendly people whom we had taken them to be. Many months later when we spoke the local language reasonably well and had made genuine friends of our neighbours we told them of our fears on that first night in their midst and caused great hilarity.

CHAPTER 6

# Village Life

COMMENTS ABOUT our move by friends and acquaintances ranged from 'throwing their lives away' or 'they will be driven out by loneliness in six months', to 'no white person can survive in this climate in a tiny mud hut attempting to live on native food'. The general opinion was that we would either quickly come to our senses and move back into the main-stream of life or be invalided out of Africa for good. Underlying all of these comments was the horror that existed in colonial circles fifty years ago of a white person 'going native'. In addition there was the serious problem of pigeonholing. 'Lecturer in agriculture at a teacher training college' is readily classified; 'white Southern Sudanese peasant farmer' is a lot more difficult.

So, what was life like in our new setting? How did we survive? On our very first night Anne had said, 'how cool it is in here. I am going to need some kind of covering in the night, I am sure'. Our house in Yei had walls nine feet tall with only a foot of roof overhang. All day long the sun beat on those walls and they stored the heat most effectively and pumped it out through the night so that any kind of bed covering was unbearable. In our new hut only three feet of wall were exposed beneath the overhang of the thatch, and so it only got warmed by the sun at dawn and dusk, which had little impact. In Yei the wall had met the roof, but now we had a nine-inch gap between wall and roof which encouraged a circulation of air. These factors were typical of all local huts but we had broken with tradition and had a large 'window' on either side of our bed. This had no glass but only stout timber bars to keep out leopards. There was, therefore, a steady flow of air across us all through the night. I imagine that we had the coolest bedroom in the Southern Sudan. Over time we were able to get a skilled local man to shape timbers with an adze and construct a bed frame with no nails but cleverly fashioned joints. This was strung with thongs of antelope hide and made the most comfortable of beds. The combination of coolness and comfort meant that we slept far better than we had done since we arrived in the Sudan.

In an extremely hot climate coolness is such a boon and simple thatched mud huts with proper ventilation offer just that. Almost twenty years after

*We had the coolest bedroom in the Southern Sudan.*

our move to the village I was head of the Ministry of Agriculture's crop section in the Southern Sudan. No houses were available because there had been so much destruction during the civil war. I therefore built a group of mud and wattle huts for our family. The only differences to our original ones were cement floors and a much larger sitting hut because we had many visitors. Other senior civil servants were critical of our living arrangements as detracting from the dignity of my position as their head. I was not worried by this but did not have to suffer the sniping for too long. President Nimeiri, the head of the whole country, came to stay with us as he inspected the agricultural developments for which I was responsible. He wore full army uniform and at the end of a long morning in the field was sweating profusely. He walked into our cool airy mud and wattle house, threw his arms out and said to the assembled dignitaries, 'Anybody want to buy a palace in Khartoum?' To any further criticism of our housing I was able to respond that 'What is good enough for the president of the republic is good enough for me.' Our housing was not therefore proving the threat to our health that our friends had feared.

And what about the hazard of living on native food? The concerns about our diet highlight the enormous shift in attitudes to diet that have taken place in Britain over the past half century. Our diet consisted of whole grains, legumes, lots of vegetables and fruit and some eggs and insects for animal protein. With virtually no animal fats or oil. There we were, eating what enlightened modern doctors would consider a really healthy diet but one which was deemed totally inadequate by our friends at that time. We found ourselves becoming increasingly healthy with a combination of plenty of physical work, sound sleep and an excellent diet and were a bitter disappointment to those who were waiting for us to fade away.

Loneliness is not really a concept which most African villagers can grasp. One is surrounded by people all day long. Houses are essentially for sleeping in or taking shelter from the rain, and life is lived outside where there is always someone to talk to or a child to sit on one's knee for a game or a chat. Our lives quickly fell into this same public pattern and it was really only in bed at night that we had any privacy. We had no children of our own at that time and so two boys of about twelve years old, Gaga and Abugo, were attached to us. They helped Anne with household chores, we built them a separate hut and they became part of our family, pushing loneliness yet further away. Watching my elderly neighbours in Malawi to-day as they sit outside their huts chatting to passers-by all day long I feel so sad for their counterparts in the Western world sitting by themselves hour after hour in a house or flat with all sorts of conveniences but burdened with a loneliness that my poverty stricken neighbours will never experience.

'Throwing your lives away' was a tougher challenge. Qualified agriculturalists were in short supply in the Southern Sudan and so were qualified teachers of teachers. Instead of putting our qualifications to the service of a large number of people we were simply living out our lives in one small community. We came under a lot of pressure from good friends to take up senior posts that were becoming vacant in different parts of Africa, and we were grateful for their concern. We remained convinced however that there was too much ignorance of what really made small scale African farmers tick which was distorting policies and leading to major failures across the continent. We felt that we should grasp the opportunity to get much closer to finding the reasons for the decisions which farmers made which often baffled agricultural staff. Many years later London University paid me the great honour of electing me as an honorary life fellow. The basis of my election was my 'unparalleled knowledge of smallholder agriculture in Africa', and it was that knowledge which led to the offers of senior national and international posts which came to me later in life. It was the teaching of my Sudanese friends in those 'thrown away' years which was the basis of that later situation, and we have never had regrets about staying with the decision that we made to become white peasant farmers.

Life in an African village is so far removed from life in Europe today that it is difficult to know what aspects to highlight to illustrate those differences. Anne's response is just how much work is involved. 'Take breakfast' she says. 'We have sorghum and sesame porridge and some pawpaw. What do we have to do? Grow the sorghum, harvest the heads, dry them in the sun on mats, thrash them on a beaten earth thrashing floor where the grain gets mixed with sand, so then it has to be washed and re-dried. Then it has to be ground to coarse flour. All the same activities are required for the sesame but that also has to be ground to a fine paste. Walk to the spring and carry back the water. Go into the forest and collect some firewood and kindling. Make a fire, boil the water and cook the porridge. And in England I would take out the packet of oats, fill the saucepan from the tap and put it on the electric cooker.' Every aspect of life just demands so much more effort in order to survive.

I would perhaps focus on the social cohesion which is so vital to survival. We lived to all intents and purposes outside the range of formal government. There were no police, no social services, no organized social support system of any kind. Under these circumstances human bonding becomes extremely important. It manifests itself in many different ways, from the communal handling of potential points of friction between families, to the great importance attached to visiting anyone within one's social sphere who is sick or in trouble, however much time and effort that may involve. Attendance at funerals to help the bereaved and provide a suitable farewell to the departed is also given high priority as a means of fostering stronger social bonds. A few months ago an elderly man died in our community here in Malawi. He was disabled and moved into this area some years ago. Because of his disability he had not been able to marry or have children so had no living relatives in the community. He had been able to do odd jobs to help him survive for a number of years but as he grew older he became totally dependent upon us for his daily needs. He was therefore undoubtedly the least privileged member of our community. When he died I purchased a coffin and four young men dug a grave for him in the local graveyard. I had hoped that perhaps a dozen kindly people might turn up to bid the poor old man farewell. In the event 85 people came to the funeral and a group of young people took the afternoon off to provide a choir for what turned into a most moving occasion. Not a single person there was related to the old man nor were any in his debt, but he had lived in their community and so must be sent on his way with dignity. This took place in the same month in 2003 when a number of elderly people in Paris died of heat stroke. Many were not found for some days and even after their bodies had been discovered nobody came forward to bury them and the task finally fell to an embarrassed government.

Bonding starts at an early age and foreign visitors to our village here have been surprised to see groups of ten or twelve children moving round together ranging in age from three months to twelve years with the older children helping, encouraging and playing with the younger. I am surprised at their surprise because this is how I have always seen children behave and find it difficult to accept that older children in a developed society do not expect to spend their days taking responsibility for their younger siblings and neighbours. In the Southern Sudan the children had no clothes, toys or possessions and this greatly reduced possible points of friction and consequently quarrelling and crying were very rare. Very few children walked the twelve mile return journey to Payawa school and so most spent part of their days helping with household and garden chores. When these were finished they moved around together singing, drumming and dancing or foraging in the forest for fruits and edible insects. Any treasure that was found was immediately shared and any attempt to keep a 'find' for oneself would have been rebuked. All my memories of those years are filled with pictures of laughing, singing, affectionate children who added great joy to our lives. One of their big advantages was their freedom from fear. It never crossed their minds that an adult would want to harm or wrong them. Wherever they went somebody would keep a watchful eye on them to see that they did not come to any harm. The children who surround me to-day have just the same trustful attitude as they run up to hold my hand, ask to be swung in the air or pile into the back of my pick-up truck to be taken for a ride.

This bonding and confidence is built up early in life as children are strapped on to the back of whoever is free to carry them around at that time. It was vividly illustrated to us when we first arrived in Yei. Every three months there was a parish communion held in the large church to which hundreds of people came from miles around. As each woman went up to take communion she handed her baby or toddler to the nearest neighbour who had already gone forward. Most of the recipients of these children were complete strangers and yet, with perhaps a hundred such exchanges taking place, there was barely ever a cry as babies settled confidently into the arms of a woman they had never seen before. Just imagine a similar situation in an English church!

What about conflicts? We were fortunate in our village of Undukori that we did not have any serious conflicts, but obviously differences took place from time to time that had to be sorted out by the community. I will use just one such case as an illustration of the skills that people develop who just have to learn to live together amicably.

'Setepano (my name locally), Setepano, I have wonderful news'. It was Maria the wife of Cornelio who came running up to me, her face wreathed in smiles. 'You know that we all agreed to dig latrine pits to help to keep the village clean? Well Cornelio finished his last night and this morning there was lots of clean water in it. Now we have a well just outside our house. I have been to tell all my neighbours that none of us will now have to walk to the stream for water. Isn't it a wonderful gift!'

Maria lived much further away from the stream than we did and so this was a real boon to her and her neighbours and we were delighted at their good fortune. A couple of hours later a very different Maria appeared at our house with her cheeks streaked in tears. 'Cornelio says that he dug that pit for a latrine and that is what it is going to be, and we will just have to go on walking to the stream for water. It's not just me. I told all my friends that they could use it and now I am so ashamed. Please Setepano go and talk to him.'

I walked the half mile to Cornelio's house, saw the pit and looked down to see about four feet of crystal clear water in the bottom. Feigning surprise I congratulated Cornelio for having discovered a well so near to his house. 'That's not a well,' he said. 'We all agreed to dig a latrine pit and that is mine, and I am not now going to start digging all over again'. I tried a bit of arguing with him about what a help it would be to his wife and their neighbours but he was having none of it. 'She's always walked to the stream in the past and she can go on doing so.' And that was the end of the conversation.

I went down, dispiritedly, to see Enosa, a wise and mature member of our church. I explained the situation to him and asked what he thought we might do. 'What's the time?' he asked.

'About two o'clock.'

'Right, leave this to me and be prepared to attend a service of thanks-giving at Cornelio's house at five o'clock this evening, I will go round and collect some other Christians.'

At five o'clock we wound along the path to Cornelio's house singing a hymn. Cornelio came out looking puzzled but started to look angry when Enosa explained that we had all come to give thanks to God for the

*Yosepa and Onesimo were skilled sawyers.*

discovery of the well and to bless it for the use of all the people in his area. Cornelio looked like thunder as we sang another hymn and Enosa led us in prayers. When the little service was over Enosa turned to his congregation and said 'Now we all know that Cornelio put in a great deal of work into digging that deep hole and it is going to be a benefit to a lot of people, so to-morrow morning I want all of you to come up here with tools and we will help Cornelio to dig his latrine on the other side of his compound'. Cornelio broke into a smile, Maria and her neighbours all started singing and clapping and a potentially divisive situation had been settled with insight and diplomacy. Nobody had been embarrassed and a possible longterm source of unhappiness was eliminated.

Our own lives became steadily more comfortable as we made use of local people's skills to add to our basic huts. Yosepa and Onesimo were skilled pit sawyers and could turn out almost perfect planks from a tree trunk, squared with an adze and then placed over a pit with one sawyer on top and one in the pit underneath. They supplied the planks with which all the doors in the village, including ours, were made. Now I asked them to cut some planks from which I could make a table and two benches so that we could eat at a proper table. When that was done we had two simple chairs made by the man who had carved our bed and we once more added to our comfort. A friend came across a pamphlet from India describing how to make a 'smokeless stove' out of clay. We found the heaviest clay that we could, followed the instructions meticulously and a few weeks later when the structure had dried Anne had a long clay tunnel with three holes on top and a clay chimney outside on which she could cook. It worked perfectly, used much less firewood, and the smoke really did go up the chimney. Out went the six stones and she was freed from the hot smoky atmosphere which is the bane of millions of rural women around the world who still cook on open fires in a small hut with no chimney.

And so we started to really settle into village life with its burden of seemingly endless chores but with all the compensations of friendly neighbours, laughing children and a tight knit and supportive community.

CHAPTER 7

# In the Sweat of Thy Brow

'IN THE SWEAT of thy brow shalt thou eat bread' says the book of Genesis in the Bible. None of us ate bread at Undukori but we certainly had to sweat to grow the sorghum, millet, cowpeas, groundnuts, cassava and sweet potatoes on which we lived. We had come to this village to learn and practise local people's methods of farming and so we were going to have to join in the sweating. There were three features of local farms that grated on Western agriculturalists and which they had spent years trying to change. The first was the untidiness of the fields. They had no defined straight edges but rather boundaries which seemed to meander aimlessly. 'Why are your fields so irregularly shaped?' I asked Aligo one day when we were working together. He did not understand the question. 'Why don't you make the sides straight, it would make the farm look much tidier?'.

'How much extra food would that produce?' came the rejoinder. 'When we clear new land several of us usually join together to share the work and we take on different parts of the field. When we get tired or it starts raining we stop work and that's the shape of the field. What good would it do to come back and straighten all the sides?' I had to confess that I did not have a logical answer, and I did not think that Aligo would have been impressed by the suggestion that it would make an agricultural graduate happier.

The second concern was with deep digging. Ploughing and double spit digging had been the sacred basis of English farming and gardening for many years. It had been the mission of many agriculturalists in Africa to convert these 'ignorant natives' from scratching at the surface of the soil to get them to dig deeply. At the teacher training centre we had done just that. Now I was surrounded by people who 'scratched at the surface'. Without turning this into a text book I would like to describe a little of how people farmed.

The process started at the beginning of the dry season in December when the seven-foot tall grass had matured and dried. People went to the site which they planned to farm in the following year and set fire to the grass. No attempt was made to control the fire which might then rage across the countryside for a day or two until it reached a river or swamp. The forest had been burned like this for millennia and so all the trees in it were fire tolerant and were not killed by what looked like a raging inferno. The next job was to cut down all the small trees and bushes and pile them around the base of the large trees. A few weeks later the wood was dry enough to burn and the resulting ring barking killed the large trees. A shudder goes down the back of conservationist readers, but this practice had been going on for hundreds of years with no adverse impact on the environment because the human population was so tiny in relation to the size of the forest. The land would be abandoned at the end of four years and the forest would re-establish itself once more. No further work was done until the rains started in late March. In a very short time the large isolated clumps of grass would re-sprout and produce a couple of feet of growth. It was then that the so-called scratching started. I joined a group of men in their field in our first year on the understanding that they would then come and help us with ours. I started to swing my hoe up in the air to dig the land but was soon stopped. 'What on earth do you think you are doing?' asked Eliabu. 'That is not the way to prepare a field, just slide your hoe under a grass clump to cut its roots and let it fall over. Don't start digging the whole field.'

'But if there is no cultivated land where are we going to sow the seeds?' I asked.

'Through the dead grass stems of course,' came the reply.

'Are we going to leave all these dried grass stems on the field?'

'Where else? If we took them off the rain would wash the small seeds away and it would pound the soil as hard as a dancing yard,' said Eliabu.

Of course that is just what had happened on our so called demonstration farm, and the students had to return repeatedly to the fields to break the surface pan with their hoes. Because their plots had been small this had not been too serious but it was obviously not practicable for a family with a couple of acres to manage by themselves. Fifteen years later Western agriculturalists 'discovered' so called stubble farming in which the land is not ploughed and the seeds are sown in the trash left by the previous crop so as to protect the soil. This is now used on tens of millions of acres on some of the most advanced farms in the world. So were our neighbours vindicated in their despised scratching at the surface.

The third criticism was of the 'jumble' of crops which were grown together rather than having different crops and different varieties in separate plots. Once our field was ready for planting I was given a large dry

*Knocking the soil off the dead grass ready for sowing the seeds.*

gourd full of a mixture of sorghum, a half a dozen different finger millet varieties, sesame and hyptis (an aromatic seed smaller than sesame used for flavouring). 'Right,' said Yosepa who was offering me the seed. 'You know how to broadcast seed evenly, don't you?'

Luckily I had acquired that skill in the Clee hills where the farm owned no seed drill and all the fields were planted by broadcasting the seed by hand. 'Yes I do' I replied.

'Right, but be careful because all these seeds are different sizes and it is not so easy to spread them evenly. Do you mind if I give you a demonstration?'

'Go ahead' I responded, but thought that in fact here was something about which I did not need a lesson. I soon found that I was wrong. Instead of scattering the seeds with a swinging motion of the hand, as in the biblical pictures which illustrate the parable of the sower, Yosepa threw the seeds hard at the side of the gourd and let them bounce off with some force on to the ground. I quickly realized that if I had used my method then seeds of different weights would have fallen together in clumps. Because Yosepa was shooting them on to the ground the mixture did not separate out. It took me a little while to get the knack of this method of sowing and our field looked a good deal more uneven than our neighbours in the first year, but I steadily improved and did not have to suffer that embarrassment in subsequent years.

But why the mixture? To begin with the four different crops matured at different times with the earliest taking four months and the longest eleven. As one crop matured and was harvested the next could take over some of the space that it had occupied, so that one lot of clearing and cultivation produced four crops and saved a lot of labour. Secondly there was the issue of security. We lived in an almost cashless society in which it was not possible to simply go to a shop or market and buy food if your own crops failed. With a mixture of crops it was extremely unlikely that all of them would be affected by a pest or disease, so that if one got damaged there were still three others to make use of the work that had been invested in the field. Finally, it meant that that the soil was protected by growing crops from the lashing of tropical rain throughout the whole of the year. It must have been at least ten years later, when living in a more sophisticated society, that I read a half page article in a major English newspaper describing an international conference at which papers were presented hailing the 'discovery' of the benefits of mixed cropping under tropical conditions. How fortunate that African farmers had ignored the advice of generations of agricultural offices decrying their 'jumble' of crops.

Despite all my good intentions I could not resist applying some of my basic farming instincts to my new situation. When our first crop of finger millet matured I soon saw that one variety had far larger heads and seeds than any of the others. I carefully selected the best heads and stored them as my seed for the following season. When the time came to plant I just sowed 'my' variety of finger millet. It did extremely well and I obtained a higher yield than any of my neighbours and felt rather pleased with myself. Once again I carefully selected seed and sowed just the one variety. The pattern of rainfall that year was quite different to the previous one and 'my' variety hardly produced any crop at all whilst my friends with their mixture of at least half a dozen different varieties obtained their usual yield. One more lesson firmly learned.

I mentioned earlier in this chapter the 'arrival' of the rains. That was not an entirely accurate statement. At Undukori we did not only have to make any material goods that we wanted, we also had to make the rain. While this was the primary responsibility of the rainmaker, we all played a part. There is a tendency to snigger when we speak of the rainmaker, but he was not only by far the most important member of the community in terms of prestige, but also in relation to our survival. He lived about seven miles from our home at the foot of the only significant hill in the area. It was called Mugwer and covered about ten square miles rising to 800 feet above the otherwise gently undulating plain. In Kakwa the rainmaker was called the 'monye mere' the father of the mountain, and he kept himself fairly aloof from the rest of us as befitted so important a man. 'What does he actually do?' I had asked when we moved into the area.

'He makes the rain of course' came the immediate reply.

'Well then how does he actually do it?'.

'Oh he guards the mountain to ensure that no fire touches it all through the dry season, and then he throws four knuckle bones from an antelope on the ground and from those he can tell when we should burn the mountain and make the rain'. Mumbo jumbo I thought, but realized that this was a subject on which any negative comment would not be welcomed.

We suffered through our first late dry season in the forest where no breath of air seemed to move and the heat became more and more oppressive. I had noticed that whereas all the rest of the countryside had been blackened by fire Mugwer was covered in dense high grass. At last a few fluffy white clouds started appearing and these soon became larger and darker as they skudded across the sky driven by the searing hot air rising from the blackened countryside. We were not the only ones suffering from the oppressive heat, and even the children mostly just sat around talking quietly. 'He has started throwing the bones' Yosepa told me a few days later, 'the time must be getting near.' By now the clouds had built up into tall black pillars but they were still speeding by and showing no signs of dropping any rain. It was the very next day that Yosepa came running to my house. 'The bones have fallen the right way!' he said. 'To-morrow we make the rain. I will come and fetch you early in the morning and sharpen your spear this evening.'

The following morning I joined with my neighbours to walk to Mugwer and we soon began to meet with streams of other men and boys all heading in the same direction. We finally reached the rainmaker's compound and found about 150 people gathered there from miles around. All were armed with spears and bows and arrows. We were divided into groups and sent off around the foot of the hill. The great majority of us formed a thin line along the leeward side of the hill while the rainmaker and a number of senior men went to the windward side. It was mid-day before we were all in position and by this time the heat was almost unbearable and there were huge black clouds overhead. 'It's going up!' somebody shouted and soon there was a roar of voices along the whole line of men as a great column of smoke started to rise from the other side of the hill. Our voices were soon drowned by the roar of the biggest fire I had ever seen in my life as the huge accumulation of tinder dry vegetation caught light. Because of the shelter and food which the hill offered, hundreds of animals spent the dry season on the hill. Now they were bolting in front of the flames and had to run the gauntlet of a line of spears and arrows. Men and boys were shouting, whooping and jabbing spears as the animals burst past them. The great majority of the animals escaped but there were a number which were killed, mostly small antelope of one kind or another. But while this was going on a vast pall of fire and smoke was rising into the sky, which was visible for miles around. It met the great clouds overhead, drove them up into the colder air at higher altitudes and seeded them with billions of smoke particles. A half an hour later the rain came down. The rainmaker had done his job well. He was rewarded with the front right leg of every animal that had been killed. The rest of the meat was divided up equally between everybody that had participated, whether or not they had killed an animal themselves. The successful hunters kept the hides of the animals, which they would use for the pouches in which babies were carried on their mothers' backs and for the seat of a chair for the head of the household. That night we all feasted on almost the only meat that we ate throughout the whole year.

Today I find it difficult to imagine how I participated in such a hunt, but that is because of the enormous change that has taken place in the relationship between man and animals in Africa over the past fifty years. We were a tiny group of humans hemmed in on every side by thousands of wild animals that threatened us, our livestock and our crops, and against which we had to defend ourselves with spears and bows and arrows. The local population made no more inroads on wildlife numbers when we lived at Undukori than they had done for the previous thousand years. It was the coming of civil war and the arrival of thousands of automatic firearms that totally changed that situation in the 1960s.

Within days of the first rain falling the whole countryside became bright green, the oppressive heat vanished and life became enjoyable once more. The rainmaker only failed once in the eight years that we lived in the district. One year he got it wrong and ordered the fire a bit too early when the clouds were not pregnant enough. It did not start raining for another month and we not only had to put up with an extra month of discomfort but were late in planting our crops. The rainmaker disappeared. He knew that he had lost prestige, but was equally aware that he faced a serious beating if he were found. A couple of weeks after he left I was asked to help a group of men felling and pulling a couple of large tree trunks across the Kaya river to replace a footbridge that had been swept away in a storm. As we heaved the trunks through the bush with thick ropes woven from bark, I realized that we were singing a new 'pulling' song. 'People have searched everywhere, BURILIWA, where has the father of the mountain gone?' The BURILIWA was meaningless but it was the signal for a combined heave. The whole song had an excellent balance about it and we were still using it three or four years after the event which it recorded. When the harvest was almost ready, after what fortunately turned out to be a good rainy season, the rainmaker crept quietly back from his exile. There was no possible way that I could probe him about his knowledge. His status depended upon the mystery of his methods, of which the throwing of the bones was the most important. How he actually judged when the clouds were ripe and whether he had any understanding of why a smoky inferno could precipitate rain I never found out.

We did have one source of food which did not require sweat and involved fun. This was the rising of the winged stage of the termites living in the great mounds which studded the countryside. They came out after the third or fourth heavy rain of the season, but it was tricky to judge when they would emerge because it depended on the actual intensity of the rainfall. As the time drew near, excitement mounted in the village. Families were allocated individual heaps according to family size, and Anne and I were given two. Days before the expected event the heap was cleared of all vegetation and a hole a bit bigger than a bucket was dug in the ground at the foot of the heap. Girls went to the swamps and selected the tall stems of a particular reed and these were bound into tight bundles to make 'torches'. Then everybody waited for the next rain.

'We think that it is going to be to-night' said Enosa as he came to tell us to get ready. 'Have you dug your holes and made your torches? And be sure to have some burning embers ready to take with you.' We said that we would and felt slightly guilty that we planned to 'cheat'. We possessed four modern items which we were going to use to help us. These were a couple of old empty kerosene tins, a box of matches, an alarm clock and a kerosene lamp. To everybody's surprise we went to bed at our usual time on the crucial night instead of going out to our heap to wait for the rise in the early hours of the morning. Nobody could see where our 'torches' were and it was assumed that we did not intend taking part in one of the great treat events of the year. Our neighbours slept so soundly that they dare not go to bed for fear of oversleeping and were not aware of the existence of a machine that could wake one up at a specific time. At two o'clock our alarm did not fail us. We lit our lamp and took our kerosene tins and fitted them into the holes that we had dug. It was a magical night. We were in the forest at a time when we had never been out before with all the insect and animal sounds that it produced, but all around us we could hear children calling to each other as they kept watch one by one at their allocated heaps. There was a lower hum of adult voices and pinpoints of light that we could see from the nearest fires that were kept alight in order to ignite the 'torches' when the critical moment arrived.

We went round our two heaps (castles of clay they have been called) which were about twenty yards apart. We peered down all the holes with which they were studded but could see no sign of life, and wondered whether this was not going to be the right night. Suddenly a young girl started calling out at the top of her voice 'Mine have started, mine have started.' If one heap was going to rise the rest were likely to follow and, sure enough, another voice soon let out a triumphant cry. We searched even harder for signs of life on our heap and then we saw heads starting to appear at the openings of a number of the shafts leading down into the heart of the heap. Soon the vanguard started to emerge, inch long insects with long silvery wings. There was no need to call because by this time 'torches' were being lit on every side as the rise had begun in earnest. The thin trickle of the vanguard got steadily thicker and then suddenly they were upon us. Thousands of 'flying ants' poured out from every side of the heap. It was like a snow storm, and they smothered our faces, tangled in our hair and covered our bodies. We held the lamp about two feet above our hole and the insects flocked to the light. They are poor fliers as they are only expected to travel short distances, so that having lost their upward impetus they fell below the lamp into the waiting kerosene tin. This took about ten minutes to fill and we dashed over to our second heap which was in full flight. The lamp went over the hole and we collected another half tin before the rise had finished. All through the forest we could see the flaring 'torches' of our neighbours and the excited chatter of the children as they scooped their captives out of the holes and into waiting pots and gourds, comparing their catch with one another. We lifted up our kerosene tins with their six gallons of flying ants and set off back to our house. The wings of the fliers fall off naturally after a few minutes so that they can mate and quickly burrow into the ground to start a new colony. By the time we reached our huts most of the wings were off, so Anne put a few handfuls into a winnowing basket to separate insects and wings while I went into the kitchen to light a fire and heat a pan. Once the pan was really hot the insects were dropped in, died immediately and fried in their own fat. As the sun came up we sat outside eating one of the great delicacies of Africa and greeting our friends as they went home to do the same thing.

Termite colonies are prodigal in the extreme. It requires just two fliers to establish a new colony and yet thousands are produced, which in their turn provide food for a myriad of creatures. As soon as the sun was up we released our dog, cat and poultry all of which rushed around gobbling up the now wingless termites which were crawling around everywhere. In the forest birds seem to have assembled from miles to feast on the termites' bounty, whilst on the ground we knew that jackals, squirrels, monkeys and baboons would all be doing the same. After completing our morning chores we had another large feast of the flying ants, but that still made only a small dent in our catch. Gaga and Abugo both had their own heaps and were well supplied so we started to think of neighbours in whose debt we were, to whom we could give our bounty as a gift. We love fresh flying ants but have never acquired a taste for them when they have been smoked, dried and pressed into balls for long term storage. We duly divided our haul into four parts and set off to offer them as gifts. We had not appreciated how welcome they would be. Everybody else collected a mixture of insects, soil and ash from their catch pits. These had to be sorted and cleaned and were always a bit gritty. Ours having been caught in a tin contained no soil and our lamp produced no ash, so they were clean and ready for eating. In the years to come our fliers were always a coveted gift. For several days women worked long hours sorting, smoking and drying their catch and making sure that the precious balls of protein were properly preserved to serve the family's needs for weeks to come.

At the end of our first year, despite the sweat, we were satisfied that we were certainly learning a great deal about village life and farming that we could never have obtained had we stayed in an institution.

# CHAPTER 8

# Song and Dance

'STEPHEN, you told me that Malawi was the fourth poorest country in the world but I have just driven 300 kilometres and all I have seen is laughing, smiling people. You must be wrong.' These were the words of the principal of a London University college, coming to stay with us on his first visit to Africa. Like so many other people in the West he had equated a lack of material possessions with a miserable, dour, joyless life, forgetting perhaps that 'poverty' is rightly a description of a quality of life rather than of monetary income. Our friends and neighbours at Undukori were certainly extremely short of material possessions, their lives were at times hard and when they were sick they could be painful. The last thing that they were, however, was joyless and miserable. Living in a supportive community, sharing the care of children, unworried about a lack of clothes or modern appliances, using conversation, story-telling and a complex game involving the movement of seeds in holes in the ground they filled their leisure hours. Above all they brought to their lives their innate sense of rhythm and song which they used to lighten the burden of many tasks and provide their main entertainment.

After we left the Sudan in 1962 we spent some months in England and during that time watched a programme on television which gave a snapshot of a half an hour in the life of a single mother living with two children under four in a two roomed flat on the fourteenth floor of a high rise building in Glasgow. She owned a gas stove, a small fridge, a radio, a reasonable range of furniture and had adequate resources with which to feed and clothe her children. But she was locked into a pattern of life in which she seldom spoke to other women, all through the winter the children could not go outside to play and they had no friends in neighbouring flats. As we watched this woman, living on her own and dealing with fractious children hour after hour we thought that here was real poverty, and realized just how fortunate were our friends in the Southern Sudan. I had a similar experience many years later walking one evening through the back streets of Monrovia in what was then a peaceful Liberia. I was with an English friend from the World Bank and we passed two women outside a shanty-like house pounding the food in mortars for their evening meal. Their children were playing happily with others round about them. They sang a responsive song in time with their work, and this was frequently interrupted as friendly passers by stopped to chat with them. 'How terrible it is that women have to live like this,' said my companion, focussing on the house.

I could not believe my ears. 'But think of all those women in suburbs in London and Washington locked in by themselves with small children with no-one to sing with, no-one to talk to and no other children to relieve them of the burden of amusing their own toddlers. Or what about elderly women sitting in loneliness in some high rise building, frightened to go out because of uncontrolled teenagers dominating the halls and lifts. Do you really think that these two women have a poorer quality of life?'

'But look at their house...' was all that he could reply. Poverty and misery might have been synonymous in the slums of Britain in the days of the industrial revolution but that is certainly not true across much of rural Africa today outside of war zones.

Dancing lies at the heart of African entertainment and this was certainly the case at Undukori. Children had mini-dances whenever they wanted using a gourd as a drum and making up songs as they went along, but for the community as a whole we had a proper dance once a month when the moon was full. The day would be fixed and preparations would be made. Every family was expected to bring food for the feast which preceded the actual dance. Women naturally vied to produce the finest millet flour and the tastiest sauces. Grinding millet on a grindstone was a skill that Anne never fully mastered. It involved rolling a rounded granite pebble over the grain, which was held in the bowl of a hollowed piece of granite rock. The work was slow and laborious. An agricultural officer had once worked out that it took more labour to thrash and grind the finger millet than to grow the crop from land clearing to harvest. We could well believe that he was right. Anne could at least make a variety of tasty dishes from groundnuts, beans, sesame and vegetables which constituted our main contribution. On our first dance night I was invited to join the other men in making their preparations. The dancing yard had to be weeded and swept. This was a large area of bare soil beaten to almost cement-like consistency by feet and rain. Then we were detailed off to cut a large volume of firewood. 'What is this for?' I asked, 'Surely it's so hot we don't need a fire, do we?'

'Then what will provide the light, and how will we tune the drums if we don't have a fire?' came the response. I did not have an answer but rather

*Grinding the millet on a grinding stone.*

dreaded having a large bonfire on a night when the temperature was already likely to be not less than thirty-three degrees.

The women did not just prepare food they had to attend to their party dress and make-up. They normally collected green leaves from any available bush to stuff into their bark belts each day, but this was not good enough for a party. They went into the forest and found the delicate fronds of the 'horses tail' plant and tucked large bunches of these in the front and back of their belt. These swung gracefully in rhythm with the music as they danced. Their make-up consisted of rubbing sesame oil over their whole body so that they gleamed in the firelight. Anne was highly relieved that it was accepted that she could wear a skirt and shirt and be exempted from smothering her body in oil. As it got dark we all moved towards the dancing yard carrying earthenware pots and gourds full of food. We sat in groups on the ground and after grace had been said (essential at any African meal) we all tucked in. The first two fingers and thumb were put into the thick millet dough and a small ball extracted. The thumb was pressed into the middle of the ball to make a depression and this was dipped into one of the half a dozen different sauces available and popped into one's mouth. At the end of the meal only the tips of the two fingers and thumb were expected to have any food on them.

We rarely had any foreign visitors but one particularly adventurous young Cambridge graduate who was studying African agriculture for a Doctor's degree came to stay with us. He had only recently arrived in Africa and as luck would have it he arrived when the moon was full and so we invited him to join us at the dance. He welcomed the opportunity and came and sat with us to eat. 'Where are the knives and forks ?' he asked. 'How primitive!' he commented on hearing that we ate with our fingers. With obvious distaste he plunged his hand into the dough, pulled out a rough lump and splashed it into one of the sauces.

My neighbour nudged me 'Has that young man got no parents?' he asked. I replied that as far as I knew he was not an orphan. 'Then why on earth did they not teach him to eat properly. His hand is covered in food and he has gravy running down to his elbow. I have never seen such disgusting habits in my life. My three year old has better table manners than that.' It was an interesting meeting of two cultures with neither party understanding either the language nor the etiquette of the other.

While we were eating the five different sized drums were arranged in a circle around the fire to dry and taughten them. The meal finished, the drummers tuned the drums by moving them nearer or further from the fire. The women cleared away the remnants of the meal and the excitement started to mount. Naked children were already capering around at the edges of the firelight in anticipation of the fun and then we took up our places within the various concentric circles, which we would maintain throughout the night. The drummers were nearest the fire, then eight or nine men who were good singers. I was in the next ring of adult men whilst Anne was with the women outside of us. Then came children of both sexes and on the very outside the toddlers. The drums started to beat out a catchy rhythm, the singers lifted their hands above their heads with the sweat pouring off their bodies, shut their eyes and started to tremble. After a little while one began to make grunting noises and then the words of a song would develop. The subject was always a contemporary happening or mini-scandal, often amusing. The drummers got the drift of the song and started to develop a dance rhythm to it. If it fitted well the volume increased, we all took up the song and began to dance. We would use the one song for about ten minutes while the drummers performed all sorts of variations and then another singer would start up. If the song did not really work the drummers would drop it, the composer would hang his head in shame and another man would start grunting and then singing. The dancing itself was simple enough. The adult men simply jumped up and down on the spot in time with the music. The women circled round us singing, clapping their hands, stamping their feet and swinging their tails in time to the drumming. Most had a baby in their womb or on their back so that children were exposed to rhythm at a very early age, and it was no surprise that even the toddler circle on the outside stamped and clapped in perfect time. Most of the men were over six feet tall and having jumped at dances for years could achieve impressive heights. I had been stunted by my childhood illness and at five foot eight inches I was by far the shortest man present. I was young and fit and learned to leap enough to avoid derision, and thoroughly enjoyed being part of this throbbing rhythmic body of people. I always suffered for it and woke up the morning after a dance with calf muscles so stiff that I could hardly get out of bed, but it was worth it. After a couple of hours of dancing some of the toddlers tired and lay down on the edges of the dancing yard and fell asleep. Slowly the number of children in the party diminished and there were small naked figures scattered on the ground around the outer circle. By one o'clock in the morning we were all running out of steam. The drumming died down, soil was thrown on the embers of the fire, pots were collected, children picked up or woken to groggily follow their parents home. They were wonderful nights with the entire community involved. The smiles, the gleaming bodies, the mesmerizing skill of the drummers, the perfect timing of the singing and the joy of the children gave them a quality that was never offered by the most prestigious balls that we have ever attended.

Singing and rhythm were not confined to dance nights but applied to any job for which they were appropriate. I had found a market for sawn timber so I bought more pit saws and a number of men started to make some money by cutting planks. It was hard work and needed a steady rhythm if it were to go well so it was always carried out to singing. On one occasion a middle aged English anthropologist came to the Southern Sudan and hearing of our closeness to village life she walked out to visit us. During the course of the day she heard the sawyers singing and asked to go and see them. As we approached the tune remained identical but the words did not.

'The white man says in church that we should have one wife,

Now he is getting another for himself.

We can't think why he chose her because she is much older than him,

And she is not very pretty'

'What a delightful song!' said my companion. I was having the utmost difficulty in keeping a straight face, especially when I caught the eye of the lead singer. I had to be extremely economical with the truth when I gave her a translation. My neighbours had not really intended to be cruel, they knew that the woman could not possibly understand what they were saying and they were simply exercising their wonderful gift of turning every possible situation into a source of pleasure and laughter.

When I wanted a plank I joined up with one of the sawyers and over the years became a thoroughly efficient pit sawyer, which led to an amusing afternoon many years later when we were living in Washington DC. A replica of the first Roman Catholic settlement in North America had been built at St Mary's City, an hour or so's drive out of Washington, so Anne and I decided to go and have a look at it one Saturday afternoon. It consisted of houses and a small farm designed as nearly as possible on the records of the original settlement contained in the national archives. We turned up in our second-hand but respectable Volvo station wagon, dressed in casual city clothes and with very English accents. As luck would have it we were the only visitors that afternoon and so received the full attention of the 'settlers' dressed in period costume. Anne was taken into a house by a couple of women while one of the men led me around the smallholding. Half way round the tour I found a log suspended over a pit with a pitsaw next to it. 'Do you do the sawing yourself?' I asked.

'Of course not. There is nobody in this country who knows how to use one of those things,' came the reply.

'Would you like me to teach you?' He considered the clothes, the accent and the Volvo and obviously thought that I was trying to be sarcastically funny. 'I really do know how,' I assured him, 'and would be happy to teach you.'

'Alright let's start,' came a very doubtful reply.

'Well we need a bit of preparation. Go to the kitchen and get a half burned piece of wood out of the fire and bring me about eight feet of string.'

While he was away I located a flat stone and a pebble and when he returned I made him grind the charred stick to black powder. 'Let's have a little water, right, now make a paste of the soot and rub the string in it'. I could sense that his patience was reaching its limit but luckily we were now able to turn our attention to the log. 'You go to the other end of the log with the string, hold it tight and I will pull the other end. Now we have a line where we want it so flick the string with your other hand'. He did as he was told and a perfectly straight black line appeared on the side of the log. 'Now let's get it over the centre of the pit and then you get down inside and I will guide the saw along the line. You are going to do the actual cutting on the down stroke and I will lift the saw up above my head so that you can get a good long pull down'.

He was a powerful young man, used to working with his hands, and twenty minutes later we had cut one side off the log. 'Turn it over and we'll draw another line and get the other side off'. He had got the hang of it now and the saw began to move much more smoothly. Anne and a couple of the women had come out and were watching us and the young man was beginning to get really pleased with himself. The second side dropped off and I reckoned that he would soon be able to teach someone else and give a rare exhibition of pit sawing in Maryland. We were given warm farewells and got back into the car.

'I've not been idle either!' said Anne. 'Their kitchen floor of beaten earth was just a mass of dust. They did not have a clue as to how to smear it properly, so I gave them a practical lesson and now it's much better.' I suspect that our visit caused more than a little stir in that small community. The only thing that I regretted was the absence of any song and laughter.

CHAPTER 9

# Something Out of the Ordinary

'SETEPANO, Setepano please come and help us, we are in serious trouble!' It was nine o'clock at night, we were in bed and just about to blow out our lamp. It was Manase at the door and we knew it must be something serious for him to be walking around in the dark when everyone else had been asleep for an hour or so.

'What's the matter?' I called through the door.

'It's Mona, a spirit has got into her.' Mona was a slightly shy but cheerful little girl whom I knew well, and the oldest of Manase's three children.

'Alright, I will just put some clothes on and I will come with you.' I pulled on a pair of shorts, picked up our lantern and set off with Manase on the half mile walk to his house.

We arrived at his sleeping hut and were greeted by his wife with her baby on her back, who was very relieved to see us. 'It's still going on,' she said. We went into the hut which was only about nine feet across. My lantern lit up the whole of it. It contained no furniture of any kind and had three sleeping mats on the floor. Mona's little brother was asleep on one and Mona was lying naked on the other. Her eyes were wide open but she took no notice of either the light or of me. Her mouth was moving and out of it were coming two quite distinct male voices. 'One is her grandfather and the other is her uncle. They are both dead,' said Manase. It was quite extraordinary. There was no possibility of anybody hiding in the tiny bare hut and the sounds were definitely coming from Mona and not from outside the building.

'Please help, Setepano' begged her mother. I had no training of any kind in exorcism but obviously something was expected of me. I got the parents to kneel down on either side of me and then I laid my hands on the child's head. She gave no indication at all that she had felt my touch and the voices continued to come. I prayed that whatever it was would stop and had a fervent 'amen' from her parents. We sat back on our haunches and slowly over the next fifteen minutes the voices became less and less frequent until they stopped. At last Mona closed her mouth and then her eyes and fell into a deep but apparently normal sleep. I stayed for another half an hour but by that time the child was obviously sleeping normally and so I said I would leave. The parents thanked me profusely. All I had done as far as I could see was offer company and support in a frightening situation. I walked home completely confused. I recounted what had happened to Anne and we were both at a loss to find any explanation of what had happened. That lack of understanding of the event remains to this day. It was one of the most unusual things that has ever happened to me.

One of Anne's ducks had just hatched some ducklings and Mona brought her little brother to see them the next morning. She was obviously totally unaware of the previous night's events and was her usual happy self. Fortunately the event never recurred.

'Setepano, I am sorry to say that Tabitha is very sick. Her legs will not work and she cannot get up from her sleeping mat.' It was Eliabu, Tabitha's husband who had come to see me.

'I am sorry' I replied, 'but we have no medicine that can deal with a condition as serious as that. We will have to try and get her to Juba hospital. We could make a stretcher and carry her to Yei and then try and find a truck going to Juba'.

'What are you talking about Setepano? This has nothing to do with hospitals. This is all to do with her quarrel with Esetere. It got so bad that Tabitha actually tried to harm Esetere's children. Thank goodness she failed, but now she knows that she committed a terrible sin and that is what is stopping her from standing up. You are the lay reader in our church and so I have come to ask you to please come and talk to Tabitha.'

It started to come back to me. Esetere was the wife of Enosa who was undoubtedly the most outstanding man in our community, and his wife was also a strong character who ran a very successful household. Tabitha was a much less effectual neighbour of theirs and had developed a deep seated jealousy of Esetere. The quarrel had become so divisive and serious that it had been brought to the church council the year before. Both women had been called and a couple of hours had been spent trying to ease the situation and had resulted in Tabitha saying that she was sorry for the way in which she had behaved and that she had now got over her jealousy and there would be no further trouble. Now I was hearing that her deeds had not matched her words. Trying to harm someone else's children was a terrible crime in our society and this had obviously become a really serious issue. I turned to Eliabu. 'Yes I will certainly come and talk to her this afternoon. Would you please try and see that there are no children or neighbours around when I come.'

Tabitha looked a sad sight lying helpless on her mat. I said how sorry I was to hear of her illness. We chatted a bit about other things and then I asked if she had anything on her mind apart from her physical condition. Nothing at all she replied, and became quite hostile when I pressed the matter a bit further, and so I said that I would leave. 'If ever you want to talk anything over with me just ask Eliabu to call me and I will be glad to come,' were my parting words. Nothing happened for a couple of weeks and then Eliabu turned up with a request that I visit her. Well, she admitted, she had not been entirely truthful during our last meeting and she would like to confess to me about her relationship with Esetere. 'Sorry,' I said, 'you cannot do that. Last time you confessed it was to the whole church council and church members. It is not me that you have deceived but the whole congregation. If you are going to confess it is going to have to be in church on Sunday in front of everybody.'

'No I could not possibly do that, I would be too ashamed, please let me just confess quietly to you.' It was a hard decision to make when the woman was in such a sorry state, but I felt that such a line of action would not get to the root of the matter, and so again I refused. She said she could not make a public confession so I chatted with her a bit more and then left. It was only another week before I was called again. Tabitha made a half hearted attempt to get me to accept a private confession but she knew that I would refuse and at last said that she would speak at church on the next Sunday,

Eliabu and three friends carried her down to church on her sleeping mat and lay her at the back of the congregation. The service was being taken by Enosa and half way through he asked that Tabitha be brought to the front of the church. There in a voice barely more than a whisper, she admitted that she had not fulfilled her promise of stopping being jealous of Esetere and that she had actually tried to hurt her. Now she really did mean to stop the jealousy and the quarrel. Enosa was warmly generous in his welcome of her confession and led us all in a prayer that she might be given the strength to keep her promise. She was carried to the back of the church and the service continued. At its close I was amazed to see Eliabu and a friend supporting Tabitha as she attempted to walk. A few days later her muscles had built up again and she returned to her normal life. At least I did know in theory what an effect deeply felt guilt can have on the physical body but I had certainly not expected so dramatic a 'cure'. It was interesting that it was only Anne and I who were surprised by this turn of events and everybody else accepted it as the expected outcome.

CHAPTER 10

# The Heritage of Babel

M Y ENCOUNTER with 'the Heritage of Babel' started at the age of
eleven, when on the first day at my new school in the Argentine I
found myself sitting in a class being taught by an Argentine teacher who did
not speak a word of English. I sat through a morning of history, geography,
literature and arithmetic, of which in only the last was I able to participate
in any way at all. Argentine law laid down that pupils at foreign language
schools had to pass the sixth grade examination of the Argentine primary
school system before they could concentrate solely on studies in their
mother tongue. At my English language boarding school we therefore were
taught all the morning by local teachers who had no other responsibilities
in the school. In the afternoons we were taken over by the British staff who
actually ran the school. Because of my age I went into the fifth grade, which
assumed that I had already spent a number of years studying Argentine
history, literature, Spanish grammar and geography. In fact, of course, I
knew nothing about any of them and I was now being taught them in a
language of which I also knew nothing. All the other boys in the class had
been born in the Argentine and were thoroughly at home with the
language. 'Total Immersion' is now an accepted method of language
teaching but nobody had heard of it at that time, but it certainly works, and
within a few months I was learning happily in Spanish. The following year
I duly passed my sixth grade exams and was able to switch to all English
teaching to prepare myself for my Cambridge School Certificate. The
French language teacher in the school learned no lessons from my
experience and, like the one who taught me in England, trailed us through
endless dull exercises. I have always bitterly regretted that when my young
brain was at its most agile I spent seven years in French classes and gained
no real fluency in the language, whereas I learned to speak both Spanish
and Kakwa fluently in a few months when I was 'totally immersed'.

Having learned to read and write in early childhood I had always listened
with incredulity to stories of the effort required for adult illiterates to
master those skills. Anne and I soon learned how true they were when we
started to study at the Arabic school in Omdurman, in the Sudan. Some

squiggles appeared on the blackboard and we were told that they were informing us that 'this is a pen'. The following day the identical squiggles appeared and we found them completely unrecognizable, to the great annoyance of our elderly Arab teacher. It took weeks of intense concentration before we could read and write in Arabic. Luckily conversation did not require the same degree of effort and, with an excellent Sudanese teacher and constant opportunities to practise, we were able to carry on a reasonable conversation when we took our final examinations, and we were extending our vocabulary every day. Arriving in Yei we found that we could converse quite reasonably with the Northern Sudanese merchants, who expressed their pleasure that we were among a tiny minority of English people who spoke Arabic in a region which the British had never intended to unite with the Northern half of the country. Both civil servants and missionaries were expected to be fluent in a local language and use English for all official business.

The shock came when we tried to communicate with Southerners. Meticulous about our grammar and trying hard to improve on our accent we were shattered when, time after time 'I cannot understand what you are saying' was the response of local people who claimed to speak Arabic. We had equal difficulty in understanding them, and so started the most painful process of undoing all those hours of hard work in the fourteen hour days that we had studied in Omdurman. Abandon all tenses and only use the present infinitive of a verb for all situations and what is the response? 'That's much better Setepano now you are speaking proper Arabic.' Do away with gender in nouns and adjectives, stop distinguishing between singular and plural and what happens? 'Setepano your Arabic is getting better every day and now we can really understand you.' So we abandoned the wonderfully structured and graceful language of which we had started to get a real grasp in Omdurman and became totally fluent in a 'pidgin' Arabic which would have devastated our excellent Northern teachers had they heard us. It must have had a similar impact on President Nimeiri when, twenty years later, he made our home his base when he visited Yei. On the first couple of occasions he spoke in English, assuming that we spoke no Arabic. Then he heard me talking to his driver in Arabic and from then on he never spoke to us in English again. It was a nightmare. Arabic, like French, is much more than a means of communication. It embodies a people's art and culture and its complete mastery is deemed one of the most valued of social assets. Here we were, desperately trying to drag up the lessons of twenty years earlier and terribly aware that what we were actually saying was a parody of the president's language. To his great credit he never batted an eyelid but it must have been an excruciating experience for him.

Once we moved to Undukori we knew that we had to master Kakwa completely if we were to communicate effectively with our neighbours. Again it was total immersion and again it worked. Within four months we could carry on a modest conversation and within a year I could preach and run baptism classes with confidence. It was not long before we both dreamed entirely in Kakwa, and barely ever used English. When we returned to England our parents were shocked at the loss of parts of our mother tongue from years of neglect, although it was nothing that could not be reversed by a bit of immersion in English society.

'Setepano, why do we pray to God each day to lead us into temptation? Life can be difficult enough without asking God to make it more difficult.' It was Eliabu speaking and I hurriedly explained that the opposite was true and that we were asking not to be put to the test. 'That's what you may do but we were all taught to ask that we should be led into temptation.' A quick survey of other Christian neighbours revealed that this was quite true. Such is the legacy of Babel, especially in a language in which the tone or pitch in which a word is spoken is crucial to its meaning. According to the tone used 'ko' either means 'do not' or 'and'. I was saying 'do not'. My neighbours had been taught the Lord's prayer by someone who had learned it from a missionary who had got the tone wrong and so they were all saying 'and'. This had led to a major change in the nature of the petition of which, one can assume, the Almighty was aware and consequently did not respond positively to their request. I embarked on a teaching programme and asked that in the next translation of the prayer book we used an alternative, longer version of the negative imperative which was less easily open to misinterpretation.

Linguistic errors were not the prerogative of other people. 'Nye jigger nan, nye jigger nan' I sang lustily in church to the tune of a popular English hymn of the time, the chorus of which ran 'He leadeth me, he leadeth me'. Lo and behold I knew, without a lesson, that the word 'jigger' meant 'lead'. The opportunity to use my new found knowledge came a few days later when I asked somebody to 'jigger' me to a homestead that I had not previously visited. I was greeted with a look of total incredulity. I reverted to pidgin Arabic and was duly led on my way. Back home I asked Enosa to explain the meaning of the word 'jigger'. 'Oh', he said 'when we are putting the goats away at night they are often reluctant to leave their grazing so we have to pull them along by their tether, while they stick their hooves in the ground to resist'. I had been asking my guide to put a rope round my neck and yank me along. No wonder he had looked puzzled. What about the hymn? I thought how much more appropriate the local words were in describing my own needs. Having to be yanked along the right path in life is all too often a lot more accurate description of what I need as compared to being gently led.

'Does a kibo tree grow along the waterside, Stephen?' asked Philippa Guillebaud at our quarterly get together. She was translating the Bible into the local language and came to me on a regular basis to check on agricultural and botanical words to make sure that her regular informant had got them right.

'Yes it's quite common along the edges of the Kaya river and I know it well,' I replied.

'Oh good I am glad that I got that one right,' said Philippa. Before we moved on I asked 'where are you using it?'

'In Psalm 137 verse 2. You remember it I am sure. By the waters of Babylon we sat down and wept, and hung our harps on the willow trees'.

'That would be a bit difficult,' I replied. 'The first branch on a kibo tree is about sixty feet from the ground. It is one of the giants of the riverside.' I gave her the name of a shrubby waterside tree and another piece of biblical confusion was avoided.

Anne was waving at me from the back of the church trying to catch my eye and mouthing 'NO, NO' with a distressed look on her face. I looked around the rest of the congregation all of whom seemed particularly alert and interested in my sermon, so I continued to hold forth to Anne's obvious distress. Several people had been asking me to preach about the significance of dreams in a Christian's life. I really was no expert on the workings of the human mind in sleep but felt that I could not just ignore their request. I took a half a dozen examples of biblical figures who had been helped to make right decisions through the medium of dreams. I thought the sermon was going rather well and was puzzled as to why Anne should so obviously disagree. The truth came out all too clearly after we had left church. 'Have you any idea what you were preaching about this morning ?' she asked.

'Well yes, about dreams'.

And what is the word for a dream?'

I responded accurately straight away, and then it hit me. I had got one vowel wrong in the first sentence of my sermon and gone on using the same word for the whole remainder of my presentation. No wonder I had a spellbound audience as I recounted how God had communicated to a number of eminent biblical leaders through the medium of the most depraved orgy that the Kakwa language could describe.

Our friends and neighbours were most tolerant of our blunders as we sought to master their language. They were typical of all our African friends who have offered nothing but praise and encouragement as we stumbled into their language. Occasionally unable to suppress a laugh with us, but never at us, as we made some truly stupendous blunder.

And blunders we made galore a few years later as we started to master our next totally unrelated African language. 'You cannot mean it,' I said to the bright young teacher who had volunteered to help us learn Runyankore in Western Uganda. 'You cannot possibly have twenty words for "big" and twenty words for "small" and ten words for "two", just to agree with the noun that you are using. Nobody could have invented as complicated a language as that.' But they had. I had followed the instructions for learning a language for which there were no text books and written out strings of sentences in which only one word was changed. 'Two big men went to the market.' 'Two big dogs went to the market' and so on. Our mentor gave me the translation of the first sentence. I then asked for the word for dogs and wrote the second.

'NO,' he said, 'that is completely wrong. You have to change the word for two because it is about dogs and not people. Now change the word for big for the same reason and the word for went.' The only word which stayed the same was 'market'. We were devastated. How could one possibly master a language as complex as this? Yet it had to be done and instead of having nice strings of sentences with a one word change in each we had them with only one word staying the same. We were grateful to have this introduction before we moved into the countryside and started the immersion. Without those three months of initial study, before we became 'immersed' in a village situation, I do not think that we would have ever understood the constant changes that people made in what to us seemed basic words which should be unchanging. Eventually we did become completely fluent but it took much longer than Kakwa, and although I could carry out my daily work with farmers before the end of a year I was not confident enough to preach for three years.

Looking at the manifold problems which face Africa to-day I sometimes feel that too little weight is given to the inheritance of Babel. Just think of the problems of welding people into a unified state when they speak not three or four languages, like Britain, but a couple of hundred, like the

Sudan. Most people never read a newspaper because they are either illiterate or there is none in their own language. On the radio they most likely never hear their own language spoken and national leaders moving around the country have to use either an interpreter, which kills oratory stone dead, or a pidgin lingua franca, in which the vocabulary is so limited that it is virtually impossible to move emotions and achieve the nuances of meaning or clever turn of phrase which are so critical to the impact of a good speech. 'Communication' has become a modern catchword, yet it is perfectly true that it is vital to shaping ideas and attitudes, as I have learned over the years in my own work both in the church and with farmers. Yet many people in Africa cannot communicate effectively with people who live just a few miles away. In the Southern Sudan there were five quite different languages spoken by the people who lived along the road from Yei to Maridi, which was a distance of less than one hundred and fifty miles. No wonder differences are difficult to iron out and that the news from Africa seems to involve more splintering of nations rather than unification. The burden of the inheritance of Babel is a heavy one to bear.

# CHAPTER 11

# In Sickness and in Health

'PLEASE COME and give me a hand with Wani, he's had a nasty accident,' Anne called from behind our hut. I went and found Wani lying on his stomach with a wound about nine inches long in the back of his leg, exposing his calf muscle. I discovered that he had been running fast through the forest when hunting, jumped over a broken off tree stump, misjudged its width and torn the back of his leg open on a jagged edge of the stump.

'I've got everything ready,' said Anne. 'I will pull the edges together and pack the wound with sulpha powder and you stitch behind me. I am sorry Wani, this is going to hurt quite a lot.' I am quite sure that it did, the stitches had to be deep to hold the gaping wound together, I was an amateur and we had no painkillers. Wani never flinched throughout the whole proceeding. We got some help to carry him to our wood store where we had a permanent bed of hay ready for such emergencies. A message was sent to Wani's family to make a stretcher out of poles and mats and come and collect him. A week later he walked down to our house with no trace of infection. We agreed when we would remove the stitches and in another week one would have hardly known of that dreadful wound apart from the scar. This case illustrated so well the two great assets that we possessed as Anne ran her dispensary at Undukori. The first was the remarkable physique and resilience of people who had survived to adulthood in this extremely challenging environment. The second was the release for general use of penicillin and sulpha drugs at a time when none of the bacteria in our area had ever been exposed to them at all and so had no resistance to them.

While we had known that we would have to be learners for a couple of years in matters of farming, house building, the use of wild plants and general survival tactics in the forest, we also realized that we could straight away be of use in helping with people's medical problems. Anne started with basic first aid with the addition of anti-malarial drugs. She soon discovered that tropical ulcers, infected wounds and pneumonia were the most serious problems and for these we did not have the resources to be of

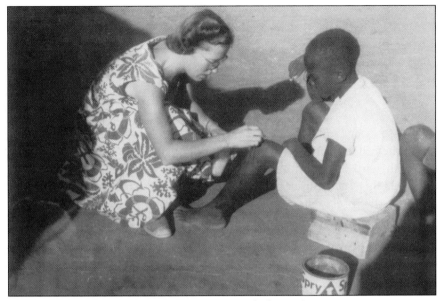

*Anne started with simple first-aid.*

help. It was nine months later that we cycled ninety miles on the very rough hilly road to the small town of Arua just over the border in Uganda. Despite being considered a remote outpost in its own colony it was far more sophisticated than Yei. We were looking for dental help and so met the English doctor at the hospital. We soon moved on from our own problems to those of our neighbours. 'How lucky,' he said, 'there is some new body come into Uganda called the World Health Organization which has supplied me with a whole lot of drugs on top of my quite adequate government allocation. They are intended to help the most needy people. I have no doubt that your people are really needy so I will have no conscience in passing them on to you'.

So it was that we cycled back to Undukori with an array of modern drugs, and started a regular pattern of six-monthly visits to Arua to re-stock.

To begin with Anne worked from a small table outside our hut, but that was soon found to be inadequate so I built a separate hut for a dispensary and Anne started a pattern of daily medical work which continued for the next eighteen years in the Sudan and Uganda. She was armed with two technical assets for this work. The first was her own grounding in veterinary medicine acquired at Wye as part of her degree. The second was my father's parting gift to us in the form of Her Majesty's Government's

'Ship Captain's Medical Guide'. This had the enormous advantage over all the other books that we had seen of never stating 'call a doctor'. It was assumed that the reader was reasonably literate, had a specified stock of drugs and that it might be weeks before the patient could be seen by a doctor. That was our situation and the book was invaluable. Over the years, seeing up to forty patients a day, Anne built up a formidable knowledge of medical practice in remote rural areas and there are many hundreds of people who owe their lives and well-being to her service. Despite those years of varied experience it was the early days at Undukori which were so satisfying.

'These drugs are miraculous,' said Anne. 'You remember those dreadful tropical ulcers that Enosa's oldest daughter had, the ones that you could actually see down to the bone? Well I gave her two injections of penicillin and they have completely healed in less than two weeks. She says that she has had two of them for over five years.' And so the scourge of tropical ulcers became a thing of the past in the surrounding community, children no longer died of pneumonia or malaria, and serious wounds, which would invariably have become infected and dragged a person down for months, were cleared up in a matter of days. Anne looked for a helper whom she could train. Wilson Lumuri offered his services, was a ready learner and soon became a skilled and valued assistant. Years later when the civil war started in earnest, he became a senior medical orderly with the Southern forces.

A lighter moment was struck at the dispensary when iodine was used for small cuts. Men who would tolerate extraordinary levels of pain following a serious accident would hop all around the dispensary verandah crying 'Oh, Oh, Oh!' and gripping the treated limb or digit when Anne dabbed on the dreaded fluid. This to the great amusement of the other waiting patients. We never really got to the root of this most unmanly behaviour from men who were so tough in every other situation. I suppose our equivalent is the reaction to the pain of the dentist's chair as compared to that of the rugby field. Anne's 'bottom records', never discussed with outsiders, also provided lighter moments for us both. Sooner or later just about everybody in the community had received an injection of one kind or another from Anne who built up a mental record of the ease with which she could get the needle into their buttocks. 'You would not believe it. There is great tough Eliabu and the needle just slips in like butter, and then there is that nice young wife of Alfred's that I had to inject to-day and it was like pushing into buffalo hide'. Her 'bottom record' was not frivolous and saved people a good deal of discomfort as she built up a knowledge of just how much punch she had to give to the needle for any given person.

Anne was not the only one who knew the consistency of all our buttocks. 'It's that time again,' Anne said one morning after breakfast. 'You were out earlier on when Enosa called to say that to-morrow is the sleeping sickness day. It only seems a couple of months ago that they tortured me last time and I have hardly recovered from the experience, but I suppose it really is six months. It always seems to come around terribly quickly'.

The next morning found the whole local community, ourselves included, laid out face down on the dancing yard with rows of bare bottoms ready for the needle. A roll call was taken and anybody missing would receive twelve whip lashes as well as the dreaded injection when they were caught. The locally trained orderlies who had arrived on their bicycles filled their syringes and worked their way along the line. Luckily it was before the days of HIV because there was no sterilization during the procedure and one needle went into a lot of buttocks. The sleeping sickness parasite is large and tough and needs a powerful chemical to kill it, and it almost killed us as well. A few seconds after the injection went in one felt one's leg go paralysed and then the faintness came on. We had to lie absolutely still for an hour then slowly see if we could stand, and if we did not faint we were under orders to walk very slowly home and lie down for twenty four hours. I was lucky and the effects had usually worn off within a week but Anne always had a sore buttock and a stiff leg for weeks afterwards. Crude it was, and I imagine that the chemical that was used would have been banned in any developed country as being too dangerous, but this preventative campaign cut the deaths from sleeping sickness in Yei district from many hundreds each year to a handful. This was the only medical service provided by the government in the rural areas but it certainly was a valuable one, controlling a disease for which the treatment a few years earlier had been to transfer infected persons to an isolation camp to die. We, like everyone else in the community, were regularly bitten by the tsetse flies which were the carriers but never had any symptoms of the disease.

With the help of the sleeping sickness injection and effective anti-malarials Anne and I kept wonderfully healthy during all our years at Undukori and never suffered any complaint for which we could not treat ourselves. This was in a part of the world where, only half a century before, eleven out of the twelve first CMS missionaries posted to the Southern Sudan had either died or been permanently invalided out within a year of their arrival. Such was the impact of half a dozen modern drugs at our disposal. Since our own arrival in Africa there has been the widespread adoption of infant vaccination campaigns which has dramatically reduced deaths from measles and the severe crippling of polio which was all too evident in all the African villages in which we lived. Despite that progress almost a quarter of all Malawian children still die before the age of five, which is a situation that would not be tolerated in any developed country where the equivalent figure is a tenth of one per cent.

It is perhaps in the field of health that the widening chasm that exists between the rich and the poor people of the world is most striking. The financial chasm has grown wide enough as illustrated by what has happened to farm workers wages in Britain and much of Africa since the beginning of the 1950s. When I first came to Africa an English farm worker was earning about twelve times more than his African counterpart. Today that figure is roughly one hundred and fifty times. But the growth in the divide in access to health facilities and modern medicine has been even more dramatic. A child dies from malaria once every thirty seconds and yet expenditure on malarial research is one twentieth of that on asthma. Of the almost one thousand four hundred new drugs released on to the market in the past twenty five years only sixteen targeted tropical diseases and tuberculosis, which between them kill millions of people each year in the poorer countries of the world. Our old enemy, sleeping sickness, which afflicts six hundred thousand people in Africa every year, has until very recently been treated with an arsenical drug developed in 1949 which caused agonizing pain over the many weeks of administration and would not have passed any of the safety regulations of the drug administrations in the Western world.

AIDS has provided a high profile illustration of the gulf between the treatment of the rich and poor, but it should not be allowed to mask all the other huge disparities in the access to health services that exist in the world to-day. We have recently been told how wonderful it is that the anti-retroviral drugs that ameliorate the impact of HIV/AIDS are now going to be available at 'only' twenty pounds per person per month. This in a country in which the total expenditure by government on its hospitals, doctors, nurses, drugs and equipment is less than five pounds per person per year, and in which sixty percent of the population have cash incomes of less than fifty pounds per year. What has been the outcome? When we lived at Undukori the average expectation of life in much of Africa was fifteen to twenty years less than in Europe. To-day the expectation of life in Malawi and our neighbouring countries is less than half of that in Europe and a Japanese woman can expect to live fifty years longer than her southern

African contemporary. We were delighted at the impact that new drugs had on our community in the Southern Sudan fifty years ago but are saddened that the early promise which they brought has not been maintained and that moving from sickness to health now depends so heavily on how much money you or your country has available.

CHAPTER 12

# Male and Female Made He Them

'WELL, NEXT YEAR I am going to have a much bigger harvest than any of you,' said Lumeri one day. 'I've found a really fertile site about fifteen miles away and I am going to move there as soon as I have finished my harvest. When you see my crops next year I expect some of you will want to come as well'. We soon learned that his wife, Poni, had no desire whatever to leave Undukori where she had many friends and where she had also become an active member of the church. She let it be known that she did not want to move, but did not actually confront her husband. Over the following weeks the rumours started to reach us that the quality of services that Poni was offering in the kitchen and in bed were slowly declining. Lumeri finished his grain harvest and we casually asked when the move was going to take place. 'The grain is not yet properly dry, but as soon as it is then I will be off' was the reply. A couple of weeks of searing hot dry weather had dried any grain that might have contained a bit too much moisture at harvest, but there was still no move. 'The thatching grass at my new site has not yet ripened' was the next excuse. So it continued for another month with one excuse after another until we all knew that it was much too late for anybody to start building a new house or opening new land because the clouds were already starting to build up. At last Lumeri admitted that they would not be moving this year after all, but he would certainly move next dry season. Once this decision had been firmly made more rumours rapidly circulated that Lumeri was now enjoying much better meals and that there had been a big improvement in his sex life.

Four years later there had still been no move. This incident provided a good example of the relationship between men and women in the Southern Sudan. They were not deemed to be completely equal but there was none of the subservience that we subsequently encountered when we moved into the great Bantu culture further south in Africa. On our first visit to Uganda we were deeply shocked to find women kneeling to greet and serve food to men. The idea of a Kakwa woman kneeling down to a man was laughable.

At church meetings women not only spoke up but would actually refute statements made by men and be quite prepared to put forward their own

suggestions to deal with a particular situation. In Malawi on the other hand
it is very difficult to hold a successful mixed meeting in a rural area because
most of the women are reluctant to speak up in front of men, even though
they provide the real backbone of village society. This ingrained attitude
that women should never argue with men or say 'no' to their demands is
now proving a deadly trait in Eastern and Southern African communities as
HIV is spread through this subservience. The independence of thinking
and acting of our friends at Undukori was typical of the Nilotic people who
occupy that part of Africa. Many years later, when I was working in the
Sudan government, an English visitor turned to me soon after his arrival in
Juba and said 'From the way these people behave one would think that they
consider themselves superior to us'.

'But that is exactly what they do think,' I replied. 'Your colour and your
official status really count for very little here, respect has to be earned'. It
was really interesting to see which white visitors were delighted and which
shocked by this attitude.

Work at the village level was clearly demarcated between the sexes, with
the heavier jobs going to the men and the lighter being allocated to the
women. The basic difference was that men had surges of heavy work,
clearing forest or felling trees to build or repair a house or grain store,
whilst women tended to have chores which had to be carried out every day
of the week all through the year. At an early stage in our time in the Sudan
an English anthropologist shared the results of his study of local society
with me. 'These men have a lot of leisure at certain times of the year,' he
said. 'One might almost call them lazy'.

'Would you really consider a thirty mile walk in the sun with a
temperature of thirty-five degrees as leisure?' I asked. He hummed and
hawed for a bit. 'Time and again men have to spend days sorting out the
problems caused by witchcraft. If some distant relation is sick in a village
twenty miles away they have to walk there to offer condolences. A death
can occupy days of discussion over who bewitched the deceased, on top of
the actual arrangements for the burial. It may not be productive work but it
certainly is not my idea of leisure.' These social obligations were seen as
vital to maintaining the bonds which held a community together in a
situation where the nominal government of the country was basically
irrelevant to most people's lives. Any man who consistently failed to fulfil
them would soon find himself isolated, which was a dangerous situation
when interdependence was critical to survival.

It was childbearing, however, which really gave status to women. When expectation of life was low and half the children born never made it to adulthood, the survival of a community depended on a woman bearing and raising as many children as she could. A brutal selection process over hundreds of years meant that only women with good genes for easy childbearing had survived, and the ease with which they gave birth came as a shock to us, brought up to think in terms of a week in hospital or in bed as the norm for an English woman at that time. Our first practical encounter with the local situation came in our early days at Undukori. Esetere, quite obviously very pregnant, came walking past our hut at about three o'clock one afternoon with a large pot on her head. 'Manase's wife, Jesika, did me a big favour last month so I have made this pot as a gift for her and I am just on my way to deliver it,' said Esetere. We chatted for a few minutes and she went on her way. Half an hour later she returned, minus the pot, but carrying a new-born baby. 'Just after I left you,' she explained, 'I felt the pains come on, so I went behind a bush and delivered the baby. Then I went on to take my gift to Jesika.' We admired the baby and started to chat but Esetere cut us short. 'I must be getting home to prepare the evening meal for my family,' she said. So much for a week in bed.

This expectation of rapid and easy childbirth could have its disadvantages as we discovered a couple of years later. A distraught young husband came to us one afternoon and begged us to go and help his wife with her first baby. 'She has been in labour since mid-day and something must be terribly wrong. Please bring some of your medicine and help us'. We had no medicine for such an occasion but took a lamp to help us in a dark hut. We arrived to find a profoundly disturbing situation. The seventeen year old young woman was in tears and terrified. There were at least eight women crowded into the tiny hut. Half of them kept on urging the girl to push harder and harder. The other half were shouting at her that she had to confess to her infidelity during her pregnancy which was the cause of her problem. She was responding that she was innocent and the women became even more aggressive. I told the husband that if he wanted the help of our medicine the first thing that he had to do was to get all of the women out of the hut without exception. We had to be on our own to use this medicine. He was desperate and despite strong remonstrations he eventually cleared the hut. We shut the door and lit the lamp. Anne told the girl to stop straining and just lie quietly. She again swore that she had not been unfaithful and we said the we believed her absolutely and that this had nothing to do with her delivery, but that it was her first baby and she was not yet used to giving birth. We desperately hoped that there was not in fact a misplaced foetus about which we could do nothing, and there was no hope of a Caesarian for her. We pushed those thoughts back and started to chat with her as she visibly began to relax. After about fifteen minutes we managed to coax a smile out of her and she looked much better. Twenty minutes later she cried out as a real contraction hit her and Anne gripped her hands. It was only another twenty minutes before a perfectly healthy little boy was born, and we let her relations back into the hut to take over responsibility. The husband thanked us profusely for our wonderful medicine, but we knew that the poor young woman was going to suffer from criticism for not having confessed to the sin which had caused her not to deliver in a few minutes as was expected of her. 'We had a white friend who gave birth to her first child recently and she was in labour for twelve hours,' I said to the surrounding women, in an effort to ease the pressure on the new mother, but my remark was met with total incredulity.

It was only in church that men and women were really segregated, with men sitting on one side and women on the other. In all the Southern Sudanese churches the 'pews' were made of hand moulded mud blocks joined with a mud mortar and plastered with the same kind of ground-up ant heap that we used on our floors. The 'pews' were about eighteen inches high and when, like good Anglicans, people knelt to pray they rested their elbows on the 'pew' in front. This brought one's face quite near to the back of the person kneeling in front. An English woman who had heard of the seating arrangements in church, but had never visited the Sudan, complained to me about this separation of the sexes. 'The Christian church should be offering an example of the equality of the sexes,' she said, 'not encouraging male pretensions of superiority.'

'I wonder if you fully understand the facts,' I replied. 'Women's Sunday Best in the Southern Sudan consists of a fresher and nicer bunch of leaves than usual, but these really do cover only a small part of their body. The elders of our church have decided that if, when a man is kneeling in prayer, his face is a mere six inches from the barely covered buttocks of an attractive young woman kneeling in front of him, this could provide a distraction from worship for even the most saintly of Christians. To avoid putting people into that hazardous situation the sensible decision was made to have us sitting separately. I can assure you it has nothing to do with male chauvinism, but is rather an acknowledgement of human frailty.' She was, I think, shocked but not mollified.

We in fact found ourselves living in a community in which men, women and children all had clearly defined roles and responsibilities. The satisfactory fulfilment of these brought respect and acceptance to young and old, male and female. Small girls would follow their sisters to the stream with a tiny pot on their head to play their part in supplying the family with water, and would have wept bitter tears if they had been left behind. Small boys were given old (and blunt!) machetes at a very early age so that they could cut off small twigs when their fathers and older brothers were clearing new gardens. Because both boys and girls could see that the work which they had to do was essential to the well-being of their family it was carried out with pride and without complaint, and the clearly defined role at each stage of their growth meant that our neighbours would have had no idea of what was meant by a 'teenage problem'. All of this was helped by the fact that whether work was done by men or women, boys or girls, it was always accompanied by song and laughter.

CHAPTER 13

# The Seeds of Change

'HAVE YOU HEARD of the big fight there was in Longamere a couple of days ago?' asked Enosa one day. When I denied any knowledge he continued, 'a man called Waro had gone down to the sugar estates in Uganda to earn money to buy a bicycle. He told his wife that he would be away the usual two years. She waited for the two years but he did not come back and she got no message from him. She waited another six months and then thought that he had either died or that he had married another woman and stayed in Uganda, so she married a man called Aligo. Last week-end Waro came home to find his wife with another man so he started a fight. Other members of both families came to try and sort out the matter but they finished up fighting as well and some people were seriously hurt. There is to be a meeting of the whole community next week to try and settle the matter.'

'If only men could make enough money to buy a bicycle here in the Sudan how much hardship and trouble it would save,' I responded.

'But how Setepano? The British tried to force us to grow cotton to earn money but we just could not manage it. Every time we were meant to be planting or weeding or harvesting cotton was just when we had to be working on our food crops. We could not abandon our food so we got very poor yields of cotton and received hardly enough money to buy a saucepan let alone a bicycle. Can't you think of some other crop that we could grow?'

'I have been thinking and reading quite a lot, Enosa, and as coffee grows well in Uganda I think that it would grow well here also. Because it is a tree it does not need planting every year like cotton and from what I can see the harvesting and pruning would take place when we had no other work on our farms. If you like we could all stay on after church next Sunday and see how many people would be interested in trying to grow coffee.'

'Well I would for one,' said Enosa. 'My cousin went to work on the sugar plantations a few years ago and told me how rich Ugandans are because of their coffee.'

The meeting was held and thirty people said that they would like to embark on this new crop. Anne and I once again laboured up the rocky hills

88

that divided the Sudan from Uganda. We left our bicycles with friends in Arua and over the next three days hitched lifts the six hundred miles to Kampala. A warm welcome waited us from missionary friends there, although they were a bit non-plussed when we wore pullovers in what they thought was a hot tropical climate but which was wonderfully cool by the standards of the Sudan. Wye College contacts in the agricultural department helped to locate the best coffee seed available and provided me with a 'crash course' in coffee growing. After two pleasant weeks in what was then a prosperous colonial city we set off on the back of a long distance lorry to bump our way over dirt roads back to Arua and on by bicycle to Undukori.

'We'll put the children in charge of the coffee nursery,' said Yosepa. 'They will look after it well.' I could not believe my ears. Here were my precious rows of tiny coffee seedlings, which had cost Anne and me so much uncomfortable travelling, and they were to be put under the control of eight and nine year olds. 'Their eyes are much sharper and their fingers are more nimble than ours,' said Yosepa, 'so they will be much better at weeding than we would be. They will love to have a special garden of their own and I am sure that they will make a good job of it.'

I was unconvinced, I had visions of what would happen to a delicate nursery of thousands of small seedlings at the hands of a bunch of young English children, but I was over-ruled. After two years I should have known better. The children not only cared for the plants perfectly, but knew the names of all the weeds that grew up in the nursery and were excellent judges of when the seedlings needed watering. As always they made fun out of the work and invented songs that they sang about their new garden. A few years later I was organizing coffee nurseries for millions of seedlings but that effort never gave me the thrill of our first small nursery at Undukori.

For the first time I became a teacher and not a learner in the local farming community. I was the only person who knew anything about growing coffee and had to initiate people into the strange world of marking out planting holes at nine feet each way on the triangle. Digging holes a couple of feet wide and deep was also a new experience for everybody, but because that was the 'rule' that I said was essential for growing this strange crop everybody did it. We refilled the holes with black friable forest soil and we were ready to move the young coffee plants out of the nursery into the thirty acres of land that we had cleared and prepared. They really appreciated the forest soil and plentiful rain and shot up. Three years later we harvested our first coffee crop and I had to embark on another teaching campaign to help people transform the fat red cherries from the bushes into the dried coffee beans that we could sell. Selling was no problem. Northern Sudanese are great coffee drinkers and the country imported thousands of tons of coffee every year. To our great advantage the government made the import duty on coffee a major source of income so that the local price was well above the world price. I find it difficult to believe that we sold our first crop for £750 per ton. This is well above the world price for Robusta coffee today when the price of industrialized goods has increased many fold. In the mid 1950s a half a ton of coffee would buy a good quality small car in the Sudan. Today it would require almost eight tons to achieve the same goal.

We were not on the look out for cars, but all the men were desperate to buy a Raleigh bicycle, the only make in which they were interested. These cost £16 and men worked for two years on a sugar estate to save that amount of money. When we shared out the money from the first coffee sale people received between £120 and £150 each according to how well they had managed their acre of coffee. The bicycle was bought, then some metal saucepans and a new pair of shorts and a couple of shirts. Wives had worked hard with harvesting and preparing the coffee and asked for a share to buy skirts to wear to church. All this added up to not more than £25, and there was still over £100 remaining. A new imported hoe and panga dealt with another ten shillings, and two empty kerosene tins, which are so much lighter for water carrying than earthenware pots, took four more shillings. Enosa was the first to buy a kerosene lantern and soon a number of others followed suit, but nobody had less than £100 left, and they could not think of anything else that they wanted to buy.

I called another meeting. 'You know how much work it was preparing the coffee by hand this year, well next year we are likely to have much more. There is a machine that will do the work quickly and easily. Who would like to contribute money to buying one in good time for the next harvest?' Every hand went up and I was given the task of finding out how much a small diesel engine and coffee huller would cost. It was still much less than the £3,000 that we had in hand, so we had another meeting. 'How many of you women helped to weed the coffee?' I asked. All the wives and older girls put up their hands. 'And helped to harvest and prepare the coffee?' every hand went up again. 'Now you men don't you think that the women deserve something more for all their work than a saucepan, a skirt and an empty kerosene tin?' There was no chorus of agreement from the men. Wives had responsibilities to help on the farm without talking about rewards. I continued all the same. 'We will only use the coffee huller for about one month each year and for the rest of the year the engine will have no work. We have enough money to buy a grain mill which could be joined to the engine for the other eleven months of the year and save so much time and work grinding millet and sorghum.' The women started shouting, laughing and singing and it would have been more than the men's domestic bliss was worth if they had said that they were not interested in a grain mill. So the order went by bicycle to Yei, by lorry to Juba post office, on a two week steamer voyage down the Nile to Khartoum and by air to England. Months later the crates worked their way back along the same route. We had decided on a site, built a special hut and finally the day came when the first millet went into the mill and two hours of work bending over a grinding stone was finished in two minutes. It was miraculous. For people who had never seen machines working before it was almost beyond imagining that flour could be produced so quickly. When the next coffee harvest came in the work of preparing the beans for sale was also reduced to a fraction of what we had done by hand the year before and the quality was better.

This early success led to more people wanting to plant the crop, but we were running into one snag. The crop enjoyed our eight and a half months of wet season but in some years the coffee suffered really badly in the intense heat of the dry season. We were still developing large sums of surplus money so our next major venture was irrigation with mobile pumps which could be moved from farm to farm along the Kaya river and give every tree a real soaking once a month, which had a major impact on our yields. New seeds were helping to solve one local problem, but there were others.

'I am so sorry,' I said to Manase as we viewed what was left of his sorghum field. Baboons had got into his garden the day before and simply ripped the unripe heads from almost every plant as they looked to see if there were any worth eating. He would hardly harvest anything from a field which should have provided half of the year's food supply for his family. 'There are still two and a half months of rain left but there is nothing that I can plant which will ripen before the dry weather comes'. Off went another letter to a sorghum breeding friend who supplied me with the seeds of a variety, Serena, which matured in three months. The flavour was nothing like as good as our local sorghums but if a crop had been destroyed half way through the season then it was now possible to replace it with another and stave off real hunger. The crop did really well under our conditions and thirty years later when our older son Christopher was the administrator in charge of the French charity 'Doctors Without Borders' in the Sudan and travelling all over the South he came across Serena in hundreds of locations.

Upland and swamp rice from Burma, a bean from India that did not get eaten by weevils, bananas from Trinidad, maize from Kenya were all supplied through the Wye College old boy network and all fitted well into the local farming pattern and soon spread far beyond the area of Undukori. These offered a greater security of production and a broader diet than people had known. All of this was made possible by the fact that we ourselves were farming and so knew where the gaps were and what could fill them. One challenge remained to be dealt with.

'Setepano, what are we going to do about our coffee when we run out of fields for our food crops in this area?' asked Enosa one day. 'We usually have to move home after about fifteen years when all the nearby land has been exhausted. We have a few more years to go but you say that this coffee should last for over thirty years.'

'Somebody sent me a book written by a man working in the Belgian Congo which says that if you just take two crops off a field instead of going on working it for four or five years until it is completely exhausted, then instead of having to wait for twenty or thirty years for it to become useful again you can cultivate it after just four years of rest. I actually left one of my fields after two years last year and you can't imagine how much bush has grown on it already. It's quite different from leaving an exhausted plot which takes years before the bush gets established again.'

'But nobody is going to leave a cleared plot after just two years when they have taken all the trouble to kill the big trees and clear all the small ones.'

'Yes, but then there will be no big trees to clear when I go back to my plot in four years, I will have fertile soil and I will not have to move house and start building all over again.'

This was a major break with tradition but the lush growth on my rested plot was certainly noticed and it would deal with the problem of the coffee. I was determined that we were not going to run our farm down to bare land but stay in one place. I added a point to this decision by budding citrus trees and planting oranges, grapefruit and tangerines around our house to accentuate our permanence. Soon requests for fruit trees came in from our neighbours and I budded hundreds of trees to provide yet another improvement to people's diet.

*Every child had a mug of milk each day.*

Anne had her own plans. She heard of cattle in the Congo which were highly tolerant of sleeping sickness so she determined to get some and start a dairy herd. A Christian Sudanese friend living on the border about thirty miles away agreed to help her and he moved back and forth into the Congo negotiating with local people until he had found some who would sell us a total of ten cows and a bull. A day was set when we would all meet at the border (an imaginary line running through the forest!) and I went with Anne with the necessary money to pay the price which had finally been agreed after days of haggling between our friend and the various owners. We employed a couple of these, who knew the animals well, to help us drive them to Undukori, where Anne developed an excellent dairy herd and initiated methods of disease control in the 1950s which we saw hailed as new discoveries by the international veterinary research institute thirty-five years later. Soon she had enough milk to give every child under five in the community a mugful each day. The animals were small but lived up wonderfully to their reputation of being able to survive in forest which was infested with the tse-tse flies which carry sleeping sickness. She never lost a calf and the herd grew steadily and local people gained experience in handling cattle with which they were quite unfamiliar.

I have always been interested in fish and fishing since I was given my first rod when I was seven years old. I was disappointed that the Kaya river appeared to contain no fish larger than sardines and provided neither angling opportunities nor much protein for the table. When we had been at Undukori for four years and I had become thoroughly familiar with the landscape I realized that a quite low thirty yard long dam at a certain spot would create a lake of about a hundred acres. At a post-church meeting I therefore broached the subject of building a dam so that we could all have fish on a regular basis. The idea of the fish was very attractive but nobody had ever seen a dam and had no idea as to what would be involved. I explained as best I could and suggested that if people would like to give it a try we wait until the end of the rains and then all contribute our work each Saturday for about three months and build the dam. On the Monday I went with a delegation to my chosen site and explained what we would have to do. They were reluctant to believe that a strip of earth could hold back so large a body of water, but I assured them that plenty of people elsewhere in Africa had been successful in doing so. More meetings and more discussions and finally it was agreed that we would give it a try. Over a hundred men, women and children turned up on the first Saturday. The men dug out the soil and the women and children carried it to where I had marked out the foundation for the dam. It took us more than three months but when the rains began and the stream started to flow strongly the dam held and in a few more months we had our hundred acre lake.

Now for the fish. On our next 'medicine' trip to Arua I met the enthusiastic young British fisheries officer who was encouraging people to create ponds in which they could raise fish. He was delighted with our initiative even though it was over the border and offered to help as much as he could. He gave advice on fish rearing and then offered to bring the kerosene tins of fingerlings to the Sudan border to save us forty miles of cycling and reduce the time that the fish would have to be on the road. We agreed on a date and I cycled up to the border with three of our neighbours and took delivery of several hundred little fish in their four containers. Most of them survived the rough journey to Undukori and they were released into their new and spacious home. It was almost too spacious and we were disappointed not to see any sign of them for a couple of months, but eventually we got sightings of them and knew that at least enough had survived to start a self propagating population. The excellent eating fish that he had given us were, unfortunately for me, purely vegetarian and took not the slightest notice of any titbits offered on a hook, so my hopes of a hobby on my doorstep were dashed. We got a net from Arua and for the first time

*A low dam would create a lake.*

local people had access to a supply of good quality fish. The dam withstood
the huge floods of 1961 and was still firm and strong twenty years later.

'African peasant farmers are intensely conservative and resistant to
change'. For forty years since we left Undukori I have had to sit through
academic presentations or read learned journals in which this statement is
repeated over and over again. Any greater travesty of the truth it is difficult
to imagine. Our experience at Undukori, where farmers grasped new seeds,
new technologies, new ideas, new foods and new ways of farming with
both hands and ran with them, has been repeated time and again in a whole
range of countries across the continent over the years. As I travel widely
around farms in Malawi today I find it almost impossible to locate anybody
growing an indigenous crop. I am surrounded by maize, groundnuts,
tomatoes and pumpkins whose seeds were brought from North America.
There are fields of cassava and sweet potatoes which came from South
America. There are people growing rice from Asia, bananas, pineapples,
oranges and onions. I can see people ploughing with oxen instead of using
their traditional hoe, applying fertilizer to their land and milking Friesian
cows imported from Europe. Elsewhere I would find small scale farmers
growing cotton, cocoa, tea and sugar cane all of which are recent imports
from other parts of the world. People have changed their food habits and

the whole way in which they farm and yet they are consistently branded as conservative and resistant to change. Where does this belief come from? It is because African farmers have consistently rejected advice which entails additional work at a time when they have no spare labour, a crop which neither stores well nor tastes nice, a variety which takes twice as long to cook even if it does grow quite well, a system that requires a lot of additional expenditure accompanied by substantial risk, a way of growing crops which could lead to total failure if the weather was not just right, and so on. It has been this sort of advice that has come from agricultural departments across Africa for many years. Instead of asking why it has been rejected it is much easier on people's pride to blame the rejection on 'conservative African peasants'. Often the word 'backward' is thrown in for good measure. At Undukori we had absolute proof that there was no resistance at all to seeds which brought about positive change.

# CHAPTER 14

# Goings and Comings

B Y 1962 Undukori was flourishing. Farmers in the area were growing a much wider range of crops, so both the quantity and quality of people's diet had improved. Large numbers of fruit trees were in bearing providing children with a plentiful supply of vitamins. Anne's dairy herd had grown greatly and she was able to supply large numbers of young children with milk every day. Coffee production was expanding rapidly as the area under the crop grew and irrigation boosted yields. Just as importantly the whole life of the community had taken on a new quality. Not only had the congregation of the church increased so much that we had to double the size of the building, but there had been a marked decline in the accusations of witchcraft, which was the most divisive and destructive force in Kakwa society. Problems were being brought to the church council instead of being dealt with through vengeful magic. We noticed a steady increase in co-operation between unrelated families who were helping each other out in times of sickness or emergency.

We found this deeply satisfying. For some years we had only thought and dreamed in Kakwa, bonds of friendship were growing ever stronger and we felt fully at home in this community. In addition people were now coming from up to 150 miles away to obtain seeds and practical teaching from us which they could carry back to their own communities. We could really start to plan for activities which would help to spread the knowledge which we had accumulated over the years over a far wider area. Unfortunately the apparent normality of our situation was belied by events in the Sudan as a whole, which were moving steadily away from peaceful and constructive development.

Following on the uprising of 1955 there had been a genuine attempt by the Northern government to win over the Southerners to the idea of a united Sudan. A number of dedicated and liberal young Northern officers were posted to the South, who had a vision of a progressive Sudan in which all the different cultures would share. Their presence led to a honeymoon period for several years with no fighting and a real improvement in relationships. All that came to an end in 1959 when a military government took over in Khartoum and imposed a harsh and repressive regime in the South. Southern resentment bubbled up and guerrilla fighting started in earnest. By early 1962 Northern officials could only move around in military convoys, while Anne and I still cycled freely around the country. In consequence suspicion of us steadily increased. The majority of officials who were sent to the South neither liked working in the region nor did they feel in any way at home in its totally different culture. They found it completely incomprehensible that two well educated English people had apparently integrated into this 'barbaric' society and therefore looked for the hidden agenda that was providing the real motive for our activities. This they assumed was to foment trouble and provide guidance to the guerrilla fighters. A substantial reward was offered to any Southerner who would give evidence against us, but none took up the offer. Finally in May of 1962 the central government issued an order that we should be expelled from the country immediately with no reason offered for the expulsion. A convoy of officials and troops came to deliver the order but the officer in charge, who knew us, was somewhat embarrassed by what was happening and said that we could have a couple of weeks to make arrangements for the future of Undukori before we actually left the country.

'Of course you cannot go Setepano. We will all move deep into the forest where the Arabs cannot find us and the guerrilla fighters will protect you.' This was the universal reaction of our friends and it almost felt like desertion when we responded that such a course of action would not really benefit anybody in the long run and could lead to serious revenge on local communities. We handed over responsibility for the church to Enosa whom I had taught and trained for several years. We had a string of meetings to work out who would be responsible for the dairy herd, the irrigation equipment, the coffee marketing and so on. We gave away our few possessions, had a deeply moving service of farewell attended by people from miles around and two weeks after the order had been received left Undukori for the Uganda border, surrounded by friends singing a haunting song which affirmed that we would meet again. We left behind our broken hearts with a village community which had enriched our lives beyond measure.

Our plans for Undukori did not have much time to be tested. The war hotted up, the fighting around Yei intensified and it was not long before we heard that our houses and the church had been burned, Anne's dairy herd had been slaughtered and all our friends had either gone with their families into neighbouring countries or joined the guerrilla forces. The coffee reverted to forest and there was little to show for our years of work. Even the best and most sympathetic of friends had a lot of trouble refraining from saying 'I told you so, wasting so many of the best years of your lives for nothing'. Were they right? Had all of those years when we forfeited our access to good books, good music and, above all, intellectual stimulus really been wasted? Had Anne given up a gracious home and way of life for the stark simplicities and drudgery of an African village for nothing? How could we answer all the criticism or pitying comments that we received? Our initial response had, of necessity, to be subjective. We knew for certain what we had gained from the years at Undukori. We had developed a wealth of detailed practical knowledge of tropical agriculture which no reading or outside observation could have given us, and which stood us in good stead for years to come. We had gained a unique insight into the motivation and attitudes of African small scale farmers, the logic of their decisions and their willingness to adopt new ideas and the rapidity with which they learned and adapted fresh skills. This knowledge was to shape much of our work for the next forty years and lead to a range of successful agricultural initiatives. At a more personal level we had discovered that we could find deep satisfaction in a pattern of life quite alien to that in which we had been raised and that we could develop close and intimate friendships with people of a totally different background to ourselves. Once again these factors have shaped our approach to the wide range of African farmers with whom we have lived and worked since we left Undukori.

We had also hoped that there might be some more concrete results of our work amongst other people, that we might have influenced the attitudes of our friends through the ministry of our church and enhanced their agricultural knowledge in a way which would be of use wherever they went. It was to be some years before we had any confirmation of the reality of those hopes. It was in late 1972 that a peace accord was signed which brought to an end the first Sudanese civil war. A few months later our friends returned to Undukori. They rebuilt their houses and the church and rescued what remained of their coffee from the forest and embarked on opening new coffee gardens. Here was an indication that all that we had done there was not lost. A heart-warming confirmation of this came to us from a document written by a British government team carrying out a survey of farming in Yei district in 1983 just at the end of the ten year peace which prevailed from 1973. They wrote 'we came across a group of people in the Payawa area who formed a deeply religious community and were the best and most progressive farmers that we encountered during our survey.

The farmers stated that they had been greatly influenced by an English missionary who lived with them almost thirty years ago.' Twenty years later there is still a Christian community at Undukori with an active church made up of the children and grandchildren of our original friends. Postal services have not existed for many years but the odd letter reaches us carried by someone travelling to Uganda who posts it from there. My Kakwa is growing rusty after years of neglect but I can grasp most of the messages and manage a somewhat stilted response.

There were other sources of encouragement. We heard in the mid 60s that Enosa had been ordained into the Anglican church and was doing a valuable job in the refugee camp where he and his family were living. When, with all the others, he returned to the Sudan after the signing of the 1972 peace accord, he was a powerful force for good for another twenty years. Another friend, Yacobo, had an almost more moving story to tell when we met up in 1973. 'Where were you during the war?' I asked. 'Did you go to the Congo or to Uganda to avoid the fighting?'

'Neither,' he replied. 'I spent the war with the guerrillas.'

'So you became a soldier?' Knowing his character I was surprised.

'Oh no, I never carried a gun and I never killed anybody. What I saw was that some of the young fighters were in danger of falling into the deadly sin of hatred. I realized that they felt that they had to fight to gain control of their region but I saw that they had started to hate the Northerners who they were fighting. That was something much more serious, so I lived with them for almost ten years teaching them from the bible and praying with them. I tried to show them that fighting for a cause was one thing but that they must never allow that to lead them into the sin of hatred.'

I was completely amazed. Here was a man of fifty who had spent ten years sleeping in the open, living off game animals and wild plants, walking hundreds of miles a year through the bush and in constant danger of attack so that he could translate his Christian faith into action by tempering the attitudes of bunch of tough young guerrilla fighters. He knew perfectly well that he could expect no monetary reward, that he had little chance of receiving any thanks or acknowledgement for what he had done, but had simply felt that this is what his Christian faith demanded of him.

When we add to these sources of encouragement the fact that thousands of farmers across Equatoria have grown the crops and varieties that we introduced all those years ago, we believe that we can truthfully affirm our own opinion that we did not waste those years in the Southern Sudan fifty years ago. But our days in the Sudan had not come to an end, and 1973 saw us back in our old haunts, but wearing a very different hat.

'Nobody from outside of this country has a detailed knowledge of agriculture in the Southern Sudan, so how can you ask me to bring experienced people in my team?' The speaker was Walter Schaefer-Kehnert the leader of the first World Bank agricultural team coming into the Southern Sudan after the signing of the peace accord, responding to the newly appointed minister of agriculture's criticism that he had nobody with him with experience of the country.

'You are wrong,' replied the minister, Dr Gama Hassan. 'There is a man called Stephen Carr who knows this country well and speaks the language fluently. We have heard that he has just had to leave Uganda because of Idi Amin and that he is now in Nairobi. You could contact him through the Church Missionary Society office.' That was a conversation which changed the whole course of our work for the next thirty years.

As soon as the peace accord was signed some Sudanese had approached CMS and asked that we be relocated to the South to help rebuild the devastated farming sector. It soon became evident that the central government, which had retained control over immigration, was not prepared to allow missionaries who had been expelled in the 1960s to return to work in the South. Following the unexpected termination of our work in Uganda by the Amin regime we were waiting in Nairobi, Kenya, to see where our skills could best be used. Out of the blue came a request for me to meet with a Walter Schaefer-Kehnert at the World Bank office in Nairobi. I had barely heard of the institution and had no idea what function it fulfilled, but as the request was linked to the Sudan I phoned their office and arranged an interview. I received a pleasant reception and after a half an hour's conversation about my experience of agriculture in the Southern Sudan I was asked if I would accompany the next World Bank agricultural mission to Juba as an advisor. I saw no reason to say that I was *persona non grata* with the Northern government and agreed to join them. CMS was delighted that I might have an opportunity of returning to the Sudan, and gave their blessing to my going with the World Bank. The application for a visa for me from that institution met with no problems as it was not assumed that they were employing expelled missionaries. So in early 1973 I was back in Yei district helping to formulate a major agricultural rehabilitation project for the new Southern Sudanese government.

'It's all very well you people popping in and out of Juba from Nairobi but what we need is one of your staff here on the ground to help us to get

things really moving.' It was Gama Hassan the minister talking again to
Walter Schaefer-Kehnert.

'I could not possibly ask one of our staff to come here,' replied Walter.
'There is no proper housing, no services, no telephone communication and
barely any shops. The conditions are just not right.'

'Have you asked Stephen Carr?' responded the Minister. 'I think that he
might be prepared to come despite the lack of facilities.'

So another conversation between the minister and Walter had a profound
effect upon our lives. I was asked if I was willing to go and live in the
Southern Sudan and replied that I would be happy to do so. CMS gave
their instant blessing and I found myself an employee of the World Bank,
seconded to head up the crop division of the newly formed Southern
Sudanese government.

'That's another thousand units ready, go over to Mr Manson at the UN
office and ask for a lorry to take them to the border.' I was in a huge old
warehouse, left over from the days when Juba had been a major source of
supply to the whole of the north-east Congo. Along three walls were a
hundred tailors with their treadle sewing machines churning out thousands
of cloth bags in which to pack sorghum, maize and groundnut seeds. On
the fourth wall were stacked hundreds of tons of seeds that I had imported
from East Africa, and the middle of the building was occupied by a string of
women scooping seed into the bags with a different measure for each type.
Refugees were due to pour back into Equatoria Province from the Congo
and Uganda at any time, as the UNHCR had declared the country to be
peaceful enough for their return. I was determined that every family would
be provided with two hoes, a panga and sufficient seed for them to establish
a large enough farm with which to feed themselves within four months.
My knowledge from Undukori enabled me to select the right varieties
whilst contacts that I had built up in East Africa allowed me to collect large
quantities of the right seed together in a short space of time. An English
charity, Christian Aid, paid for the seeds, a Scandinavian charity paid for the
tools imported from Kenya, the Director of Agriculture made himself
responsible for obtaining thousands of yards of cheap cotton cloth from a
Sudanese factory and employing the tailors, while Doug Manson of the
United nations had come up with the transport.

Doug was a man after my own heart, much more concerned about
getting things done than about bureaucratic correctness and we worked
well together over the next couple of years. I was an innocent in
government service and failed to recognize just how lucky I was with the

ministry staff, the charities and the UN as we all pulled together quickly and efficiently and were successful in distributing tens of thousands of 'farm packs' to the refugee families as they returned, thereby making an enormous difference to food production in the first year of the peace.

That initial emergency over, I had to start on the long term planning for developing an effective Ministry of Agriculture from scratch. The few modest facilities established by the British had been destroyed, there were only a handful of qualified staff and most farms had been abandoned because of the war. 'Juba is in the middle of a hot dry gravel plain which really is not good for much agriculture, sir, and the old British headquarters in Yambio is so remote that it would not be at all suitable, especially as the road system is almost non-existent.' The minister and I were discussing where we should base the headquarters for the crops division with a research farm, seed farm and staff training centre and central office for the division.

'You know that I would like it to be near me here in Juba,' replied the minister, 'but I can see your point about it being a poor farming area. Where do you suggest?' This was the opening that I had been hoping for.

'There is a 500-acre site just outside Yei that used to belong to the forestry department, but all the trees have gone. It is only three hours drive from Juba, is in the middle of an excellent farming area, and Yei should soon have good schools again which would help to attract staff to work there.'

My argument was accepted and a couple of weeks later I was laying out the plan for our mud and wattle huts, stores, staff houses and offices just about a mile from the old Village Teacher Training Centre where we had started work twenty years earlier. The Centre had been abandoned for some years and most of the buildings had been destroyed, but part of John Parry's kitchen was still standing and I felt that he would not begrudge me the bricks from his chimney so that I might provide a decent chimney for Anne's new kitchen, thus providing a tiny link with our past. Anne joined me as soon as I was in Yei and our two sons, Christopher and David, came there for their holidays from their school in Kenya. I moved into top gear and in a few months we had coffee nurseries scattered along southern Equatoria producing hundreds of thousands of seedlings for local farmers. The research farm started to function as I once again plugged into the old Wye network for material from around the world. Within a few months we were bulking up seeds which I knew would be acceptable to farmers and turned a fifteen-ton truck into a mobile shop to distribute them around the

*We laid out the plan for our mud and wattle huts.*

country. Anne designed and supervised the building of a residential training centre for fifty students and the ministry started to really function. I was not able to spend much time with my old friends at Undukori as I combined my supervision of the work at Yei with long trips across my allocated patch, which was a quarter the size of India with rudimentary dirt roads on which it was a major achievement to average twenty miles an hour in a good Landrover. Three-week journeys were not uncommon. When our boys were on holiday they came with us on the shorter journeys. Their attitude to the pleasures of travel differed markedly from my own. 'Mr. Cornelio, we have had a really good trip to Maridi and back. We had four punctures, which Dad had to mend himself, and at one place it took us seven hours to dig the Landrover out of the mud! It was a really interesting journey, not like the last trip to Mundri when nothing went wrong the whole way there and back and it was so boring.' So said Chris to our excellent senior Sudanese staff member on our return from a particularly trying and exhausting journey.

There were no hotels outside of Juba at that time and so on most of our journeys we camped in unused government buildings wherever we could find them. Anne quickly developed a 'camping package' which would fit in the Landrover and provide basic food and comfort for our long journeys.

*It was a major achievement to average twenty miles an hour.*

The vehicle itself was a mobile bomb with up to 100 gallons of petrol strapped around it because of the complete absence of petrol stations outside of Juba. Luckily the roads were almost completely empty so that the likelihood of crashing into another vehicle was extremely remote. There were times when no government building was available and I would look for one of my old trainee teachers in a village for hospitality. One such stay provided me with what I think of as the longest night of my life. The sleeping accommodation which I was invited to share was a small round hut with mats on the floor. I was offered a place between the parents on one side and five children who lay between me and the door on the other. In the absence of any form of lighting the family settled down at eight o'clock and their deep breathing soon indicated that they were all fast asleep. I was beginning to doze off when I felt a burning sensation on the back of my leg. I knew all too well what bed bugs felt like and just hoped that there were only one or two of them. My hopes were in vain and soon they had started on my back. The initial fiery bite soon turned into the most terrible itching, and as I quickly stood up I had difficulty in stopping tearing at my flesh. A family living with regular bed bug bites develop a factor in their blood which repels the insects so that they will not attack them. This makes the small blood suckers all the more eager for a new

source of supply, such as that offered by my nice fresh body. My path to the
door was blocked by five sleeping children and so I stood in their midst on
one leg at a time brushing off the bloodthirsty horde. The hours passed
with excruciating slowness until finally at about one o'clock one of the
children got up and opened the door to go and relieve himself. I stepped
quickly over the remaining children and gained my freedom from attack. I
sat on a log outside with my whole body on fire until dawn came at last.
Luckily this was not a common experience.

The discomforts of travel in the Southern Sudan were more than offset
for me by the opportunity which it gave me to meet with smallholder
families all over the three provinces which fell under my jurisdiction. I was
amazed at the resilience and fortitude of people who returned from exile
with virtually nothing, did not wait for any outside help but got on and
built houses, cleared bush and forest to make farms and developed their
community life once more. In many cases I found that as soon as they had
put up a rough shelter for themselves they threw their energy into building
a new church cum school. Within months of the refugees' return I found
village schools and church congregations in full swing. I soon discovered
that these schools had virtually no books at all. I found teachers who had
preserved the two basic readers and arithmetic books in the vernacular and
in that easygoing pioneering environment I was able to move out of
agriculture into education and make a push to get books into children's
hands. I obtained a grant from a Scandinavian church group, got a waiver of
copyright from the original publisher, had a good friend in Nairobi who
located a first class Indian printer who offered a competitive price, and
within two months I had the pleasure of using our agricultural vehicles to
distribute ten thousand of each of the four books to village schools.

Perhaps one of the main lessons that I learned in those heady early days
was just how much a small group of enthusiastic people can achieve when
they are unfettered by standard civil service procedures. Nobody was
fighting for their own turf, nobody was standing on their dignity or
claiming that some vital action was not in their terms of reference or that
chapter six, paragraph five (a) of the civil service code did not allow for this
particular activity. So it was that half a dozen enthusiastic and able Sudanese
staff, Doug Manson in the UN office, a handful of young volunteers and
myself, with the help of some generous and flexible charitable donors were
able to achieve some remarkable results in the first couple of years after the
peace treaty was signed. Those conditions inevitably come to an end and
more normal civil service activities take over. With World Bank funding the

Yei site had been greatly developed and the British government supplied half a dozen senior technical staff to run it. A senior expatriate administrative officer was appointed to handle the organization of the ministry headquarters and it was clear that the day of the pioneers was over. Doug Manson found himself another UN post in a really tense situation and I prepared myself to move back into conventional missionary work wherever CMS felt that I was needed. So Anne and I in 1976 left the Sudan for the last time.

It was not however the end of our family involvement with the country. Our son Chris returned to the South in the early 1980s. He went first with the Episcopal Church of the US, but as the war started again that organization pulled out and Chris spent four years as the administrator for the Sudan of the French medical charity *Medecins Sans Frontières*, with responsibility for some fifty expatriate and almost two thousand local medical staff. Although his headquarters was in Khartoum he spent much of his time in the South. At one point he had six French staff in Yei hospital whom he visited regularly, using a small plane given him by another French charity. He not only revived the memories of his boyhood, but amazed us with descriptions of a medical service in a time of civil war which was infinitely better than anything that we had ever known in all our years of peace.

At a large conference in Birmingham a couple of years ago, when I was introduced as coming from Malawi, a loud voice from the body of the meeting called out 'No he doesn't, he's a Kakwa from the Southern Sudan!' It was an old friend from many years ago, now in a senior international position, and to some degree he spoke the truth. We have spent many happy years in a number of different countries but I suppose none has marked us as much as those when we were white Kakwa at Undukori.

# CHAPTER 15

# A Fresh Start

'MAY I CALL YOU STEPHEN?' asked Bishop Shalita of Ankole as we settled down in the comfortable sitting room of his pleasant bungalow in Mbarara in Western Uganda. It was two weeks since we had left Undukori in May 1962 and we had just driven 180 miles from Kampala in a hired car on a superb new highway to meet with the bishop. The difference with the Southern Sudan could not have been greater and was further accentuated by the bishop himself with the light brown skin of the people of the cool mountain areas of this part of Africa, his flawless English and his gracious home, all contrasting vividly with our jet black friends in their mud huts in the Sudan with whom we had lived so recently.

'I have asked CMS for the services of an agricultural missionary because we face two new problems in this country and I believe that the church should play its part is looking for solutions to them. The first is that the huge expansion in the number of schools in the past few years has resulted in large numbers of young men with a secondary education being unable to find work. Only ten years ago any young man who had been to secondary school was sure to find white collar employment. Parents were prepared to make great sacrifices to send a son to school in the certain hope that he in his turn would bring money back into the family from his employment. Now that is no longer the case, and the change has come about so quickly because of the speed with which schools have expanded, that both parents and children are confused. When young men cannot find work in this district they flock down to Kampala and Jinja convinced that there must be work in the big city. All too often they are finishing up on the streets eking out an existence washing cars or acting as porters in the market. They are ashamed to come home and admit defeat to their parents, and sooner or later they are in danger of slipping into crime. I am convinced that we should start an agricultural school to give such young men a couple of years of agricultural training so that they can become farmers. That is why I have asked you to come and see me, because from what I hear you would make an excellent principal of such a school'.

'You can certainly call me Stephen, and I have some experience of the situation that you describe because it was arising in Nigeria when I worked there ten years ago. In response to that challenge CMS founded a well staffed and funded agricultural school offering a two year course. It had excellent facilities and provided a high standard of training. Unfortunately hardly any of the young people who graduated from it went into farming. There were two main reasons for this. The first was that the school did not succeed in changing the image of farming as a dirty, sweaty occupation for illiterate people, because the students simply did not see any well educated people actually farming. The second was that virtually all the students signed up for the course in order to gain two more years of formal education which they felt would improve their chances of getting the white collar job which was their ambition in life. I had friends teaching at the school and went there quite often and was really well aware of the failure of what had looked like an appropriate response to the situation that you are describing here. I am sorry therefore that I really would not be willing to establish a similar project in your diocese.'

The bishop looked deeply disappointed as he had obviously started to plan for this initiative. 'Do you have any alternative suggestion then, or do we simply wash our hands of these young people?'

'I would certainly like to help but I would want to try and get at the root of the problem. If educated young men in your area see farming as a dull, dirty and inappropriate occupation for them then no amount of extra schooling is going to change that perception. I would like to help a couple of hundred of such people to become successful farmers and offer a real example of how a man with secondary education can make a satisfactory living out of farming, and that such a farmer would have nothing to be ashamed of for his chosen occupation.' After another half an hour of discussion the bishop was finally convinced, although it was obvious that he would still have liked to have an imposing institution rather than a group of successful young farmers who would be more difficult to show off to visitors.

'But you said that there were two problems, sir, what is the second?'

'Ah yes, well the very high price of coffee in recent years has led to a large gap developing between the prosperity of the coffee growing areas and those in which it will not grow. We have the extraordinary situation of large numbers of coffee growers in the centre of Uganda owning cars whilst in parts of my diocese there are still people dressed in goat skins. I am keen that we should try and show that in these poor areas farming could also be profitable. How about you selecting a really poor area for your experiment with secondary school leavers?'

'Well you are certainly offering me a challenge, I have to show young secondary school leavers that farming can be profitable and worthwhile, and do this in a really poor farming area. I don't know enough about your diocese to be able to make a decision just now, but I do enjoy challenges. All of this will depend on the decision by CMS as to where they will send me, but even if they agree that I come to you I have to go and work for them in England for five months, so I would not be able to start until almost the end of the year.'

The bishop looked disappointed and asked 'What on earth work do you have to do for CMS in England, I thought that all their work was overseas.'

'Well CMS depends on British people's donations to keep its thousand staff in the field, and people will only go on giving if they hear how their money is being spent. I will be travelling all over Britain in the coming months speaking at one or two meetings every day and sleeping in a different home every night. I can tell you it is much more tiring than working in the bush in Africa.' With that we parted, and Anne and I returned to Kampala and then flew on to England.

CMS had requests for my services from Nigeria and Kenya, but eventually decided that we should go to work with the Bishop of Ankole in Western Uganda. We arrived back in Mbarara, the district and diocesan headquarters, late in 1962, a couple of weeks after the country had gained its independence from Britain. The transition had been entirely peaceful and there appeared to be no ill feeling against individual Britons, many of whom stayed on in both the public and private sectors. There was a great deal of understandable euphoria and excitement combined with the anticipation that the country would now make great strides forward. We received a warm welcome from the bishop and started work straight away. He had identified the poorest county in the whole district and was anxious for me to go and have a look at it to see whether I thought that I could do anything with it.

'I don't think that I have ever been so cold in my life' I said as I pulled my stiff limbs off my camp bed and stood shivering in the chilly dawn air. I was with a young agricultural assistant in the high hills of Buhweju county, sleeping in a small thatched shelter with no door. All my experience of Africa had been in the hot tropics and I was totally unprepared for the cold nights at almost 7,000 feet, and my canvas camp bed and a single blanket had proved entirely inadequate for the climate of Buhweju. My companion had been born a couple of miles away and had been much better equipped. We had been to see the county chief the day before to ask if I might look into the possibility of a new farming initiative in his area. He was dubious that anything could be done with these cool, acid, bracken covered hills, but was perfectly happy for us to look around. Here we were on our first working morning ready to explore on foot the almost empty precipitous hills which stretched roadless for miles in every direction. We used elephant tracks whenever we could but when the animals were not going where we wanted we had to force our way through dense waist high bracken. We actually only walked about 250 miles in the next month, but the density of the vegetation and the steepness of the hills made it seem at least twice that distance. The widely scattered households that we encountered were indeed very poor and, true to the bishop's words, many of the children that we met were clothed in goat skins. I did have one enormous compensation for what was otherwise tiring and uncomfortable work. I could see for miles. In the Sudan our view had seldom been more than a couple of hundred yards. Now I spent my days looking out over lakes, mountains and magnificent sky-scapes, and I revelled in it. At the end of a month of surveying, the agriculturalist, with his local knowledge, and I with some sense of farming potential had selected a couple of thousand acres of land which looked to have possibilities. We walked back to the county chief and reported to him and then drove down to Mbarara to discuss the future with the bishop. Even fairly empty areas had names and our selected sight was called Nyakashaka, 'the place of little grass'. It is a name which brings back wonderful memories for Anne and me, but a lot had to be done before those memories could develop.

'Oh no!' I said under my breath as the bishop stood up in front of the two hundred strong audience of the diocesan synod and asked if anyone had a question for me. I had spent two weeks practising my speech in the local language, Runyankore, to present to this important meeting. I described my plan to start the first smallholder tea scheme in the area, initiate commercial strawberry growing for the first time in Uganda, and introduce the first pedigree Friesian cattle from Kenya to be the basis of a dairy industry, all of these making use of the cool moist climate of Buhweju. I had written it in English and then had a friend translate it into Runyankore. He then recited it in short bites into our newly acquired tape recorder and I sat down half a dozen times a day and mimicked his recording. I had then stood up in front the assembled senior dignitaries of Ankole and given what I was subsequently told was a lucid and fluent speech in their language. I sat down to a satisfying round of applause and then the bishop asked if there were any questions. Hands went up and I had to stand and recite almost the only phrase of the language which I knew, which was 'I am sorry, I do not speak Runyankore'. The audience murmured in total disbelief. They had just heard me deliver a fifteen-minute speech in that language! The bishop explained that I had learned to read the speech but that after less than two months in the country I did not speak Runyankore. Unfamiliar with the new invention of the tape recorder the audience was puzzled that anyone could accurately pronounce a language of which they knew nothing, but really appreciated my effort to avoid the tedium of a translator. Years later I would meet local leaders who would laughingly remind me of my embarrassment when the questions started coming at that meeting.

The bishop had been right to make me outline my plans in that audience which included local members of parliament, senior chiefs and prominent community leaders. Their support was crucial in surmounting the various bureaucratic hurdles which presented themselves over the following months and to make our plans known to potential recruits for this new initiative. The bishop was now enthusiastic about my plans so we could start looking for the resources and permission to embark on our scheme. We needed access to the land at Nyakashaka, the blessing of the Ministry of Agriculture for a quite fresh initiative in terms of crops and livestock, and we needed money to pay for the project.

'Rent? Rent? What are you talking about man?' The speaker was the elderly, senior Ugandan who chaired the Land Board. 'We should be paying Mr Carr to take this completely useless piece of land off our hands.' The English Lands Officer who was secretary to the Board looked duly mollified. I had just presented a map of the land that we wanted at Nyakashaka together with a description of how it would be used and an application for a twenty-year lease. The chairman had been in the audience at the synod meeting and had made up his mind before the current meeting had even begun. He was highly respected in Ankole society and so the lease was granted free of rent without any further ado. Forty years later the transformation of Nyakashaka has resulted in there being cases in court to dispute ownership of as little as a quarter of an acre of what was then described as totally useless land. One hurdle had been surmounted, now for the other two.

'Anything that will slow this party down would be welcome,' said the senior soil scientist sent by the Ministry of Agriculture to check and see whether Nyakashaka was suitable for my proposed plans for extensive tea development. All the morning we had been climbing up and down Buhweju's precipitous hills led by a twelve year old boy in a goat skin who had been detailed off by the local chief to carry the soil samples that were being collected. The child positively skipped up and down the hills, lying in the sun at each summit to wait for us to catch up with him. I had been climbing around for some weeks so that both my legs and lungs were holding up well. The heavily built English soil scientist was making much heavier weather of the whole exercise, and hence his remark when Anne met us at a pre-determined spot for a picnic lunch. She had said how much she would have liked to join us but she was concerned that she might slow the party down. 'Please, please join us' was our visitor's response. Despite his exhausting experience he wrote a favourable report and I was called to the Ministry Headquarters to provide more details of what I planned to do. There was considerable scepticism about my being able to attract secondary school leavers to live and work in such a remote area and one British officer said 'Well I hope that you will enjoy sitting in solitary splendour on your hill, Carr, enjoying the scenery.' They had no technical objections to my proposals and so gave their permission for me to go ahead. Two hurdles surmounted. One to go.

With land, official permission and local support in high places I put forward a budget to CMS as to what my costs would be. I wanted £3,000 to cut sixteen miles of road from Nyakashaka to the nearest existing road and £62,000 for all my other plans. Virtually all of this would be in the form of loans to farmers so would be repaid and could then be used for another purpose. CMS responded that they certainly did not have that kind of money available but that another Christian organization called Inter Church Aid (later Christian Aid) might be of help. My whole plan and budget covered four pages and produced the money that we needed. These days I never seem to see any application that covers less than fifty pages and some are a good deal more verbose than that. The donor world could benefit from the contribution of a large number of Readers Digest condensed books précis specialists. We soon learned that an enthusiastic vicar, John Bickersteth, in the Medway towns had offered to raise the entire amount, and with this assurance we were ready to make a fresh start.

CHAPTER 16

# Into the Hills

'I HAVE NEVER, never, had such a cold wash in all my life,' shivered Anne as she got a taste of the Buhweju evening chill. We were back at the same hut that I had camped in five months before and were sharing the cover of a bush for an evening wash down in icy water from a nearby stream and with a cutting wind biting into our naked bodies. We had moved up that day into Buhweju to start work, accompanied by two young men whom we had recruited to help us. We had hiked up with basic camping gear and were trying to get the sweat and grime off before we had a simple supper and bedded down for the night. The other two were behind their bush on the opposite side of the hut and from the sounds that were coming from their direction were enjoying their first bath in Buhweju no more than we were. A half an hour later with a good fire burning, a hurricane lamp lit and the smell of Anne's cooking in the air we all felt a great deal more cheerful. I had made very sure that we had enough bedding on this trip, and a good night's sleep had us all eager to get started on our new venture at dawn the next morning.

The previous three months, as we waited for lease documents, formal letters of permission and the assurance that we had funds, had been mostly spent with our ears glued to our tape recorder as we struggled with the complexities of Runyankore. We were now reasonably fluent and I was confident that I would be able to handle a large labour force. We had also recruited our first two Ugandan helpers who would be crucial to our success. They had come to us through an old friend from our Sudan days who was now the headmaster of a Ugandan school. He was anxious that we should have the right people and chose Jackson Kataraiha and Yotham Motoka from among his former students to come and meet us. They spent a long weekend with us in our temporary rented home and we got on well together. On the basis of that meeting and the reference of their headmaster we asked them to join us and embarked on a friendship which has lasted for forty years, mostly maintained by frequent letters but refreshed from time to time by joyous re-unions. It proved a source of some amusement that three of the four founders of Nyakashaka should be called after motorized

*Motoka (left) Carr and Jackson.*

transport. I had got my Carr by birth, Anne by marriage but Motoka much
more spectacularly by being born in the back of the lorry that was taking his
mother to hospital.

Our most urgent task was to get bivouacs built at Nyakashaka and so
avoid spending two hours each day walking backwards and forwards to our
present camp. Anne helped us select a suitable site and then the three men
set about cutting the saplings and grass that we needed for our temporary
shelters. It took us a couple of days to get two small huts built and on the
third day we moved over to live at Nyakashaka. We extended these shelters
in the following days but still expected to occupy them for only a short time
while we built more permanent houses. Little did we think that seven
months later we would still be in grass bivouacs. We found Anne three
good stones on which to cook and with the help of an empty kerosene tin
and some sand from a stream she was soon baking a delicious loaf every day
to supplement the limited rations that we had been able to carry up. How
different a move to that which we made to Undukori. No village in which
to settle, no dog, cat, chickens or bees and no near neighbours to whom we
could turn to for help and advice. What we did have was a cool climate,
mountain air like honey and the most glorious views we had ever seen in
our lives. These gave us boundless physical energy whilst the idea of

*Little did we think that seven months later we would still be in a grass bivouac.*

pioneering something quite new which nobody else had tried before gave us a zest for action which we remember with a mixture of disbelief and gratitude in our creaking old age.

'The first job has got to be the road,' I said as soon as we had some shelter. 'I have been looking for a likely route each time I came up here over the past months so I have a good idea of where we have to go. Now we need to mark out the first couple of miles before we recruit a labour gang. It's going to be a fairly winding affair to get down the first steep 1000 feet, but there are no serious rock outcrops in the way. The real problem comes after four miles when there is that almost sheer rock face that we have had creep along on our way here. It's going to take a lot of explosives to cut a ledge along it, but let's get started on the easier part first.'

We walked down the first couple of miles of my chosen route marking out one hairpin bend after another with saplings cut from the surrounding bush. 'Do you think that you could manage a gang of fifty men to start digging this road, Jackson?' I asked. He was confident that he could. A message to surrounding chiefs that we were offering paid work to men who would come armed with a hoe soon had a goodly sized labour force moving in from miles around in an area where paid work had never been available before. Some walked a number of miles each day while others built

*The rocky ledge was blasted out with thousands of charges of gelignite.*

themselves bivouacs around our boundary, returning to their homes for the week-end. I helped Jackson work out appropriate piece work rates for each depth of bank that had to be cut, and soon he was working confidently with a cheerful and enthusiastic gang which rapidly hewed a red, twisting, snake-like cut down the steep hills. Road making in so much of the world today conjures up pictures of large pieces of mechanical equipment, and it is easy to forget what men can achieve with a few simple hand tools. Our sixteen miles of mountain road was almost entirely built with hoes and shovels. The rocky ledge that we had to cut for six hundred yards was blasted out with thousands of charges of gelignite, but even the holes for the charges were drilled by hand using sharpened crowbars and sledge hammers and a lot of human sweat. It took thirteen months and thousands of man days before we could drive our Landrover up to our house, but forty years on the road is still in daily use.

With Jackson well established we could turn our minds to building. We were now experienced with mud and wattle construction after our Undukori efforts and with a substantial piece of forest within our boundary we were not short of materials. 'There's no need to worry about through draughts and keeping cool in this climate, and with the amount of rain there is I want my bedroom and living room under one roof' said Anne.

The result was a rectangular two-roomed mud and wattle cottage with the usual cow-dung and ground-up termite heap floor. The Ugandans had developed a skill that did not exist in the Sudan and could provide a really attractive finish to a mud house with a plaster made from cow dung and sand. There were local lime deposits and so we finished up with a white, thatched cottage with rambler roses and fuchsias growing round it. Although the structure was almost identical to our huts at Undukori the end result looked a good deal different. Like everyone else in the area we had no glass in our 'windows' but wooden shutters to keep out the worst of the rain, which also plunged the house into darkness when shut. They were therefore only closed during the day out of dire necessity in a big storm. They thus remained open on the many days each year when we were in the clouds and these drifted in through one 'window' and out through another which gave the cottage its name of 'Clouds Drift'. Expatriates' opinions of our home depended almost entirely on the weather at the time of their visit, as became very clear after the first time that the CMS Secretary for Uganda came to see us.

'Norman said that he would be here by ten and it's now half past eleven. The road is really slippery after all this rain and I think that he may have got stuck. Don't you think that you had better go and see if he's alright?' said Anne on the day of his scheduled visit. Our road was completed by this time and so I set off in my Landrover and sure enough a very miserable Norman Campbell was sitting in his car completely stuck in the mud on one of our steep hills. 'Just leave the car here, Norman, and bring your stuff into mine. There is absolutely no crime around here so you need not worry about it. I'll come with some men tomorrow and get it out.'

We drove through thick cloud and drizzle to our house and suggested that he get his sweater out before he joined us for lunch. Sheepishly he admitted that he had not brought one.

'But Norman I made a special point in my letter of saying that you really would need a good thick sweater,' I said with some exasperation.

'I know you did but I have lived in this country for over twenty years and I have never been anywhere that was cool enough to justify a sweater.' He was a big man and I am small and no pullover of mine would begin to fit him so as the clouds came drifting through the room and the rain dripped steadily off the thatch Norman spent the afternoon sitting huddled under a blanket as we did our work. At least we could ensure that he was warm in bed, but the next morning the weather was identical. There was no view of any kind, water dripped off every branch and roof and it was cold. I took him back to his car with a gang of our workers and saw him safely on his way. Two weeks later the post produced a gracious 'bread and butter' letter thanking us for his pleasant stay in our delightful cottage. Six weeks later his wife wrote to ask if their sixteen year old son could come and work with us for his school holiday as he got so bored in Kampala. We said that we would be happy to have him, and after a few weeks I drove the fifty miles to Mbabara to pick him up off the bus. It was a glorious day with fluffy white clouds sailing across a clear blue sky and as we turned the last corner and our white thatched cottage came into sight with its spectacular backdrop of mountains and lakes, he blurted out 'Well I don't think this is a ghastly, god-forsaken hole at all!' So much for the sincerity of 'bread and butter' letters, but typical of the range of opinions held about our home.

There were not only staff houses, office and stores to be built but dormitory blocks for the young men whom we hoped would join us. We put together another gang of workers and quickly got a number of buildings up and mudded. Then the problem began. In the Sudanese dry season the mud on a wall would dry in a week to ten days in the searing hot dry weather. Here at Nyakashaka we would have a few sunny days when the mud would really start to dry and then four days of cloud and drizzle when the mud would seem to re-absorb more moisture than it had lost. We started to become desperate, not only were the four of us still in grass bivouacs but we were expecting to start recruiting farmers and had nowhere for them to sleep. We had been building with such confidence and showing so much detailed knowledge of this method of construction that none of our local workmen had thought to offer any advice, but at last one of them came to me and said 'But Bwana when are you going to start the fires? This mud will not dry in years if you do not have a fire in the house.' The next day a small gang was detailed off to cut firewood and maintain fires in the dozen buildings that we were waiting to use. Within three weeks the whole situation had changed and we could at last start using our buildings.

The tea plant loves acid soil, needs a steady supply of moisture, improves in quality with cool weather, provides an income on a regular basis throughout the year and lasts for over a hundred years. These were all factors which made me decide that tea would be the crop which could transform the economy of Buhweju and also provide a worthwhile enterprise for our school-leaver farmers. We therefore had to start straight away with establishing a nursery for the millions of tea trees that we would need. There was no flat land anywhere (our nearest football pitch was twelve miles away!) and so I showed Yotham how to terrace a hillside into a

*Hundreds of thousands of healthy young tea plants.*

series of giant steps and he soon had a gang of eighty men doing just that. I brought in tons of seed from the best estates in East Africa and had the pleasure of seeing acres of bracken-covered hillside transformed into level beds of hundreds of thousands of healthy young tea plants which thrived on our soil and climate. When I visit the hills of Nyakashaka forty years later it is deeply satisfying to see those same seedlings as mature trees which will provide a livelihood to their owners for another seventy years.

Road, buildings and tea nursery on their way, now we needed farmers. Would we sit in solitary splendour looking at the view or would educated young men be prepared to take the risky plunge and come and join us? The moment to find out had come. We had put the message out through the widespread network of the church, and local chiefs had been co-operative in letting people know what we had to offer. Soon a steady trickle of applications started coming through the post. A date was set for interviews in Mbarara and to our relief some fifty young men turned up.

'I want to be quite honest with you,' I said. 'Buhweju is not an easy county. There are no buses, very few shops and it is extremely hilly. You will have to do a lot of walking and the weather is cool and wet. I will provide a dormitory to sleep in but you will have to look after yourselves as far as food is concerned. In the long term I hope that I can help you to become successful tea farmers, owning your own land and with a greater income than most of you could hope to get in the sort of jobs that are available. Tea lasts for more than a hundred years so that once you have planted it you will get an regular income from it for the rest of your lives. If you decide to try us out I will ask you to come and work as a general labourer for six months. This will give you a chance to see whether you do want to make Buhweju county your permanent home, and it will give us the chance to see whether we think that you will make a good farmer. You will receive the same wages as all the other workers which will enable you to pay your own way and possibly save a bit of money to help you when you start up on your own farm.'

The questions came thick and fast, and then I was helped by some local leaders to talk individually to each young man. At the end of the day thirty-seven men said that they would give it a try and they were told when to report for work and how to reach us. They moved into either the road or nursery gang, Jackson and Yotham kept a special eye on them and I made a point of spending evenings at their dormitories to get to know them personally. We had budgeted for thirty farmers in the first year and after a bit of further sorting of our recruits that is what we got. It began to look as if Carr would not have to sit in solitary splendour looking at the view.

With potential farmers on trial we had to get down to surveying the five-acre plots which each one was to be allocated. The nature of the country was such that they could not all be in one place, as we reckoned to give each man a plot of land on which all the land was of reasonable quality. I was back to a lot of pushing through the bracken and clambering up and down hills. As the work became more widely scattered, with the road gang working some miles away and the prospect of disbursed farmers to be supervised, Anne and I decided that we had to have an alternative transport to our own legs. A letter to an old Wye friend in Kenya produced an offer of two suitable horses and a few weeks later I was at the nearest railway station seventy miles away awaiting their arrival. The train was ten hours late so that instead of unloading them in the afternoon the job had to be done at one in the morning. The station had no lights and when we opened the horsebox door we could just see the outline of the two horses but no details of which was which. The Kenyan groom who had accompanied them on their three-day journey climbed stiffly down into this strange environment. He spoke no English and I spoke no Kiswahili so we had to communicate by sign language. He handed me a letter, which I stuffed into my pocket, backed up the lorry that I had hired and loosed the first horse and tried to

*The horses improved our efficiency beyond measure.*

lead him onto the lorry. The groom helped but it was a half an hour battle
and we both nearly got kicked quite badly. We finally had him on and tied
up. The second horse then simply walked on by herself with no problem at
all. When I opened the letter the next morning in the daylight I read 'On no
account try to unload Tommy first as he will be almost impossible to move.
Get the mare Dalliance on to the lorry and then Tommy will be no trouble.'
Had they come in daylight I would have read the letter and we would have
avoided a very unpleasant battle in the dark as we tried to unload Tommy
first.

Within days of our getting the horses to Nyakashaka, where they proved
ideally suited and improved our efficiency beyond measure, the processions
started. These were the first horses in that whole area of Uganda and
thousands of schoolchildren were walked by their teachers for up to fifteen
miles to come and see them. 'If we charged sixpence per child we could pay
for the horses, tack and transport,' Anne said as we made our way through
another throng of children. The novelty lasted for about a month and then
life returned to normal. I had selected an older man, Kapitani, from among
our workers, who had a reputation of being excellent with cows, and
invited him to be the groom. He said that he would be happy to do so.
Good grazing was only found in isolated patches in the hills and so

whenever the horses were not in use he was to take them to where he knew there was good grass. 'These are not cows, Kapitani, you cannot drive them around. You will have to keep this halter on them and lead them with a rope and then give them a long rope when you get to the grazing.' Kapitani said nothing and for the next few days would be seen with the horses on a halter. It was after about a week that I saw him walking back carrying the halters on his arm and with two completely loose horses in an area with no fence within a hundred miles. It was an unusual procession. Kapitani was in the middle with a very lively Arab pony with his head over one shoulder and the more stolid Somali mare with her head over the other. As they drew nearer I could hear that Kapitani was talking to them without stopping. He never again put a halter on them and two horses wandered the hills of Buhweju with a man who had never seen a horse in his life acting as the most successful of 'horse whisperers'. He developed a deep affection for them and turned into a superb groom.

East African estates at that time used a system of bringing tea into production which took seven years from seed to first plucking. This was much too long for a smallholder to wait. I planned to give the farmers two year old plants to get them started and I had been introduced to a totally different method of shaping the tea bushes which would bring them into bearing after a further two years. This still meant that I had to provide farmers with a source of income for those two years. We offered them the choice of growing strawberries, having a hundred laying hens or becoming vegetable growers. None had done any of these things before and it took many evenings of talking for them to make a final decision. For whichever they chose they were given a loan which was going to have to be repaid from their production. The thousand day-old chicks came in from Kenya, the strawberry plants came from Cambridge in England and the vegetable seeds came from South Africa, so a lot of letters and travel was involved in getting them started. Each new farmer was also given a twenty pound loan with which to build himself a house and then he had to get down to the serious business of planting his tea, the 'green gold' which was meant to support him for the rest of his life.

'Damn that alarm!' I said as I dragged myself out of sleep at half past three on a cold wet morning. We were in the middle of our first tea planting season. The plants in our own nursery were only one year old and so I had to buy tea plants from an estate a hundred miles away for our first farmers to plant. These were being delivered every other day to a point just below the rock face which we were now blasting out of the way, but which was still a barrier to motor transport. The lorries arrived in the evening and I had to set out at four in the morning for the hour and a half walk to where they were parked accompanied by thirty farmers and the labourers they were hiring to help them. I had to check off the thousands of plants and sign for them and then divide them up between the farmers who in turn had to sign for what they had received and carry them back up the long steep hills to their farms. Each man needed 6,000 plants for his initial planting and they could only plant 200 a day, so I had thirty days of 3.30 alarm clock calls. The second intake of farmers simply had to collect their plants as they needed them from our own nursery, and to this day the first group still consider themselves better men because of the struggle they had to get their tea planted.

'Stop, stop!' The young man ran out from the cowshed and came dashing up to the car. 'One of the new heifers is calving and she is in real trouble, you must come and help.' It was Sunday morning and Anne and I were in our best clothes with Yotham, Jackson and a couple of other friends on our way to the parish church twelve miles away for the christening of our son Christopher, who was perched on Anne's knee in his very best outfit. I got out of the car and went to look at the heifer. An hour later my best clothes were ruined beyond redemption, we had abandoned any attempt at going to the service, but our first Friesian calf had been born. The vicar waited in vain for our arrival, was not at all pleased with our excuse, and Chris was not baptized for another six months.

The Friesian herd was a separate experiment. There were no high producing cows in the area at the time and yet the conditions seemed excellent for them. I had fenced off forty acres of grazing and improved on the local grasses and then Anne and I had driven down to Kenya and gone to the farm with the finest herd of pedigree Friesian cattle in East Africa. We selected ten beautiful in-calf heifers and, after a lot of humming and haaing, had finally settled on a fine eighteen-month-old bull with an excellent pedigree. The animals came up on the train and I loaded them on to a lorry and brought them as near as I could to Nyakashaka and drove them up to their new pasture. Two school leavers from cattle keeping families had been selected separately from the main group and were going to become dairy farmers. As soon as the cattle arrived I was faced with a serious problem. What should I do about the bull? Local cattle were extremely docile and treated almost as members of the family and hence the bulls were never aggressive. I was introducing half a ton of notorious Friesian aggression to people who had no fear of animals at all. What should I do? Say that this is a dangerous animal, and induce fear in the men, which the bull would immediately sense and respond to, or say nothing and let them treat the animal like one of their own and risk having somebody gored? After a lot of thought I opted for the second course of action, given that the bull would be running with the heifers which would tend to keep him quieter. The men immediately started talking to him and petting him as they would one of their own animals. I remained nervous until a couple of months later when I went over to the cowshed and found the naked five year old brother of the cowman driving a large Friesian bull out of the yard with a twig. The bull grew enormous and never showed the slightest indication of hurting anybody.

Our dairy experiment was not without its problems. The other farmers growing tea and strawberries were dealing with crops they had never seen before in their lives and so had to learn totally new skills and techniques. They reckoned that I knew what I was talking about and followed my instructions. The two young dairy farmers on the other hand had been working with cattle since early childhood and reckoned to know all that was necessary about keeping cows. The fact that the management of a cow which gave twenty litres of milk a day had to be different to one that gave two was not that obvious to them. A cow is a cow and we know how to look after cows was their motto. We did have problems, but we also demonstrated that Friesian cattle could thrive in this environment and produce twenty litres of milk a day. People came from far and wide to see this amazing sight and soon more prosperous farmers from the lower land on the borders of Buhweju came to me to ask how they could obtain similar animals. I put them in touch with a thoroughly honest livestock dealer in Kenya and slowly the number of Friesians in the area began to grow. To-day they number 5,000, belonging to a large number of small scale dairy farmers and making this the largest single milk producing area in Uganda.

Eighteen months after Anne's freezing bath on a deserted hillside we had started to see the transformation for which we had come into these hills.

# CHAPTER 17

# Results

'PLEASE WOULD YOU let me continue. I am trying to help some young Ugandan farmers and if you send me back to Mbarara their produce will be ruined.' I was desperate. I had set out from home at three in the morning with our first consignment of strawberries for the Kampala market. I was in a new one-ton pick-up that we had fitted out specifically to carry the strawberry punnets so that they would arrive in perfect condition. The car had run well and I had motored through a sleeping Mbarara at half past four and completely forgotten that, following on an assassination attempt on the president, all travellers had to collect a movement permit from their local police station. Here I was just 50 miles from Kampala and the policeman on the road block was telling me to drive back 130 miles to Mbarara and then come back to Kampala. That would mean delivering the strawberries in the heat of the day and losing all the advantage in terms of quality on which we were depending.

'What you are carrying is none of my business, but you have to go back and get a movement permit.' The policeman was large and apparently adamant.

'But you don't understand, the crop that I am carrying is not bananas, just a few hours of hot sun and the fruits will be spoilt and the young farmers will lose their market.

'Let's see what you are making all this fuss about,' he said. I opened the back and there were the beautiful strawberries in the half pound punnets that had been made for us with Nyakashaka's name and a nice mountain picture. 'And how much are you going to sell one of these little packets for?'

'We will get four shillings and fifty cents each,' I replied.

'What? I can buy two huge bunches of bananas for less than that. Who pays that sort of money for a handful of little red fruits.'

I started to be economical with the truth. 'It's white people and Indians. If a man eats a packet of these then his experience in bed with his wife at night is something quite different.'

'Oh now I understand why people pay so much. When do they eat them?'

'Well about seven o'clock in the morning is the best time. Then they have plenty of time to work properly. Would you like to try a couple of packets?' He accepted them, decided that I was not a threat to the nation and let me go. As far as I am aware it is the only time that I have knowingly bribed an official in Africa and my conscience did not trouble me greatly. As most aphrodisiacs depend on psychology rather than physiology I hope the strawberries worked for him.

I had run into unexpected problems in getting a market for our strawberries. I knew just what the Kenyan product looked like after a twenty-four hour train journey for which they had often been poorly stacked. I knew that we could offer a far fresher and better quality product, yet when I went round the top hotels and supermarkets I ran into a wall of prejudice. 'Black farmers could never produce good quality strawberries, apart from which only the Kenyan climate is any good for the crop.' In one way or another that was the message that I had received from rather superior sounding white managers. It was only after a lot of persistence that I had finally obtained modest orders from several customers for a total of one hundred and fifty pounds, which was a small part of our expected production. Hence my concern, when I was personally delivering our first consignment, to ensure that they arrived in perfect condition. After my encounter with the policeman the rest of the journey went well and by eight o'clock I was delivering flawless fresh strawberries to very surprised customers. Within a month all imports from Kenya stopped and we were selling a ton of strawberries a week to Kampala. Situated a few miles from the equator our hours of daylight did not change and consequently we could produce strawberries throughout the year. The farmers were delighted to be receiving more money than they had ever had before. While the pick-up set out three mornings a week at three o'clock to go to the capital there was also a five-ton truck going in the opposite direction to deliver vegetables, potatoes and fresh eggs to the hotels, lodges and a large copper mine that lay within an eighty mile radius of Nyakashaka. To add to our satisfaction as to how the first part of our strategy was working was the fact that the new young tea was growing better and faster than we had dared to hope. More farmers had joined the scheme and the surrounding hills were turning a different shade of green as tea replaced bracken.

It was in fact only a little over eighteen months after the first tea was planted that 'two leaves and a bud' became our motto. It is just the young shoots of tea that are picked and the standard for this is the two youngest leaves and the little shoot. All the farmers had it rubbed in to them that if

*The new young tea was growing better than we had dared to hope.*

they tried to cheat and pick three leaves in order to sell more tea then their produce would be rejected at the factory. The great day arrived at last when it was announced that all the first farmers could start plucking and a buying centre was established from where the green leaf would be taken to a tea factory 25 miles away. There was huge excitement and people started plucking as soon as there was a chink of early dawn light. By one o'clock when the tea had to be brought for weighing all of that excitement had evaporated. A good tea plucker can gather 50 pounds of tea in a day. He or she works simultaneously with both hands and with all four fingers of both hands. A beginner almost always has a lot of difficulty in plucking with both hands simultaneously and so picks off one shoot with the thumb and index finger of one hand and then does the same with the other. The result is a total harvest of four or five pounds at the end of seven hours of work. That was what happened to all our farmers when they started and there were some very long faces at the buying centre as they found out how little they had earned from a long morning's work. They simply would not believe that it was possible to pluck ten times more than they had achieved, but sure enough in a couple of months that is exactly what they were doing. In the climate of Buhweju each bush was ready for plucking every eight days so with a three acre plot to cover the farmers have to pluck five days a

*The great day arrived when the first farmers could start plucking.*

week throughout the year. If the tea is not plucked for a couple of weeks it overgrows and requires a lot more work to get it back into the right condition once again. This steady flow of tea does ensure a regular income but it does also mean that people have a full time job with no significant gaps in the work. Our farmers were absolutely delighted to see money coming in every day for the first six months to a year but then they woke up to the fact that tea did not allow for holidays. It was some time before their families grew and the burden could be shared between different members while the money still came in.

Farming was not our only concern and we had started a church service at our house for the first small group of farmers. The numbers soon outgrew our accommodation and so we embarked on building a church to serve the area. 'That's a question for which I have been waiting for years,' said my architect friend when I asked him if he had any ideas for a simple rural church which was not just a rectangular box. 'There is only one logical shape for a church and that is a triangle. How many churches have you been to in Africa where two leaders occupy one third of the building and a couple of hundred people are squeezed into the remaining two thirds. Now, in a triangle, the leader occupies a tiny area at the apex and ninety five percent of the space is available for the congregation. What's more with a triangle you can have a very wide building with no internal pillars because the roof trusses only have to go across the angles of the triangle and not the whole width of the building.' He promptly sat down and drew the detailed plans of a church which had three sides of 70 feet each. Building was done on Saturday mornings and participation was entirely voluntary, but virtually all the farmers turned out. We built the walls of mud and wattle but the roof had to be of corrugated iron because thatch would have been too heavy for so large a structure. It fulfilled all of my architect friend's expectations, provided an original building and has certainly stood the test of time. Virtually no work has had to be carried out on it and today it looks almost exactly as it did when it was built almost forty years ago. Over time several of the farmers were ordained into the church and one of those is the vicar of the parish today.

After four years we felt that Nyakashaka could prosper without us being there all the time and so we moved to another part of Uganda to start again. By this time there were a hundred school leavers farming tea and I had employed staff to help other people who had moved into the area to plant their own tea. A co-operative society handled the marketing and I returned every month or two to sort out any problems. The tea area steadily expanded and all went well until 1974 when the regime of Idi Amin brought development across the country to a halt. The tea estates were shut down and there was no factory to which the farmers could sell their crop. It was no longer possible to buy the cattle dip crucial to keeping Friesian cows alive and the dairy farmers had to travel hundreds of miles to the neighbouring country of Rwanda to buy it. I had been forced to leave the country and could be of no help. The tea was abandoned but the farmers did not leave Buhweju. They searched out small patches of more fertile soil on which to grow food and settled down to six years of subsistence farming. Amin was overthrown at the end of the seventies, I returned with a different hat and was able to use my influence to get their factory rehabilitated and restarted. The ten-foot tall tea plants were cut down to two feet and six weeks later they were back in production and the 'green gold' started to flow out of Buhweju once more.

Anne and I were invited back to Nyakashaka in July 2003 to celebrate the fortieth anniversary of our founding of the scheme. We received a tumultuous welcome to a very different place to that in which we had camped forty years before. The thousands of acres of tea stretch out for miles. No longer is the only shop run out of one of the farmers' houses but there is a trading centre with a dozen or more shops. Anne's mud and wattle dispensary has been replaced with a pleasant small modern hospital with a fully qualified resident doctor. Farmers no longer come to my cow dung floored little office for loans but to a proper bank. Two primary schools and a secondary school deal with the educational needs of the children and two buses a day into town have eliminated all those miles of walking. A huge marquee had been erected and we were set in the midst of members of parliament, the Director of Agriculture and a bevy of local dignitaries while some eight hundred members of the farmers' families filled the rest of the tent. Songs of praise for us from different children's choirs were followed by praise dances by women's groups and then the serious business of lengthy and fulsome speeches occupied the next couple of hours. We were regaled with gifts by different groups and then moved on to a photographic session with all our old friends which was only brought to an end by the onset of darkness. To my amazement, for one who can no longer remember the name of somebody I worked with yesterday, I managed to recall the names of virtually all the farmers, now all grandfathers who had matured from the young school leavers who so bravely pioneered the hills of Buhweju forty years earlier.

In my own speech I tried to accentuate the fact that, while we were deeply grateful for all the nice things that had been said about us, Anne and I had only spent four years getting Nyakashaka started and that most of the credit of reaching the point where tea production was up to £2 million a year had to go to the farmers who had worked and struggled through good times and bad to maintain and build on the foundations that we had laid. Our Buhweju experience had more than confirmed what we had learned at Undukori about the adaptability and skills of African small scale farmers. We had introduced a range of different crops that nobody had ever seen before. Both tea and strawberries required methods of production which bore no relationship to anything in farmers' previous experience, and yet in a matter of months they had mastered the technology and been able to pass it on to other people. Even maintaining a steady supply of high quality peas, brussels sprouts, beetroots, cauliflowers and carrots had involved crops and growing methods which were quite unfamiliar to the farmers. By the time we left Nyakashaka we had helped farmers to plant about 400 acres of tea. The expansion of that area to the current 3,000 acres took place as one farmer taught a neighbour what to do. The original growers were indeed school leavers with a reasonable level of education but the people who moved in subsequently were a mixture of literate, semi-literate and illiterate smallholders all of whom were ready to experiment with a quite new system of farming and adopt the complexities of managing a strange and demanding crop.

This experience has been replicated across the continent as new cash crops and farming methods have spread with remarkable rapidity. The strange new crop of cocoa was brought from Central America to the Gold Coast (now Ghana) at the very end of the nineteenth century. It bore no relationship to anything that farmers had seen before and the preparation of the crop for sale requires a system of fermentation which tallied with nothing in their previous experience. And yet in less than twenty years smallholders were exporting 176,000 tons of the crop, and before long had become the largest producers in the world. Cotton was brought from America to Uganda early in the twentieth century. Once again a strange crop, unfamiliar to the local small scale farmers, but within twenty years they were producing 200,000 bales of cotton and they doubled that figure over the following twelve years.

Their adaptability has not just been shown with new crops. For reasons I have never been able to discover a Scotsman was selected to come to Uganda in 1921 to teach people how to train oxen for ploughing and then how to actually use that technology for land preparation instead of using a hoe. He started work in the cattle keeping area of Teso and selected half a dozen chiefs' sons as his pupils. After only two years of work the colonial office had an economy drive and closed that scheme. The Scotsman returned home and nobody else took up the work, and yet the technology spread from those few young men to thousands of farmers. Traders brought ploughs in from India and by 1938 there were 15,000 ploughs in use by people who had never before trained an ox to pull anything and never seen land ploughed. Within a few years ploughing had become almost the sole method of land preparation in Teso district.

I was fortunate that none of the work that I did over my years in the Sudan and Uganda involved any significant amount of farm machinery, because it was with machines that African workers gained their worst reputation. 'Everything they touch they manage to break' has been the complaint of large scale commercial white farmers in different parts of the continent for many years as they talk about their local staff, but perhaps the fault is not of one party only. A good friend of mine farmed in Kenya some years ago and sang this same song about the incompetence of his local staff when handling machines. 'Can't they see that the nut is coming loose or the oil is getting low?' he would ask with exasperation. 'Why am I blessed with such ham-fisted staff ?' Then the Mau Mau rebellion broke out. His workers belonged to a different tribe to the rebelling Kikuyu and so were formed into a platoon to track down rebels in the forest with my friend as their commander. 'Why on earth are we blessed with this completely useless European?' was now the complaint of his workers as they moved silently through the forest at night while his own progress sounded more like a charging buffalo. 'Didn't you see that broken twig? The starlight is quite bright,' they would ask as he completely missed what to them was an obvious sign that they were on the track of somebody. Now the roles were reversed. He was the one who could not get anything right and was constantly messing up their work. Slowly he began to realize that just as he had no background experience and upbringing whatever in night tracking in the forest and could not therefore just 'pick it up', so his workers had absolutely no background experience in using machines and could likewise not really be expected just to 'pick up' those strange skills. He started an intensive training programme for all of his staff and the level of breakages and of his frustration soon dropped sharply.

Generalized reputations deserve to be questioned before they are accepted too readily, and the same applies to the label of 'lazy' that I have heard applied to my friends and neighbours over the years. The accusation is all too often made by people who have virtually no real contact with those whom they are criticizing. I hear the accusation being made by white women in Malawi who have little idea of how local people really fill their days. In the village where we now live there are a group of women who, in addition to all their farm and house work, go into the neighbouring forest to cut firewood for sale each afternoon. They get up soon after three o'clock each morning, load 20-30 kilos of firewood on to their heads and walk seven kilometres to our nearest town of Zomba. Traders are waiting for them in the market at five to buy their bundles and to sort and prepare the wood for retailing in small lots. The women then climb back uphill to their homes, where they arrive at about the time that the women who talk of lazy Malawians are just getting out of bed.

At other times the accusations arise because people simply do not think through the reasons for other people's actions. 'Why don't farmers do this, that or the other?' I am often asked by people who have not started to work out what the rewards for doing 'this, that or the other' would be. Often the returns to the extra labour involved are so small that it is entirely understandable why people are not adopting some activity that an 'expert' is proposing. It is quite certain that the critics would not dream of working for such insignificant rewards. Likewise, with the current official agricultural wage in Malawi being less than four English pence per hour as compared to six pounds in Britain, it hardly surprises me that farm labourers here do not demonstrate all the industriousness and commitment that their employers might desire. We have always found ourselves to be living with people whose energy and capacity for hard work when on their own farms, or when offered the right incentives has never ceased to amaze us.

'Why are you helping people to grow tea or coffee for foreigners to drink or strawberries for the local elite instead of concentrating on improving people's food supply?' This was the question that critics of our work raised from time to time, and it was one that I found difficult to understand. At Undukori coffee had brought about a general improvement in the whole standard of living of the community as well as providing an invaluable cash buffer to serious hunger if a crop failed or was destroyed. At Nyakashaka we took land which could support small crops of low yielding millet worth ten or twelve pounds an acre and planted it up to tea which gave an income more than ten times greater. Surveys of cash crop farmers in Malawi have consistently shown that they are better fed than those who produce food crops only, because the cash offers security in times of poor harvests. I find the question somewhat arrogant in its assumption that someone sitting in an office thousands of miles away should dictate to African farmers what or what not they should grow, when they would not dream of doing the same to one of their own compatriots. The overwhelming majority of small scale farmers in Africa who grow a crop to sell rather than to eat do so as a matter of their own choice and not because someone is pressurizing them into a particular type of farming. My response to the question was basically that I have tried with some success to help farmers to embark on an enterprise which meets their needs rather than fulfilling the ideology of armchair critics.

It strikes me that anyone reading this chapter with its accent on the innovativeness, adaptability, skill and hard work of small scale farmers in Africa would be justified in asking 'if they have all these attributes why have they stayed so poor?' That is a very fair question and the answer deserves more than a foot note at the end of a chapter, but will be given much fuller treatment later in the book. In the meantime we rejoice at the progress made by the farmers at Nyakashaka as a result of our venture into the hills all those years ago.

# CHAPTER 18

# Our Family Grows

'THERE'S A TELEGRAM in the mailbag, I wonder what on earth can be wrong?' We were in our early days at Nyakashaka and took it in turns once a fortnight to walk the eighteen miles to the house where the bus driver left our mailbag. Today had been Yotham's turn and in among the letters Anne had discovered the telegram, the first that we had received in Africa. She tore it open and then gasped. 'What's happened, what's wrong?' I asked anxiously.

'Well nothing's wrong, but it is still a bit of a surprise. It is from the archbishop's wife and she is asking if we would stand by our original agreement with her and come to the Mission Hospital as soon as possible and collect a baby.'

Remote rural Africa did not offer much help to couples who faced problems with having a child, and after ten years of marriage we had been forced to face up to the fact that we would not be having children of our own. The wife of the Archbishop of Uganda, Mrs Brown, heard of our situation and asked whether, should the need arise, we would consider adoption. We gave the matter a lot of thought before replying because of the pioneering nature of our work, but then had decided that if our neighbours could perfectly well raise children under remote and rough conditions then there was really no reason why we should not be able to do the same. We therefore told Mrs Brown that we would be interested. That had been six months ago and now suddenly Anne was faced with a twenty-four hour pregnancy. Early the following morning we walked down to the Landrover and set out for Kampala. We confirmed that the baby was waiting in the hospital so I went to the market and bought a locally woven Moses basket and Anne bought milk, a bottle and a book on how to raise babies. We then went to collect a nine-day-old son whom we had already decided to name Christopher. We stayed in Kampala for a day to make sure that we could manage the feeding and that there were no other problems and then set out for our grass hut in the hills. We left the Landrover in its usual place at the end of the road and then I carried the baby in his basket for the long miles to Nyakashaka to receive a warm but puzzled welcome from Yotham and

Jackson. They were entirely used to a family taking in a needy child from a relative, but had never met a situation in which people adopted the child of total strangers. This in no way detracted from their delight at having a baby around the camp.

'It is not a very good house is it?' asked the young child welfare officer who had been appointed to supervise us until the formal adoption procedures had been completed. We heard subsequently that he had refused the order to come and inspect a white family until he was told that in newly independent Uganda he would have to deal with any race that needed his offices. He set out from Kampala expecting to drive up to a large modern bungalow with an aloof white family and was wondering how on earth he would make his assessment in so forbidding an environment for a young Ugandan graduate. Then he found that he had to walk 16 miles to reach us and that our single-roomed grass shack which the baby was sharing with a cat, dog and farm tools was more primitive than any home that he had ever visited. 'We are building a permanent house and this will be Christopher's room,' we told him as we showed him the skeleton of our new home.

'Well I certainly hope that next time I come I will find the baby in more suitable accommodation,' he said, and we assured him that he would. That was before we knew how long it would take for the mud to dry in our mountain climate, and to our embarrassment he found us in our grass hut for two more visits. He had to admit that the baby seemed both happy and healthy and so he allowed the adoption procedure to continue.

Formal legal adoption had been confined to white families only in Uganda and had been so rare that there were none of the necessary forms in print when we made our application. In consequence Chris was an articulate two year old when we were at last called to the High Court in Kampala for the final adoption hearing before a judge. We were accompanied by the child welfare officer, who had become a good friend, the head of the adoption agency and Norman Campbell, a close friend who had agreed to fill the required position of *pater ad litem*. As the bewigged and berobed judge entered the small courtroom, we stood in what was intended to be respectful silence. 'Look at that funny man, mummy, what's he got on his head? He does look funny doesn't he?' Our companions were having the utmost difficulty in keeping straight faces but the judge showed no sign of having heard the comments and ordered us to be seated.

'Do you take this child…' the sonorous voice started to enquire.

'He's got a very funny voice hasn't he, mummy? Why doesn't he talk like other people?' interjected Chris. Despite Anne's efforts and Chris being a well behaved child, we still had a running commentary throughout the proceedings and the child welfare officer spent most of the time pretending to blow his nose as he used his handkerchief to cover his laughter. The judge continued to ignore the comments completely and to our great relief finally signed all the necessary documents and Chris became legally ours.

We soon appreciated the advantage of raising a young child in a rural African setting where we were surrounded by friendly and helpful people on all sides. We had watched the success of our neighbours in the Sudan in raising happy, secure and affectionate children and we now started to experience the same environment ourselves as Chris was absorbed into our community. I never ceased to wonder at the patience and skill of our staff and neighbours in dealing with him. When an inquisitive and talkative two or three year old son came to watch me struggling underneath a broken vehicle it would usually be not much more than ten minutes before I would assure him that his mother needed him urgently. My mechanic, Benoni, doing a better job than me on a more complex problem, would answer Chris's endless questions for the entire morning and thereby win his passionate devotion. The same applied to our drivers, headmen, and neighbours. The outcome of this attitude to children is very easy to see. I can sit in a room with half a dozen men, each of us with a young child on our knees, and carry on a perfectly reasonable conversation. Every now and then a child asks a question. Our conversation is stopped, the question is considered seriously and the child is answered and then adult talk is resumed. At no time do any of the children find it necessary to misbehave or show off in order to attract attention to themselves, and so they absorb information while we enjoy their company.

When Chris was old enough he could go and play with children of his own age belonging to the young farmers. The nearest of these was Fred Nkuruho, who was just the same age as Chris. It is a source of great pleasure to me that this child of one of our first tea farmers whose early education was at a simple, vernacular primary school with few facilities, no teaching aids and young untrained teachers now has a dozen letters after his name and is the chief executive officer of a large organization. Few people in England seeing an African student in a university town can have any idea of the kind of education which some of these young men and women received in their early years. During the visit of the principal of an English college to our home in Malawi I pressed him to come with me to visit our local primary school before he embarked on his work at the national university. The school has over 2,000 pupils housed in a small group of classrooms. In the lower classes there are over one hundred children to a teacher. The children sit on the floor jammed together so tightly that the teacher has no hope of moving between them and has simply to teach by rote from the front with no access to teaching aids. Higher up in the school the drop-out rate reduces class size to 60 and the children sit on benches, but, all the same, learning is virtually all by rote. The school is blest with an outstanding headmaster but half of his staff have no formal qualification. My friend spent two hours in the school and claimed to have gained a totally new perspective on the background of the African students who came to his college and had to compete on equal terms with English students whose schooling had been so dramatically different to that which he had seen in Malawi.

'Oh well, this time it's a letter,' said Anne as she opened our mail when Chris was almost three years old and a source of daily joy to us. 'It's from the English chaplain in Jinja. He says that a fatal motor accident has left a two-year-old boy without a family. He is looking after him for the time being but they have four children of their own and they feel that they cannot take on another just now and wonder whether we would like to have him.' It took us very little time to make up our minds and we wrote back to say when we would travel to Uganda's second city, Jinja, some 250 miles away, to collect him. The child, David, had been involved in the accident but had come out comparatively unscathed, but it had still been a traumatic experience. Now, just as he had become used to his new home, he was whisked off again by a couple of complete strangers. We were amazed at how well he settled despite these harsh blows, although inevitably his anger at the sudden disappearance of his parents came to the surface from time to time. We had been in Uganda for over four years when David joined us and were soon due to go to England to carry out our responsibilities to CMS there. We therefore decided to formalize David's adoption in England. The judge in the court in Oxford wore no wig or gown and spoke in an everyday manner so the proceedings went through with none of the hilarity which had marked our Kampala experience, and with a minimum of formality David became a legalized member of our family.

The four of us returned to Uganda in rather spectacular manner when the ship in which we were travelling was trapped in the Suez Canal during the 1967 war between Egypt and Israel. We finally emerged, delayed but unhurt, and made our way back to Uganda and a new home in which the boys spent the next four years. In a virtually uninhabited area we were extremely fortunate to find that one of the three families who lived anywhere near us had a small boy who was two years older than Chris. He had no playmates and soon came to our camp looking for company. It was not long before this particularly bright six year old, called Bagada, became almost a family member as he stayed with us from morning till night every day. Our boys spoke Runyankore, which was near enough to his language to enable easy communication, and very soon there grew up a close friendship which lasted until we left Uganda. Bagada was typically 'bush wise' and his company provided our boys with a wonderful freedom as he led them off on one expedition or another. We were sure that no adult would harm them, and confident in Bagada's local knowledge. We were therefore unworried when the trio disappeared to the farm or workshop for a morning. Only once did they cause us any concern. 'Where were you this morning?' Anne asked the boys one day when they were aged eight, six and five.

'We went to see Bagada's grandmother,' replied Chris.

'That was nice of you, and how is the old lady?' asked Anne.

'Oh not that one,' came the reply.

'But he only has one, his other one is dead'.

'Yes that's right,' said Bagada, 'but now she lives in a big snake and that's who we went to see.' Four parental ears suddenly pricked up sharply.

'And where did you find her?'

'She was in the forest, curled up near the bottom of a great big tree. She really is huge,' said David.

'How did you know where she was, Bagada?' I asked.

'A hunter told me and showed me a path that the buffalo had made so that we could get to her' came the reply. The forest of which they were speaking was the last edge of the vast Central African rainforest, which in those days stretched almost unbroken from the Atlantic ocean to within 300 yards of our home. From it came the herds of elephants and buffalo which caused us problems from time to time on our land and the troops of chimpanzees that swung around the trees at the edge of our garden. In it also were the giant forest hogs which could tear a man to pieces, and on the floor were three inch long thorns which could easily impale the foot of a shoeless small boy. I decided that I would say no more until we had sorted out fact from imagination by a personal visit. 'Do you think that your grandmother would mind if we all visited her?' I asked Bagada.

'Oh no, I am sure she would like it very much.'

'Alright then, finish up your lunch and then we will all go and pay her a visit.'

We soon found that we were dealing with fact and not fiction. The three of them had followed a buffalo trail for about three-quarters of a mile into the forest and between the vast buttress roots of a forest tree lay a python as thick as my thigh and about 15 feet long. Fortunately it must have fed well in the recent past and so had made no attempt to attack the children. The three boys went near to the snake and bid her good afternoon and asked after her health. It lifted its head and began to move a little so Bagada said that perhaps she now wanted to go somewhere else and we should sweep a path to make the first part of her journey more comfortable. The boys duly broke branches from a shrub and swept about 20 yards of path. We all then lined up to bid farewell to 'grandmother'. Once again the python raised its head but showed no signs of aggression and so we returned home. I was unprepared at this point to query Bagada's tribal belief that the spirits of the dead reside in pythons, but I did make it abundantly clear that there would be dire consequences if he ever again took the boys into the forest unaccompanied by an adult.

It was only later that we fully appreciated what an easy time we had with our children. Bagada owned no toys and there were none in the shops in the small town in Hoima which we visited from time to time. We were therefore spared any competitive clamour for an ever increasing collection of toys. Bagada wore a simple pair of shorts and a cotton shirt and no shoes and so our boys were perfectly happy to do the same. They ran barefoot until they went to boarding school where they had to suffer wearing sandals until lunchtime but were wisely allowed to remove them after lunch so as to preserve the tough callus on the soles of their feet. No clamour for fashionable trainers or designer clothes ever marred their childhood years. The same applies to the children who surround me in the village in which we now live. They are all dressed in ragged secondhand clothes and wear no shoes, but because all their friends are in exactly the same situation there is little sign that their clothes are a source of serious heart-ache or diminish their enjoyment of life.

We were also lucky that we had a volunteer, Malcolm Alexander, who had come to help with our work, whose wife Helene was a teacher. She kindly took on the teaching of our two boys and enabled us to keep them at home for their first two years of schooling. Malcolm's term with us came to an end and they returned to England and so, with no English language school anywhere in our vicinity, the boys had to go off to a small boarding

*A simple pair of shorts and cotton shirt (David and Christopher).*

school in South West Uganda some 250 miles from our home. It was a particularly happy school with a mixture of African, Indian and English children. We soon learned how much effort has to be expended by adults to make their children race conscious. The boys would come home with accounts of children's exploits or of their new 'best friend' and would tell of the child's prowess in sport, their quality of friendship or their ability to make people laugh but would never mention the colour of their skin and thought it most odd if asked to what race a child belonged.

By the time our boys had gone to boarding school Bagada was nine and he claimed that he was now quite able to manage on his own so asked to go to school in Hoima. We rented a tiny house and Bagada started to live on his own, cooking for himself and attending a good primary school in his own language. On Sunday he would walk the 23 miles to Hoima carrying his food for the week and on Saturday he would walk home to collect the next week's rations. He had learned a lot of English from us and had also been taught to read and write so he did well at school and is now a successful businessman with a number of different irons in the fire. We have kept in close touch over the years and are grateful for all that he gave to our children when he was young.

Our boys enjoyed two happy schools in East Africa until they were thirteen, when they had to go to boarding school in England, which they enjoyed much less. Chris went straight on to university in England and was back in Africa as soon as he graduated, organizing the feeding of the Tuarag people of the West African Sahara during the terrible drought of the early 1980s. This was followed by some years of work in the Sudan and Mozambique before he married Sandra, who was a senior official of the International Red Cross. Chris moved to Geneva and worked himself for the Red Cross for a number of years before starting up his own company, which also has strong links with Africa. David opted to join us in Washington after he left school, graduated in the States, married an American, Lori, and is now a gifted ceramicist and art teacher. We are a scattered family living on three continents but we make a point of meeting every year, and Anne and I are deeply grateful for the telegram and letter which came to us at Nyakashaka all those years ago and gave us the opportunity of having a growing family.

# CHAPTER 19

# Expanding Opportunities

I HAVE NEVER been very good at worrying. I have tried from time to time but with little success and in any examination on worrying skills I would score poorly. I have often felt somewhat guilty when a friend has said how worried I must be about so and so and I have had to confess that I actually had not thought of worrying about it. But tonight all is different. I would gain top marks in any worrying exam. I have been sitting in my small car since two o'clock this afternoon at the side of a deserted road waiting for the arrival of Anne and the boys from Nyakashaka. They had planned to leave at dawn with the small lorry, bringing our possessions to start a new life in another part of Uganda. We had reckoned that they should be at this junction where I am waiting not later than three o'clock and now it is eight o'clock at night and there is no sign of them. I heard a vehicle at half past four and my hopes soared, but it was not our lorry and drove straight past me. Since then there has been no other sign of life on the road. At six the sunny afternoon gave way to a heavy storm and so now I am sitting in the dark with the rain pounding on the roof of the car. Had the lorry skidded on the dirt road and rolled over the side of one of the steep hills along which they had to travel? Had they had a crash, was one of the children sick so they had never left Nyakashaka? The questions are going round and round in my head and I am really learning very quickly what worrying is all about. I will give it until nine o'clock and then I will go back to the camp.

It was half past eight when lights appeared through the rain and came very slowly along the road. I switched on my own lights and in a few minutes the Nyakashaka lorry with our dependable driver, Eliabu, had drawn up alongside me. They had suffered two blow-outs on the way and it had taken Eliabu hours to get help on this very empty stretch of road and then, with makeshift repairs, he had driven at snail's pace to avoid another flat tyre. Now I have really learned the meaning of the word 'relief'. Anne with her usual efficiency had put together a box of things that we would need straight away and Eliabu and I got these into the car followed by Anne and the children. The lorry then set out for the small town of Hoima where Eliabu would spend the night parked at the church awaiting the help of

*Driving along a green avenue.*

friends who had agreed to store our things in their garage until we had built
a house.

The rain was still pouring down as we set out down the seven miles of
dirt track leading to our new home site. On either side was elephant grass
with stems an inch thick and reaching up 15 feet into the air. I had driven
up along a green avenue but now the rain had bent the grass down so that
the tops met over the road creating a narrow green tunnel down which we
slid through the mud. I could not see the road for water and had to drive
very slowly, so that the journey seemed to go on for ever. The family's
delight at being reunited steadily evaporated as even Anne began to wonder
whether I had not missed the camp and that we were now lost in a deserted
and inhospitable countryside. I was sure that I had not gone too far but was
profoundly relieved when I saw a gap in the elephant grass and knew that
we had arrived. My relief was more than matched by that of my companion
Kapoco. He was one of our workers at Nyakashaka who had shown himself
not only skilful and resourceful but cheerful and willing. He was
unmarried, so I had asked him if he would like to come with me to start my
new work in Bunyoro district. We had come a week ago and between us we
had cleared a quarter of an acre of an old abandoned banana garden which I
had seen on my first visit to survey the area. Although it was completely

*Our beehive hut in which we spent a very wet first night as a family.*

overgrown it was still a lot easier to clear than forest. There we had built two 'beehive' huts from saplings and grass. He had just had his dose of worry as he sat by himself a couple of hundred miles from his home, in an area with more wild animals than he had ever seen before and with no neighbours to whom he could turn. I had assured him that I would be back with the family before four o'clock and now it was well after nine and he had been really frightened. Not only that but our camp was under water. We had made our bivouacs well and they had not leaked. What we had not done was anticipate the volume of water that might run down from the hill behind us. Now, with the first big storm since our arrival, there were four inches of water in our huts. Anne was used to roughing it but our first night as a family in Bunyoro really put her loyalty to the test. I had cut and dried a large pile of grass on which I had planned that the children would sleep while Anne and I used the camp beds which she had brought. Now the grass was soaking wet and sitting in a puddle of water, so the boys went on to the camp beds while Anne and I lay down on the sodden grass for one of the more uncomfortable nights of our lives. The rain stopped in the middle of the night but that was little comfort to us, and it was a stiff and exhausted couple who crawled out of our hut in the morning. Kapoco had tied some dry wood in the roof of his hut and soon had a fire going, and by the time that the sun came up and the smell of coffee was in the air we were all a lot more cheerful. The boys had slept well on their dry beds and emerged to be delighted by their new environment. Huge tropical butterflies flitted through our clearing, a hornbill with a beak larger than they had ever seen went trumpeting from one forest tree to the other, whilst a flock of parrots flew noisily overhead. In addition there was the novelty of camping instead of living in an established household. Breakfast finished Anne went off to Hoima to find Eliabu and deal with our luggage and the replacement of the tyres before he returned to Nyakashaka while Kapoco and I set about the crucial task of digging a deep storm drain right around our camp site.

Supplies from the lorry made our camp more comfortable and as Anne took over the housekeeping Kapoco and I were able to turn our time to locating a site for a permanent home. At Nyakashaka I had to push my way through dense bracken but at least I could see where I was going. In this hot tropical environment the vegetation was not only impenetrable but towered above our heads so that visibility was never more than a few feet. 'How are we ever to see where we are going?' asked Kapoco. 'We are not going to,' I replied, 'but I have a little tool called a compass and we are just going to rely on that to be our eyes.' There was just one hill in the area with two peaks and a saddle in between and that is where I wanted to investigate. I climbed a tree to get a compass bearing on it and then Kapoco and I started on the sweaty and hard work of slashing our way through the 15-foot tall elephant grass. Nearing the top of the hill the soil grew poorer and rockier and the grass was shorter until at the top we could see above it. Behind us lay the endless rolling dark green sea of the tropical rainforest stretching to the horizon. In front of us lay large 'meadows' of elephant grass interspersed with patches of forest, the land that we had come to develop. Widening our path as we walked back to the camp for lunch we both agreed that the hill would make a good place for all of our houses. As the worst of the heat wore off in the afternoon we all set out to look for a house site. Kapoco and I carried one boy each and Anne followed in our footsteps. The top of the saddle had a wonderful view on both sides but it was stony and infertile so we opted to move down from the crest to the first spot where the soil was deep and the land not too steep. We had no view of the forest but could see the whole of the area on which we would be working. Choosing a new house site in empty, undeveloped country has a certain magic and we all returned to the camp in high spirits.

Having land and a chosen site was one thing, but where was the labour

*Slashing fifteen foot tall elephant grass.*

that would do the clearing and building, make the roads and establish the huge tea nursery that we would need? Of the four families who lived within a couple of kilometres of us there was only one man who wanted work, which would not get us very far. I had seen the problem before we came and had been to speak to the leaders of a refugee camp for Rwandans about 50 miles away. They had said that plenty of the refugees would welcome work and the authorities had agreed that they could leave the camp and come to our site. 'They will never do any work,' said Kapoco. 'Don't you know that they are Tutsis? All they have ever done is herd cattle and rule over other people. Even if they did agree to work they would not know which way up to hold a hoe.'

'Now that they are out of their own country and culture I think that they will be much more willing to work with their hands, and we will have to teach them how to hold a hoe,' I replied. Kapoco was not at all convinced and was sure that we were going to have a lot of trouble.

'It is going to be heavy work of all different kinds from digging to clearing bush. There is no housing and no shops so life will not be easy, but you will be earning proper wages. Have you any questions?' The refugees were in their large meeting hall and they did have questions, which I answered as best I could. 'Anybody who is interested in coming to work, stay behind at the end of the meeting.' There was a surprisingly large number who did stay and over the next couple of hours I was able to make a list of a hundred men. The UN staff in charge of the camp were delighted that some of the refugees should be getting a chance to do paid work, and offered to use their lorries to deliver them to our camp and give them a month's rations to get them started. 'Please bring them early in the morning to give them plenty of time to build themselves bivouacs for the night,' was my only request.

In common with their fellows in Rwanda and Burundi many of the Tutsi refugees who joined us were well over six feet tall, and Kapoco had been right about their lack of skills with common tools. He was however quite wrong about their willingness to work and they threw themselves into every task that they were given. I was particularly impressed that the hardships they had suffered had welded them into a tight-knit group and for the first time in Africa I saw younger men helping older ones to finish their piece work and stronger ones helping the weaker. I was used to wide variations in the time that members of a gang finished their allotted tasks, but now gangs finished at the same time as the quick workers helped the slower ones. There was an abundance of building materials and they had soon built a string of huts to replace the bivouacs in which they started. With land and labour we could now really start to have an impact on this wild piece of Africa.

I am sorry that I have wandered on about how we got started without saying what on earth we were doing camping on the edges of the hot, wet rainforest of Bunyoro in Western Uganda. Following the success at Nyakashaka of using secondary school leavers as agents of development I had been asked to make use of the same approach for a different purpose. For historical reasons parts of Uganda were densely populated while others were virtually empty. Population movement was discouraged by tribal boundaries. The Prime Minister, Milton Obote, was determined to overcome tribal barriers and accentuate that any Ugandan could live in any part of the country. I had been asked to start a movement of people from the most densely populated district of Kigezi to the least populated but highly fertile district of Bunyoro. This seemed to be a sensible initiative, and so the church authorities under whom I worked agreed that is what we should do. They also wanted to expand smallholder tea in Bunyoro so we had to focus on an area which was empty, but that was not too far from an existing factory. A good map and some pushing and slashing through the bush had led us to select the site that was to become the focal point of our efforts. Like most parts of 'empty' Africa the locality had a place name and was marked on the map as Kidoma, and so we proudly announced the birth of the 'Kidoma Development Scheme', and Anne spent a good deal of time painting a notice board to that effect which we placed at the junction of the main road with our track. It was some weeks later that a well educated local person whom I met in Hoima town asked 'Why have you called your new initiative "the place of idiots"? It does not sound a very attractive title.' Whilst the local language was similar to the Runyankore, which we spoke, it was not identical, and I had not known the meaning of the word Kidoma. My informant explained that a hundred years earlier a chief from the general area in which we were settling had made a particularly silly remark at court and the king had ordered that the name of his area be called 'the place of idiots'. I quickly asked if there was any unfortunate connotation to the name of the river Wambabya which flowed through our land, and having been assured that was quite harmless Anne had to do some more work and repaint our notice.

'We will have to go back to separate sleeping and living houses with this hot climate,' said Anne, 'then we can be sure of at least some breeze through the rooms.' Unlike at Undukori the sleeping hut had to have two rooms to accommodate the boys and the living hut had to be large enough to cope with the far greater numbers of people that we expected to have around us as compared to our small village in the Sudan. Our one local worker helped us to identify the right timbers for the walls and roofs and we soon had skeletons of houses poking up above the elephant grass. Luckily with the hot climate the mud dried quickly and we did not suffer the frustrations which had marked our house building at Nyakashaka. While Anne took over the building programme I had my hands full with other developments. A tea nursery for an initial 400,000 plants was my first priority, but that required the making of three miles of road to the river where the nursery would be sited, and a detailed survey for the best site. At the same time I had started on the recruitment of the first settlers and they had began to arrive to work out their six months of probation before they would be allocated plots. They came from settled homes in thickly populated country with schools, churches, shops and an active social life, to live with strangers in temporary huts in a strange environment and with none of the facilities to which they had been accustomed. They soon made friends, settled in to heavy work and made a particularly cheerful group who once again filled our days with their laughter.

★

'This piece work is impossible!' said the leader of the refugees on the day that they started to prepare the tea nursery for planting. 'We will be here until after dark to finish it.' We were adopting a completely new method of raising tea, using cuttings in polythene pots instead of seeds in beds. 'But I have done it myself and I know that you can easily finish in good time,' I replied. There was obviously a lot of discontent as large men who had never filled a flower pot in their lives struggled to get soil into a small plastic bag, so I reduced the piece work for two days but assured them that it would go back to the original level as soon as they had some practice. Sure enough within a week many of them were finishing their task in four or five hours and soon thousands of pots were stacked in neat rows ready for planting. Then it was my turn to complain. 'Another four o'clock morning,' I groaned as the alarm clock dragged me out of sleep. I rolled out of bed, had a quick breakfast and set out on a 70-mile drive on a rough dirt road to collect the tea branches from a specialist grower from which we would produce the cuttings for planting. Back at Wambabya by half past ten a large gang would sit in a big hut and cut off single leaves with two inches of stem and put them in baths of water to keep them fresh. At six in the evening the cuttings were all ready and I went home to collect the kerosene pressure lights by which the gang would plant out the thousands of cuttings in the waiting pots. Bed at two in the morning if I was lucky made for long working days, which continued until we had reached our target of 400,000 plants.

I was not without help. Malcolm Alexander from Wye came out as a volunteer to assist us. He soon found that despite his agricultural training his real interest was in accounts and records. This suited me well as these essential functions were my least favourite work. Wambabya changed the course of Malcolm's life and he has spent the past thirty five years as an accountant in senior management positions. He was not the only one for whom Wambabya marked a change of career. I had recruited an experienced headman from Hoima district, Christopher Kirimunda, to help supervise the labour but also to be a mentor with regard to local feelings and sensibilities. After a few years with us he offered for ordination in the church and retired last year as the Archdeacon of Bunyoro. More striking still was one of the Rwandan refugees, John Rucyahana, who quickly showed himself to be a good leader with a great gift with people. I made him an extension worker but soon found that he was combining this agricultural role with pastoral work among the settlers and the refugees. His skills came most strongly to my notice on a Christmas Day and resulted in a dramatic change in his life.

'I really have stopped getting drunk,' said Kapoco for about the sixth time since he had been with us. Excellent helper that he was, his one weakness was locally brewed gin, supplied by a woman who had opened a 'bar' a half a mile away, under the influence of which he could become violent. After each particularly bad bout he had always expressed his remorse and promised that it would never happen again. The promise lasted for a couple of months and then there would be another drunken brawl. As he came to us on that Christmas evening with yet one more promise of reform Anne and I had to suppress our scepticism and be as encouraging as we could. Kapoco obviously wanted to elaborate. 'After the Christmas service this morning I went straight down to the bar. As I arrived there were two men rolling on the ground hitting and biting one another, already drunk at ten in the morning. I remembered all the laughing, friendly people outside the church that I had just left and thought, what am I doing here? I went to John Rucyahana's house and he spent the whole afternoon talking to me and helping me to see that I needed God's help to overcome my problem, because I will never manage by myself'.

I was really impressed that one of our staff should have sacrificed his whole family Christmas Day to helping Kapoco. We were even more impressed when month followed month with no sign of a relapse, and in fact Kapoco never got drunk again. I found that John had a real sense of vocation for ordination but because his qualifications were from a French language school in Rwanda he was not eligible to enter the Ugandan theological college. I am never quite sure where the boundaries of nepotism are, but I had no conscience in using my friendship with the college principal to gain John's admission. He became an outstanding pastor in Uganda and when peace returned to Rwanda after the genocide he was asked to be a Bishop in Rwanda. It was a moment of the greatest pleasure when we listened to a broadcast of part of his induction service on the World Service of the BBC sitting in our home in Malawi.

Four years after our arrival there had been a dramatic change at Wambabya, with large areas of cultivation, roads lined with houses and a couple of churches serving the ever-expanding population. Thirty five years later the change is even more striking. A total child population of our two boys, Bagada and his little sister has been replaced with six large primary schools with hundreds of children who provide the band and guard of honour for our visits. The little track to our camp has been transformed into an excellent road with lorries taking produce to market every day. Anne's little dispensary has given way to a modern health centre and my layman's efforts in a mud and wattle church are now handled by an ordained man with a large parish church and six satellite congregations. But that is not all, because the several thousand people who now live around Wambabya were the vanguard of a far larger movement of population from Kigezi to the general area of Bunyoro into which we moved. Driving to-day down the 70 miles of what used to be almost completely deserted road leading into Bunyoro is a quite different experience, with villages, farms, schools and churches lining much of the road, all occupied by people who have moved out of the over-crowded hills of Kigezi. As with Nyakashaka we had spent just four years at Wambabya, had provided a plan of action which we believed fitted in with people's needs, and all the subsequent development has been entirely the result of local hard work and initiative.

We were now about to make a reverse move to that of our settlers. With Wambabya well established and another volunteer, John Markie, in place to help with the assistance of new settlers for another two years, I had been asked to go and help in the densely populated hills of Kigezi myself, to research new plants for the area and then to spread them among the population. So we found ourselves back in mountain air at 8,000 feet above sea level and with wide sweeping views of mountains and lakes to replace the dense bush of Wambabya. Once again we camped, once more we built houses, but this time there were no settlers and our initial efforts were concentrated on a small forty-acre research farm which we established at a site called Karengyere.

'How bitterly disappointing it must be for you,' said my friend as we looked out over hundreds of dead and rotting potato plants.

'Not at all,' I replied. 'This is exactly what we have been waiting for. Do you see that bright green plant over there, and another one to the right and there is another at the far edge of the field. That is what we are looking for, plants which can resist the disease which has killed off ninety-nine percent of the field.'

'What's the disease? It certainly smells bad whatever it is,' responded my friend.

'Potato blight, which caused the Irish potato famine and changed the face of that country. It came to Uganda in the 1920s and drastically reduces the yield of smallholders' crops in this area where potatoes should thrive. Farmers cannot afford to spray with chemicals, so we are looking for plants which have a natural resistance to the disease. These plants come from a range of South American sources and, as you can see, it looks as if they include some winners.'

And winners they were. I multiplied up five plants which I then moved to an isolated seed farm that I established on the edges of the Impenetrable Forest reserve, well away from any other potatoes. Just as the first acres of seed were maturing a misunderstanding with the Amin regime forced us out of Uganda. I thought that all my work had been wasted, but I thought without my excellent headman. He went on looking after the seed farm, sold some of the crop to raise money and then planted more. On my first return visit to Karengyere after Amin's overthrow I was amazed to see that all the potatoes on sale at the side of the road were of the varieties which we had developed. Today, I am assured by the staff of the Ministry of Agriculture, seventy-five percent of all the potatoes grown in Uganda are of those varieties. Once again an initiative which went to the heart of farmers' needs was picked up and carried by them with a minimum of outside help. We were just grateful that we had been given these expanding opportunities to make the initiatives which triggered the changes that we now see as we visit Uganda.

CHAPTER 20

# Creatures Great and Small

SOME YEARS AGO the phrase 'When I was in Poonah' was the standard opening line of a lampoon of a retired army colonel whose conversation was dominated by an account of his attempts to decimate the wild animals of India. I do hope that by providing an account of our own encounters with creatures both great and small I will not be classified as being in the same mould. I include this chapter not only because animals, both domestic and wild, have played an important part in our lives, but because it will highlight one of the greatest changes that has taken place in Africa over the half century in which we have lived here.

'Now I really feel that I am in Africa,' said Anne when we had both stopped trembling. We were at a mission station called Panekar on the hot flat plains of the Dinka tribe in the Southern Sudan a month after we had arrived in the country. We had been asked to go and prepare an agricultural plan for the station and were staying in the house of the missionary who was on leave. His servant was very competent and had the house running well and in the evening confirmed our own feelings that it was much too hot to be able to sleep inside and that he would make up the bed, with a mosquito net, in the garden. We duly settled down for the night, to be woken later by grunts around our bed. There was a full moon and it was all too clear from where the noise was coming. Seven adult lions were prowling round the bed and occasionally nosing the mosquito net and then backing away as it swayed in the breeze. We really did feel that our end had come but could do nothing except lie as far from the net as possible and keep absolutely still. The inspection continued for ten interminable minutes and then the lions moved away and started roaring. As the roars grew more distant we bolted into the house quite sure that heat was less of an impediment to sleep than lions. At least Anne was now really sure that she was in Africa! The Southern Sudan teemed with lions at that time. In the main town of Juba the night was not punctuated by dogs barking but by lions roaring as they wandered around the town. They were classified as 'vermin' by the government and could be shot without any permit. There were endless stories of Dinka men who had faced up to a lion all night

154

crouched behind their seven-foot long spears on to which the lion would have to impale itself to get at them. The lions circled round and round in the hope that the man would relax or not move his spear quickly enough. Just yesterday I read that it is now thought that there are less than 20,000 lions in the whole of Africa and that they are endangered outside of three large game reserves.

Our other very close encounter with a lion was totally unexpected. It was when we were in our grass bivouac at Wambabya in forest country which was certainly not lion territory. Once again we were woken by grunting and it was soon apparent that a lion was circling our 'beehive' hut. The grass walls were three inches thick and we could easily hear the animal breathing as it sniffed at us through the grass. A single swipe of its paw would have ripped the wall apart and left us completely exposed. As it moved round the opposite side of the hut we slid down our camp beds so that our heads were more than their original nine inches from the lion's nose. The boys on their grass bed were further from the wall and we did not attempt to wake or move them. Once again the lion circled round and round the hut, went off for a few minutes and then returned. We realized that it was on the move from one plains area to another and would have been unable to hunt for food in the thick forest on its forty or fifty mile journey. It was therefore likely to be hungry and we just had to hope that the grass wall would baffle it. Fortunately that did seem to be the case and after a frightening half hour it moved on, leaving us shaken and hoping that there were no other members of its pride in the area. There were not, and we never again saw any sign of a lion at Wambabya.

Undukori was also in the forest and we never saw any sign of a lion, but the area had an abundance of leopards which were a constant source of menace to our livestock and occasionally to people. 'Wake up, it's at the door again,' said Anne as she shook me. I could hear the leopard digging in the soil below the door of our hut as it tried to get in to take our dogs which slept with us. I got my spear and waited until the paw was well under the door and gave it a jab sufficient to discourage the animal without injuring it. With an angry grunt our visitor left and we went back to sleep. The more usual and frequent alarm came when our chickens or goats made it very clear that they had a problem. I would have to move quickly, pick up my spear and then a stone from the pile that lived outside our door. Up on the roof of one of the livestock houses the leopard was tearing at the grass in order to gain entrance. Loud shouts and a well aimed stone usually dealt with the situation and we could go back to sleep. That was not always the case, and once nearly led to a nasty end. The chickens woke us and I went through my usual ritual noticing that it was a particularly large male animal clearly outlined on the roof by the light of the moon. It jumped down and went off into the bush and I returned to bed. A few minutes later the chickens were at it again and a couple more big stones drove off the leopard. 'Now it's at the goats,' I said as I leapt out of bed for the third time and had even more trouble in dislodging the animal from the roof of the goat house. 'It's no good we will have to have a fire and sit watch,' I said. 'I will help,' said Anne. 'I'm not having that leopard kill any of my poultry.' We always had a fire laid for such occasions and soon had it blazing. After three lots of stoning and a fire I was convinced that the leopard would not return and we sat quietly on each side of the fire throwing a piece of wood on to the blaze from time to time. Suddenly there was a deep growl not more than three yards behind Anne. Without hesitation she jumped straight over the top of the fire to join me. She was wearing her wedding nightdress provided by an American uncle when nylon nighties were unobtainable in Britain after the war. She landed safely on my side with a minimum of burns but the nightie had virtually evaporated and Anne was far from adequately covered. I quickly added my gun to my spear and we spent an anxious few hours until dawn aware that we were up against a particularly aggressive animal.

The abundance of leopards with which we were surrounded was a great help in limiting the wild pig and baboon population but constituted a constant source of worry and loss to local people. We lost goats to them ourselves, taken from their tethers near the house in the middle of the day, and children were killed from time to time as well. Yet to-day the sighting of a leopard in a game park in Africa is considered the highlight of a safari as they become rare and endangered animals.

'Quick, some more brands!' I shouted as I threw my last flaming torch at the screaming elephant a few yards away. The noise was deafening as a herd of fifty or more trumpeted in anger because we had inadvertently built our house on a route that they had traditionally used to move from one feeding area to another. Kapoco and Anne were beating empty kerosene tins while Benoni our mechanic who had run from his house to help when he heard the noise was lighting the long tightly bound grass brands that we always kept ready for these events. We could only see the half dozen lead animals by the light of the flares but we knew that there were plenty more behind them. More staff came to our help and with drums, flares and shouts the advance was stopped. Complaining loudly the huge animals moved off to take another route. The herd had obviously been a long way away when we were building and we had moved into our house before we realized that we had blocked their path and were unwilling to start building all over again. We therefore had these noisy and frightening confrontations every few weeks for eighteen months before the elephants finally made a new permanent path about a mile away. Away from their legitimate complaint about our intrusion they were remarkably lacking in aggression. I would meet them on my way round the farm on my motor-bike and they would show no sign of wanting to do me harm. Their tolerance was put to a severe test by one of our Rwandan workers. 'Where is your receipt for the delivery of the tea cuttings?' asked the foreman at roll call in the morning when a worker had been sent to one of our sub-nurseries the previous afternoon. 'I haven't got one,' came the reply, 'because I did not deliver them. I bumped into an elephant on the way and dropped them.' A hoot of derision from the other workers met this remark. 'You had better think up a better excuse than that before the boss comes,' said the foreman. When I did come the man held to his story and so I asked to be led to where the event had taken place. Sure enough the evidence was perfectly clear. There were all the signs of elephants having passed through and right next to their footsteps were human imprints and a whole mass of scattered tea cuttings. Carrying the basket of tea cuttings on a very wet day the man had put an old fertilizer bag over his head to keep off the rain which severely limited his vision. As he walked down a narrow path through the elephant grass looking at the ground to avoid slipping and spilling his precious load he had suddenly bumped into a solid object. Looking up he saw a rough grey wall in front of him and realized that he had walked into the side of an elephant. Throwing his basket down he had run for his life, but the elephant had made no move to follow or harm him. I have no doubt that he has repeated the story many times. Seeing elephants at the side of the road or walking across a farm was a normal part of life in Africa fifty years ago. Today, with their numbers decimated, one has to spend a lot of money at a game park to catch sight of these wonderful creatures.

Buffalo are not so tolerant and the large herds at Wambabya did give us cause for concern on a number of occasions. Fortunately they also found it difficult to move quietly through the dense elephant grass so the noise of their approach would produce a shout of 'Look out here they come' from a survey or road gang and everyone would shin up a tree. It is surprising what skill and speed in tree climbing is stimulated by the sound of a charging buffalo. We never had anybody gored, but did have one very narrow shave which I witnessed. The warning shout went up, I joined in the general run for a tree and saw one worker slip as he reached the second branch of his tree. 'Hold on,' I yelled as the buffalo broke out of the tall grass, snorting and stamping. Desperately he held on but slipped round the branch so that he was hanging upside down by his hands and legs. His unbuttoned shirt hung down below him and a buffalo made a beeline for it, hooked it in its horn and tossed its head. I shut my eyes as I envisioned the man pulled out of the tree and gored in front of our eyes as we remained completely helpless. There was no scream and so I looked to see that a very aged shirt had ripped away from the man's back and the buffalo was now shaking his head to disentangle itself from the cloth. A desperate swing from the man got him back upright on the branch and we all heaved a sigh of relief. But even buffalo do not all conform to their reputation and we had a huge aged bull which lived around our tea nursery for a couple of years and never attacked anybody. The nursery was next to the dense forest along the river which provided his home. Its great attraction was the fifty-yard wide firebreak all around it which was kept slashed and provided the old man with tender and plentiful food throughout the year. The first time that he appeared was at night when we were planting cuttings. Everybody fled as he walked carefully along one of the narrow paths between the rows of pots. From inside the cutting shed we could see his enormous bulk move slowly through the nursery taking no notice whatever of us. He reached the opposite fire break to that from which had come and started to graze. I was desperate. Thousands of cuttings worth hundreds of pounds would be lost if not planted that night. 'Right, you can see that he is eating quietly and is not interested in us. I will stand between him and you while you go back to work. If anybody gets hurt it will be me. You can see that he is old and so you will be able to run faster than him.'

After watching him quietly graze for a few more minutes I led some of the best workers out to the planting beds and went and stood between the buffalo and them. He took no notice whatever and slowly the whole gang returned to planting. This became a regular happening and he never showed any sign of aggression. What always amazed me was that his huge hoof marks always meticulously followed the narrow paths and in his nightly wanderings he never trod on a single seedling. I realize now how privileged I have been to have such close contact with magnificent animals in the wild. An experience which has become ever more confined to reserves and parks to-day.

★

'Daddy can we shake hands with him?' asked Chris as a huge male chimpanzee stood in the doorway of our living hut one afternoon. I replied that chimpanzees did not have the same habits as us but that he could call out a quiet 'Hello' to him. In fact I was not at all happy about the situation. Chimpanzees in our garden were an almost daily occurrence. They sometimes swung on the boys' swing on a tree near the house but had always kept a distance between themselves and any humans. Attractive and intelligent as they are they can also be aggressive and I had no desire to be trapped inside a room with a large male. He surveyed us, our house and possessions for a few minutes, dropped back on to all fours and sedately walked off across the garden. I heaved a sigh of relief but was also glad that we had experienced so close an encounter with our nearest relative and that the boys had been so totally unafraid that they had actually wanted to greet it. Yet again there are few people left who can watch wild chimpanzees in their gardens on a regular basis as we did at Wambabya or see them frequently in the trees around their farm as we did at Undukori.

'I can't believe my eyes,' said Anne as we drove down across the Athi Plains in Kenya forty years ago to visit a mission initiative on which I had been asked to comment. 'There are thousands of them, I have never seen anything like it.' And she was right. There were thousands of gazelle, zebra and buck grazing the plains as far as the eye could see. We reached the missionary's house, which was up on stilts to preserve it from termite damage, and from his veranda we looked out again at hundreds of wild animals. This was not in a game park or reserve, this was simply the open Masai plains across which the local people grazed their cattle, and yet there are very few game parks left in Africa where one could see a comparable sight today. Thirty years later we drove down the same road and in fifty miles we did not see a single plains animal. That really summarizes what has happened in the past half century as human populations have quintrupled. We have watched a situation in which tiny groups of people sought to defend themselves from an encircling horde of wild animals, to a situation in which tiny pockets of wild animals have to be protected from the constant threat of humans.

'Two people killed by hippo'; 'Woman taken by crocodile'; 'Hyena bites off man's leg in his hut'. So read the headlines, and it is natural that the threat of large animals should attract attention despite the small numbers of casualties they cause in a year. It is the small creatures which have always been the real threat to our lives. The mosquitoes that passed on the malarial parasite which had developed resistance to the prophylactic that we were taking and reduced us to shaking misery for a few days, only to be saved from something worse by our access to a newer drug. The ticks which have twice passed on a gift of parasites that almost killed me. The water snails that harbour the bilharzia that invaded our livers and sapped our energy. These are the real danger and the real killers, not of hundreds but of millions, by their insidious activities, even though they lack the drama of a goring by a buffalo or trampling by an elephant. One small creature that played an important role in our lives for many years was the little flea called a jigger. It lives in dusty floors, of which we encountered plenty, and lays its eggs under toe nails. If removed immediately when pin-head size the operation is not too painful, but if its presence is not detected because of the anaesthetic put out by the egg, then the digging out of an object the size of a pea from under a toe nail can become a particularly unpleasant experience. Part of our evening ritual for many years was to inspect each others' toes and dig out the small eggs. It would be classified as grooming by anthropologists and should have a bonding role, but I am not sure that we always saw it in that way. I remember after a particularly long session in which she seemed to have had to dig an egg out of each of my toes, Anne said that she should have had an alternative to the marriage service in which she would have promised 'to love, honour, obey and de-jigger me on a daily basis.' But we have survived, and look back with thankfulness for all that creatures both great and small, wild and domesticated have contributed to the richness of our experience.

CHAPTER 21

# A Change of Tactics

ON LEAVING Uganda we had returned to the Southern Sudan, as recorded earlier in the book. Now that our work in the Sudan had come to an end we had to think about how best to use our experience. I was keen to return to village work, but Uganda was still under Amin's rule and closed to us. No obvious openings came up through other churches so that when I was invited to join a small team to provide agricultural advice to the Prime Minister's Office in Tanzania, CMS encouraged me to accept the offer. We were posted to the country's second city Mwanza, on the shores of Lake Victoria, and soon settled into our new environment. Tanzania was considered a hardship station by expatriates at that time but Anne, coming straight from Yei, thought that she had arrived in the Garden of Eden, with a wonderful market filled with every kind of fruit and vegetable, fresh fish, daily supplies of meat and a dairy which sold milk and butter. The fact that there were no imported foods, that electricity supplies were highly erratic and public services inefficient really did not worry us, because we had not expected to have them. We had never had it so good.

It was a pleasure to live in a country where the head of state, Julius Nyerere, was not corrupt, refused to live in a palace, dressed simply, did not permit the flaunting of wealth and had a genuine desire to develop the country for the benefit of the poor. Unfortunately being honest, modest and altruistic does not automatically lead to sound government policies. When I worked in Tanzania the President was concentrating all his efforts on to two fundamental policies which had a profound impact upon my own work as well on the prosperity of his people.

The first of these came to our notice as we flew to Mwanza from Nairobi in Kenya. Anne looking out of the plane window at the Tanzanian countryside said 'Look at all those fires, they are not bush fires, they look like burning houses. There are hundreds of them, how can so many houses all have had an accident at the same time?' We were mystified but soon found the answer after we had landed. Nyerere was convinced that there could be no progress in rural Tanzania until people were consolidated into large villages which would stimulate political and communal activity and

161

development. He had spent years trying to get people to move voluntarily but without any success. At last he had lost patience and embarked on a massive programme of compulsory villagization. People were taken to an empty site and told that they had three weeks in which to build a new house and move to their designated 'village', after which their old home would be destroyed. Many people just did not believe that this would happen and took no action, but whether they had moved or not their houses were destroyed after three weeks. These were the fires that we had seen as we flew in. Each new village had between four and five hundred families and this is where my problems started. I soon found that in the livestock areas anything up to 5,000 cattle, which had previously been scattered across 400 farms, were now concentrated in one place and in no time they destroyed all the grazing within four or five kilometres of the 'village'. Young stock could not walk far enough to reach any reasonable grazing and calf mortality soared. In arable areas with fragile soils there was no possibility of resting the land without pushing the fields so far from the 'village' that people would have to spend more time walking themselves and their working oxen to the fields than they would be able to spend doing any significant amount of work. I immediately started work on designing patterns of satellite villages based on what I was hearing from farmers. I calculated the numbers of people in a 'sub-village' which would allow for proper grazing of cattle and soil management, and linked them to a central village headquarters as the hub of the political unit. This did not tally with the ideology and all my proposals were rejected. The large artificial villages remained until Nyerere stepped down from office when many people returned to their old areas and rebuilt their homes.

The President's second concern stemmed from his belief that people should not work for their own benefit but for that of their community and their nation. A belief with which many of us would sympathize but one which ignores the universal experience of human weakness. Agricultural production was therefore to be based on a command structure in which every village in the country was told what each family had to produce, irrespective of their personal choices or the profitability of the proposals. Not only did this go against farmers' natural instincts but was so poorly thought through that an elderly widow was expected to produce the same amount as a healthy middle-aged man with five family members to help him. This soon led to some incongruous situations as farmers sought to avoid the rules. 'What cash crop do you have to grow in this village?' I asked on one of my regular visits to farmers around the country.

'We are a tobacco village,' came the reply.

'And how much does each family have to grow?'

'One acre each.'

'You said that there were four hundred and twenty five families so you have four hundred and twenty five acres of tobacco?'

'Yes that's right,' came the reply.

'I would really like to see it,' I said.

'Oh no, that would not be possible, it is very far away and you could not get there with your Landrover.'

'Luckily God gave me two good legs and I enjoy walking.'

'Ah but there are many snakes in this area.'

I assured them that I was very used to walking where there were snakes and that they would not worry me. In the face of their growing consternation I hastened to say that I was not there to spy on them or report on their performance but was just really interested to see what they were doing. With a good deal of reluctance they led me to the tobacco field less than half a mile away. At a quick guess I reckoned there were 35 acres of tobacco. 'This is your only field of tobacco?' I asked. Yes it was. 'And this covers four hundred and twenty-five acres and everybody has an acre?' Yes they did. 'Would you please take me to your acre?' I asked the leader of the group. 'Certainly, no problem, follow me.' We went to a plot about five yards wide and forty yards long. 'This is my acre,' he said.

'But an acre is 22 yards wide and 220 yards long, this is not even a tenth of an acre'.

'You're talking about an English acre, but our tobacco is grown on Tanzanian acres,' came the immediate reply with a twinkle in his eye and loud laughs from his companions. And so the nonsense continued. I looked up the records of this village at the end of the season and saw that they were recorded as having planted 425 acres of tobacco but they had suffered a poor year and the total production had worked out at an average yield of only 20 kilos to the acre instead of the planned 400!

I was asked to prepare a paper for the Prime Minister on why cotton production had collapsed but with no mention of pricing 'because peasant farmers have no economic sense and so price is not an issue'. It was an exercise in fatuity and the collapse of the agricultural sector continued. Rural families accepted this mismanagement and hardship with their usual courage and resourcefulness and survived one way or another. When Nyerere, unlike most of his contemporaries, willingly and graciously stepped down from the presidency the majority of his people remembered him with respect and affection for his honesty and modesty and for his outstanding achievement of drastically reducing tribal divisions and welding the country into a unified nation with one national language. They forgave his economic blunders which had been perpetrated with the best of intentions. This was after I had left the country, and my own eighteen months in Tanzania had two outcomes for me personally. The first was that it provided me with the only period of my 52 years in Africa when I can think of nothing that I did which had any positive impact upon small scale farmers in that country. I have been very blessed that in every other job I have done I can see evidence of the effect of my efforts, but not in Tanzania in the mid-nineteen seventies. The second was that as a result of my regular contact with World Bank staff in the course of my work I was invited to join that institution as an agriculturalist in the Eastern African Region based in Nairobi. Once again there were discussions with CMS and the outcome was that I was seconded from CMS to join the World Bank, thus providing a rather incongruous combination in the eyes of some of my friends.

Until I came across the World Bank during our second spell in the Sudan I really had no idea about what the institution did nor where it came from. As the next couple of chapters are going to be about working for that organization I feel that it may help some of my readers if I provide a little background material. Established in 1944 with the rather ponderous name of The International Bank for Reconstruction and Development (IBRD) it was intended to provide the credit for the reconstruction of Europe after the war. Once this work began it was obvious that the main function of the IBRD was in civil works where it could lend for the rebuilding of railways, harbours, roads, airports and dams. It soon established a reputation of excellence in this field and, when Europe was back on its feet, started to spread its efforts to other countries. Whilst many of the projects that it funded were large the work of IBRD was not really complicated. It was able to recruit a cadre of senior, experienced engineers and economists who could go and assess whether a country's application for a loan for an extension to a railway or harbour made technical and economic sense. If it did, then the work went out to international tender, major companies readily bid because they were absolutely sure of trouble-free payment through IBRD. Consulting engineers certified the work and were cross-checked by the staff of the institution and the bill was paid. The work spread out from rich countries to middle income countries and finally to poor nations such as India. Still the main accent was on civil works and IBRD was judged an efficient and successful organization. Slowly pressure started to mount to move into health and education in poorer countries. Even here civil works played a major role as new hospitals, schools and teacher training colleges were built using IBRDs existing experience and skills. Then came agriculture and the picture changed. It is one thing to let a contract to a major engineering firm to build a hundred miles of road. It is something totally different to try and help fifty thousand peasant farmers improve the yields of their small plots. Under the irrigated conditions of Asia, which lend themselves to a unified approach, there was considerable success, but with the millions of small scale farmers in Africa, depending upon rainfall and often in risky and fragile situations, the picture was different. There was a struggle to identify investments which would really bring about significant change. By that time the institution had an additional low interest arm for poorer countries and had become more widely known as the World Bank. Its efforts in every field were still concentrated almost entirely on lending for specific projects and not venturing into the realm of policies. It was therefore into agricultural project work for the thirteen countries on the Eastern side of Africa that I started in the middle of 1978.

I have no intention of giving a blow by blow account of the projects with which I was involved but a description of a few will give a flavour of the sort of work for which the experience of our years had prepared me. After my first assignment to look at the request of the Zambian government for a loan to re-vitalize an agricultural research station and the associated extension service, I was assigned to look at a proposal from the tiny kingdom of Lesotho, which is tucked into South Africa. The government there had borrowed money to help farmers to gain access to better seeds and fertilizer. It had proved highly successful and fertilizer sales in particular had rocketed. Everybody was pleased and a similar loan was being requested which I was to check out with the government. One of the real shocks for me about working for the Bank was the volume of paper involved. My applications and proposals to CMS and Christian Aid had occupied three or four pages. Now I was faced with fifty or sixty wherever I turned. I had to be reminded that lending 50 million dollars did need a bit more detailed study than my concerns with a few hundreds or thousands. Settling down to work my way through the 50 page report on the recently completed project in Lesotho I conscientiously read it right through to the small attachment at the very end. Written by an economist it stated that 'as a result of the poor soils which gave fairly low responses to fertilizer, and the cheap price of maize from neighbouring South Africa, our surveys showed that the value of extra maize which farmers are harvesting is often less than the cost of the fertilizer'. Here was a bombshell. We had been patting ourselves on the back for the rapid increase in the use of fertilizer and yet this overlooked appendix was claiming that farmers were not really benefiting by using it. Apparently nobody else had got as far as the last page of the report. I went up to my division chief, Bob Dewar. 'There is something very wrong about this report or this project,' I said as I showed him the offending section. 'I have checked the data and figures that the economist used and they all seem sound enough. The inference is that tens of thousands of small scale farmers are making an illogical decision. In all my years of working with smallholders in Africa I have never known them make illogical decisions. They are too vulnerable to be able to afford them.'

'Not everybody in this institution would agree with you there Stephen. After all we are mostly dealing with illiterate women farmers who have no training in cost:benefit analysis. But what do you think the problem is?' asked Bob.

'I really do not know. I am quite frankly mystified. What I do know is that we should not go ahead with another project until we have sorted this problem out.'

'There is no doubt about that,' responded Bob. 'The Bank will never agree to make a loan if there is no proven benefit to farmers.'

It was therefore agreed that I go to Lesotho a week earlier than planned and that I focus on this anomaly before discussing another loan. I saw this as my first challenge in the Bank to support my belief in the ability of small scale farmers in Africa to make sound choices, which I was determined to make the basis of my work in the institution. But I was certainly puzzled as to why thousands of them had made a choice which outsiders would undoubtedly construe as stemming from their lack of appreciation of the relationship between costs and benefits.

Landing at the capital Maseru I thought that the plane had somehow jumped a continent. I had lived all my time in Africa within a few degrees of the equator and was totally unprepared for swaying daffodils under blossom covered apple and peach trees with patches of snow on the hills above the town. Unprepared also for the fact that all the immigration and customs officers were women, something that I had never seen before in Africa. Nor was I ready for the fact that many of the senior staff that I met in government the following day were also women. I was really in a quite new situation and wondered whether all my experience in Eastern Africa would actually apply here or whether it was too localized. I was glad that I had the extra week to study this radically different country before I had to start on the serious work of assessing a new loan proposal. I hired a car, was given a guide cum interpreter, and set out for one of the areas where there had been the greatest surge in fertilizer sales and where my guide had personal contacts.

'Come in' beamed the large lady whom we visited first, standing at the door of her typical round mud and wattle thatched hut. I stepped inside and once again was in for a surprise. Well furnished, with good quality items and a large radio, this was a far cry from the huts of the Sudan and Uganda with which I was so familiar. I was obviously going to have to do a lot of adapting. Courtesies over I asked whether she had bought fertilizer in recent years. 'Oh yes, it's wonderful. I have used it for the past three years and it has helped me so much. Last year I got a hundred kilos and that gave me four bags of extra maize'. A quick bit of mental arithmetic told me that she had not got a very good bargain as the value of the maize had barely covered the cost of the fertilizer. Here was the first confirmation of the economist's figures. So why was she so enthusiastic about fertilizer? 'Might I ask from where you got the money to buy the fertilizer, did you get a loan from a club?' A loud laugh greeted my question.

'Oh no, I did not have to do that. I told my husband about the fertilizer when he came back for his month's leave from the mine in South Africa three years ago. I repeated what the agricultural advisor had told us about the help that it would be for our farm. The price was ten Rand a bag and so he gave me twenty Rand and told me to buy two bags. Mind you he warned me that I should have the receipts ready for him when he came home again and there would be serious trouble if I spent the money on anything else.'

The light began to dawn. The whole basis of analysing costs and benefits is that the person who gets the benefits pays the costs. Here we had a situation in which one person paid the cost and another reaped the benefits, so why bother as to whether the gains were commensurate with the expenses. She assured me that she had a good husband who had bought all the furniture that I saw and sent her housekeeping money on time, but he would never have given her twenty Rand on top of her normal housekeeping in order to buy more food. She had got four extra bags of maize via the fertilizer at no cost to herself. But that was not all. 'Because of the fertilizer the maize grew much taller and greener so there was more food for my two cows and the children and I had a lot more milk than usual. You have seen that we have no trees here so we use a woody plant that grows among the maize like a weed for fuel, and that grew much more strongly with the fertilizer. I also grow all my vegetables among the maize plants and they also do much better now that I use fertilizer.' Problem solved. Nothing at all illogical about this woman's decisions. She doesn't count the cost because she doesn't pay the bill and she gets several valuable benefits that the economist had never looked at. My belief in African small scale farmer wisdom fully vindicated. We visited another half a dozen women and the story was always the same. I could report that the fertilizer did bring real benefits to rural households and go on to concentrate on finding out a bit more about this unusual country.

I soon discovered why I had encountered so many women in official positions. According to the census there were 200,000 families in Lesotho and the official figure for the number of men working in the South African mines was over 150,000 with more than another 50,000 working in other industries over the border. For once African women given responsible jobs had a chance to show what they could do. The following weeks of meeting farmers in different parts of the country confirmed many of the differences from East Africa that I had noticed on my arrival. It also confirmed that the small scale farmers whom I was meeting were just as resourceful, resilient and capable of making sound decisions as those with whom I had spent the previous quarter of a century. This was a comforting discovery. If my experience could serve me well in the unusual conditions of Lesotho it was likely to prove equally as useful in the other countries in Africa to which the Bank was going to send me. Over the coming months I was sent to a number of countries with tasks of varying usefulness. I now had to face up to the fact that I was an employee and not a free agent and so I did what I was told to the best of my ability and with as good a grace as possible. I was learning that the World Bank was an institution which could offer me opportunities to use my experience in a way that I could not possibly find elsewhere, but was also capable of setting me tasks which made little use of my skills. I had to balance one against the other and after my first year with the organization I decided that I was still prepared to give my new tactic a further try.

CHAPTER 22

# Back to Familiar Territory

'KAIJE! KAIJE! Buhoro Buhoro Gye'. The welcome greeting in Runyankore for those whom you have not seen for a long time went on and on as I was picked up, embraced, and held at arm's length for inspection by forty or fifty powerful young men. I was back at Nyakashaka for the first time since Amin had forced me out of Uganda. The Tanzanian army had invaded the country and finally overthrown Amin who had fled to Libya. Two weeks after some degree of normality had returned to the country I had been selected to lead a group of World Bank staff into Uganda to assess the priorities for rebuilding the country's agriculture. We split up into groups to visit different parts of the country and I chose the South West because I knew it so well. I was equally sure that my close friends there would give me insights that I would never obtain from official sources.

'How is Anna? How are Chris and David? You still look strong, so have you come back to live with us?' The questions flowed as more people heard of my arrival and came running to greet me. The glorious Nyakashaka air smelt just as good and the scenery stunned me afresh with its beauty after years of absence. The farms however looked very different. Tea up to twelve feet tall covered the hills as far as I could see. Amin's government had been uninterested in development and eventually the lack of foreign exchange and spare parts had forced the factory to close and the tea had not been plucked or pruned for five years. It was in its natural environment and so had grown strongly with no attention at all. If we could get the factory going then the tea could be pruned back and production would commence within weeks. The first crop would be particularly good because the trees had been rested and their roots would now be much deeper than before. 'Please Stephen, get the factory opened again. We have just been surviving with home grown food crops for all these years with no money coming in at all.'

'I will do my best,' I replied, but I was not sure how. Re-starting smallholder tea factories would not provide a large enough investment to justify all the work and negotiations required for a World Bank loan.

I was accompanied by a woman member of our team who had been rather sidelined amidst all the excitement of the reunion, but now we were both invited into one of the farmers' houses for lunch. A crowd of people squeezed into the room and, in a mixture of English and Runyankore, we began to get a better idea of what life had been like in recent years, how they saw the current situation and where their priorities lay. After a while I noticed my companion slip out of the room and assumed that she wanted a breath of fresh air. A half an hour later I realized that she had not returned, and I was rather concerned. A couple of us went out to look for her. A question to some children elicited the fact that she was in the kitchen at the back of the house where the lunch was being prepared. Into the smoke filled building we went to find the World Bank specialist on her knees on the earth floor doing a commendable job of grinding finger millet on a granite stone, to the immense delight of the farmers' wives. This is not perhaps the mental picture that people have of World Bank staff visiting a member country. I constantly hear references on the radio to 'dark suited World Bank staff' jetting around the world, and yet on more than a hundred Bank missions I have never worn a dark suit and hardly ever remember any of my many fellow staff doing so either. What I do have is many memories of tramping through muddy fields, sitting in cramped, stuffy local agricultural offices and sleeping in cheap and dirty rural lodgings. It is amazing what a false picture the simple phrase 'dark suited' can give.

We had begun our trip in the extreme South West in the town of Kabale, where our children had started their schooling and which was the nearest town to our last home in Uganda at Karengyere. 'It is an ill wind' goes the saying, and it was certainly true of Kabale. I had left it a small town in a poor area with few resources. I returned to find it transformed into a prosperous centre with a mass of new buildings. The contrast with the Kampala that we had left in the morning could not have been starker. The once clean and attractive capital city had been bombarded with heavy artillery and there had been street battles which had pockmarked many of the buildings. Tanks had driven through the streets and ripped up the tarmac. Rubbish was not collected and had blocked off some streets completely and there was no water supply in the city so that it stank. Yet here we were in Kabale with clean streets, flowers in the park, well kept houses and an obviously thriving community. Our children's school looked just like the day that we had last visited it and the expatriate missionary staff were all still in position. What 'ill wind' elsewhere had blown so favourably here? The lack of damage was easily accounted for because Kabale had never had an army presence and had not been in the path of the invading Tanzanian soldiers. But what about the prosperity? That took a little longer to work out, but the truth finally started to creep through friends' conversations. Kabale is on the border of Rwanda and the Congo, and the ever increasing shortages in the centre of Uganda had made smuggling a highly profitable enterprise, which had produced the wealth which in turn had transformed the town. News of national gloom frequently misses these pockets of prosperity which can develop when local people seize an opportunity presented by unusual circumstances. Africans are frequently accused of lacking the entrepreneurial skills required to compete in today's world. It is true that many lack experience in managing large businesses, but they show quite remarkable ingenuity in quickly identifying any situation which may offer the opportunity to turn a profit. The population of Kabale had demonstrated this capacity to the full.

To my amazement I found the agricultural staff the same as those that I had left ten years before. The Amin government had not really taken much notice of civil servants as long as they kept their heads down, and over the following weeks I came across old friends who had been neither transferred nor promoted in a decade. This made my own job easier, as it meant that I was working with people whom I knew. It was therefore with a former friend that we went out to Karengyere to find the station a bit run down but with my old staff producing and selling large quantities of good seed potatoes. Again there were warm greetings followed by requests for what they needed to get back into full swing. Once more I tried to give a positive response but with no clear idea as to from where I would elicit that help. One thing that did become clear from our journey was that farmers were short of the most basic tools.

'Look at our hoes!' had exclaimed our friends at Nyakashaka, holding up the worn out stump of a tool.

'Think of me clearing bush with this panga, Stephen, it's more like my wife's kitchen knife!' said another. We had come to Uganda with instructions to look at how best we could get the Ministry of Agriculture functioning efficiently again. My close connection with farmers quickly convinced me that smallholders had much more urgent needs that required action before we thought about re-habilitating the civil service. I realized that this might involve a battle at headquarters with its natural concern with national services but I was prepared to fight hard for this one.

Back in Kampala we all compared notes and I got people to focus on what they had seen of smallholder needs rather than institutional issues. Stories started to emerge of farmers in the East who had no spares for their ox ploughs and had to revert to much slower hoeing for land preparation. Hoes, axes and pangas everywhere were worn out. Fishermen were using tiny sections of net and their catches had dropped dramatically whilst everywhere people were desperate for bicycles because of the lack of any other transport. Most of the team returned to Washington while I stayed on in Kampala to start work on a strategy for helping farmers. One happy outcome of the difficult conditions in Kampala in that immediate post-Amin period was the way in which donors were prepared to co-operate in an unusually helpful manner. I became friendly with the representative of the European Union and put to him the plight of the smallholder tea growers. He was attracted by the challenge and quite quickly raised funds and staff to rehabilitate the factories to the great rejoicing of my Nyakashaka friends. Another included Karengyere in their plans and I could then concentrate on my own priority of putting tools back into farmers' hands. I quickly ran up a twenty million dollar project to supply three million hoes, half a million axes and pangas and thousands of fishing nets, plough spares and bicycles. Everything was to be bought for cash so I did not have to worry about credit and that helped to push the plan ahead quickly. I met with much less opposition than I had anticipated after offering assurances that I believed that work could start straight away on the next Bank investment focussing on research and extension.

A British company won the contract to obtain and wholesale the goods and it was not many months later that I had the pleasure of inspecting their work as they took over huge empty warehouses and sold essential tools to retailers around the country to take back to their villages. My pleasure was even greater as I started to see large hoes, long sharp pangas, mended ploughs and shiny new bicycles popping up all over the countryside through which I drove. I had made one serious miscalculation, for which the British staff teased me a good deal. I had budgeted for a big and expensive safe for each of the warehouses in which they could keep the large sums of money that they would be collecting each day. What I had not done was to think what three billion shillings would look like when the largest denomination note was one hundred shillings and most people were dealing in tens and twenties. The English accountant at the first store that I visited asked if I would like to see the arrangements for accounting. I naturally said that I would and was taken into a room where sixteen teenage girls with nimble fingers and sharp young minds were counting mountains of money under the strict eye of an older 'matron'. At the end of each day the stacks of cartons of notes were put into a large room and a five-ton lorry took them to the bank every three days. The accountant was totally dependent on the teenagers for the accuracy of his records, and the famous safe was used to keep the staff's whisky. Apart from that slip the project was immensely popular and I have no doubt that it made a major contribution to getting Ugandan farmers back into production once more. It also helped to convince me that this institution was enabling me to help small scale farmers in a way in which I could not possibly have done through a voluntary agency.

'I will have you crucified outside the World Bank building if you are wrong,' said the senior executive of the International Monetary Fund (IMF) as we left a meeting of Ugandan permanent secretaries and their senior staff. I was having my first taste of policy issues after being lent by the Bank to the IMF for two weeks work in Uganda. The background to this work was the exchange rate. Amin's government had kept the official exchange rate at eight shillings to the dollar for years. Because of the collapse of the economy the real rate of exchange on which the whole of society worked was 110 shillings to the dollar. Farmers had to sell their produce to government marketing boards, which paid them at the official rate. With that money they then had to go and buy basic goods at a rate fourteen times higher. The outcome was that it took kilos of coffee to buy a bar of soap, or a sack full of cotton to buy a bottle of kerosene. The natural result was that farmers had stopped picking their coffee or planting cotton. From being the largest producer of robusta coffee in the world Uganda was now a minor player, and from having exported half a million bales of cotton the country now had to import cotton for its spinning mill. The elite had no problem with this situation because they could use their influence to buy dollars at eight shillings each and go straight out and sell them for one hundred and ten! Enter the IMF with a demand that the official exchange rate be made one hundred and ten. This was obviously not popular with people in high places who saw their money-making machine being removed. But pressure was applied and the rate was changed. The whole idea of this was that farmers could now be offered attractive prices for their crops and so stimulate production. The IMF had reckoned without the long established practice of milking farmers through the government marketing boards. Despite the huge devaluation the marketing boards only made minor changes in the prices offered to farmers. The boards then expected to make massive profits from the revised exchange rate which could be filtered off into ministries for whatever purpose they chose.

The IMF was frustrated and came to the Bank asking if there was any staff member who really knew about the pricing of export crops in Uganda. My name was put forward and I was lent to the IMF for two weeks. I could not just multiply the old prices by fourteen to accommodate the change in exchange rate because quite a lot of the marketing costs were in foreign exchange. I therefore had to work the costs back from Frankfurt, Liverpool and New York and other potential markets, to the farm gate. I had already done quite a bit of this work and so quickly provided the IMF with appropriate farmgate prices for coffee, cotton, tobacco and tea. It is with these that the IMF executive and I had gone into the government meeting. 'These figures are quite ridiculous!' came a chorus of comments. 'We cannot possibly pay coffee farmers 85 shillings a kilo for coffee or 25 shillings for cotton.' These views were echoed by a number of participants, at which point the man from the IMF turned to me. 'Did you say that there was a plane at two o'clock this afternoon, Stephen?'

'Yes, there is a flight to Nairobi that connects quite well to Washington,' came my reply.

'Excuse us then, gentlemen, we must go and get ready to leave.'

'But what about the 50 million dollar loan that you had come to negotiate?' came the urgent question.

'I am afraid that there is no possibility of that if you are not willing to offer your farmers a proper price and get agriculture moving once more, so please excuse us.'

Hurried whispering followed and we were asked to please not leave until they had a chance to discuss the matter with their ministers. Could we please gather again in the afternoon? It was as we walked out of that meeting that I was threatened with a grisly death if I had got my figures wrong. I was sure that I had not and in the afternoon they were accepted by a reluctant gathering of officials who saw an anticipated flow of funds into their ministries being removed by the IMF. We were guests of the Governor of the Reserve Bank and had the satisfaction of watching the six o'clock news in his house when a senior official announced my figures as the new prices to farmers. The impact was amazing. Coffee sales shot up as farmers once again gathered the crop from their bushes and attractive prices stimulated the necessary work to get the other main crops back into full production. My decade of village level work in Uganda has possibly put quarter of a million dollars into farmers' pockets over the years. My two weeks with the IMF mission put tens of millions of dollars into the pockets of hundreds of thousands of farmers.

I was not allowed to spend all my time on Uganda however, and I was soon back into other countries with work which had its fair share of rewards and frustrations, but also its lighter moments. I was asked to go to the little kingdom of Swaziland to inspect a project that the Bank had funded to improve on the quality of agricultural extension. I was accompanied by Frank Thomas, who had been a contemporary of ours when we were students at Wye College. He had gone to Australia when we went to the Sudan and as we worked our two acre plot we read of the hundreds of thousands of acres of sheep ranch that he was managing. He was head-hunted on to an even bigger ranch in South America and was then invited to join the World Bank as a livestock specialist. Our normal pattern of project inspection was intended to assess whether the purpose for which the money had been lent still made good sense and whether the project was achieving its goals. We did not usually focus on small details, but on this occasion we could not help but notice that the cars that had been supplied to all the agricultural extension officers were looking remarkably the worse for wear after only 18 months. A few quiet inspections of the mileometers of a number of vehicles soon revealed that they were doing up to 4,000 miles a month when each officer had an area to cover of not greater than twenty miles in diameter. Some more careful investigation told us that the vehicles were being used as long distance taxis all day with the money being pocketed by the officers who were meant to be using the cars for their visits to farmers. We could not ignore this misuse of funds and so brought up the matter of excessive mileages with the permanent secretary when we met him in the capital.

'The trouble with you people who were born and brought up on that tiny little island of England is that you just cannot imagine the vastness of Africa. It is because of the vastness of Africa that we supplied our staff with cars and not bicycles.' We were submitted to another five-minute lecture on the smallness of our own world view and the vastness of Africa, when there was a slight break in the flow and Frank intervened.

'With respect Mr. Permanent Secretary, sir, I have never managed a farm as small as Swaziland.' I had to disguise a laugh and the flow on 'vastness' came to an abrupt halt. We were able to discuss the misuse of vehicles and ask for the official's intervention to stop the current practices and get his staff back to work as extension officers rather than cab operators. There are not too many English people who could truthfully make a similar claim and I was delighted to have had Frank with me.

Another lighter moment was provided when I had to return to my old stamping ground of Mwanza in Tanzania to assess the application for a large loan being requested by the regional government for agricultural development. On this occasion I was with another Englishman, Andrew Mercer, who had lost one leg at the hip during the war. He had mastered his artificial leg superbly and, a tall man with long strides, he often left me lagging behind on field trips. But artificial limbs can sometimes be a problem and this was one of them. 'I just cannot do it Stephen. The pain is almost killing me and we have not even taken off. There is no way that I could stick this for another three hours.' We were in a small plane at the end of the runway at Dar es Salaam airport in Tanzania on our way to Mwanza. I was sitting next to the pilot and Andrew had the double seat behind. The pilot stopped the engine and we both got out. We eased Andrew's tall frame on to the ground. He removed his trousers, undid his straps and handed me his leg. 'That's better,' he said as he now sat comfortably with his leg standing up beside him. 'Let's go!' We had been at the far end of a very long runway and nobody had seen our unusual arrangements, but Mwanza was a totally different story. A short runway led up to an airport building which was the size of a small domestic house. As we landed we saw a dozen dignitaries emerge from the building and line up at the end of the runway to greet this important mission which they hoped would bring a lot of development funding to their region. The engine stopped and the pilot and I got down and opened the door for Andrew and helped him on to the ground. The group surged forward to greet us but Andrew held up his hand and asked them to wait a moment. Standing, slightly puzzled, about ten yards away they watched in stupefaction as Andrew undid his belt and removed his trousers. I reached into the plane and passed him his leg, which he strapped into place. I gave him an arm as he replaced his trousers, did up his belt and advanced with a beaming smile to shake hands with a group of profoundly shaken dignitaries. I knew most of them from my previous work and a quiet word about wartime heroism and the cramped space in the small plane brought understanding nods and a warm welcome to an enjoyable visit.

CHAPTER 23

# Not All a Bed of Roses

'THERE IS A tendency to shoot the messenger rather than face up to the facts of the situation. So Mr Carr has not had an entirely easy time of it.' So read part of my Annual Performance Review in 1985. After six years working on the countries of Eastern Africa I had been asked to move to the West African division and take special responsibility for a billion dollar portfolio of lending for rural development in Nigeria. This money was being used in part to sink 1,500 boreholes fitted with hand pumps, which have undoubtedly been a great blessing to many women. It was also used for the construction of hundreds of miles of rural access roads, which have also been valued by local people. The heart of the projects, however, was the transformation of local farming from mixed cropping with sorghum, millet and cowpeas to one in which new varieties of these same crops were to be grown in pure stands. It was the increased production from these new varieties which was used to justify the loan and which would produce the revenue with which it was to be repaid. These were the largest loans that the World Bank had made for an agricultural project in Sub-Saharan Africa, and therefore had a high profile within the institution.

'Why do you grow your crops in a mixture?' I asked one farmer after another as I travelled round the project areas on my first one month long visit to Nigeria. The answer was always the same.

'Because we get three crops off the same piece of land with just one lot of cultivation. The millet ripens first and once we have harvested that the sorghum hidden underneath can shoot up and produce. When we have harvested the sorghum that lets the light in to the cowpeas which are crawling across the ground and then they give us a crop.' Not only did the system make the best use of land and labour but the varieties used by the farmers had been selected over hundreds of years and were ideally suited to the environment and farming system in which they were being used.

'Have you seen a demonstration of the new varieties that are grown on their own?' Some had but nobody was interested in using them. Not only had the farmers good reason for not adopting these new varieties, but some quick calculations showed me that they would certainly lose out in terms of production if they did change their system. Here then was the Bank lending millions of dollars to multiply huge quantities of these new seeds, demonstrate them to hundreds of thousands of farmers and establish stores from which they could be purchased. Here was I saying that farmers had excellent reasons for not using them. At the end of a couple more visits I reckoned that there would be a few mechanized commercial farmers who would be interested to use the new material, but that uptake over the five year project period was likely to be less than five percent of the projections on which the profitability of the exercise had been calculated. This in the event proved to be the case. No wonder senior management was inclined to want to shoot the messenger.

How had the Bank ever got itself into this situation? The senior, highly qualified plant breeders at the main Nigerian research stations had spent twenty years producing higher yielding varieties of the three major food crops. All of this selection and breeding was done in pure stand, which was the farming system for which their years of training had prepared them. The varieties that they developed were actually tailored so that they could not be used in mixtures. Many considered the mixed cropping used by all the farmers as being a primitive form of agriculture and the one scientist who had highlighted its value had been ignored and sidelined. After years of work they had varieties ready for distribution to farmers but did not have the resources with which to bulk them up, demonstrate them and distribute them across the huge numbers of farmers in Northern Nigeria. Hence the approach to the World Bank. The man sent to assess their proposals was an Indian who had held senior positions in his own country and had a reputation as an outstanding agriculturalist. This was to be his first visit to Africa, and so naturally he went to the major centre of research excellence at Samaru in Northern Nigeria and met with a group of highly qualified and experienced Nigerian scientists. They showed him all their data, their field experiments and their seed multiplication plots. All very impressive, and their new varieties substantially out-yielded local crop varieties when both were planted in pure stand. No mention was made of the fact that none of these traditional varieties was ever, in fact, grown in pure stand, nor of the commendable features of the traditional system of agriculture. The Indian was impressed by the qualifications and presentation of the local scientists and, as a newcomer to the continent, found no reason to query their facts, and gave the favourable report which resulted in the granting of the loan. Once the reality of farmer lack of interest was fully appreciated, we were able to divert a substantial amount of the loan to developing small scale irrigation through the sinking of shallow wells and the sale of tens of thousands of small petrol powered pumps. This proved popular and productive and was some compensation for the failure to dramatically change the rainfed farming system of millions of farmers as had been planned.

Nigeria was certainly not the only country that I came across in which the work of the agricultural research stations was not closely related to the real situation facing farmers and in particular their labour constraints. 'If farmers are to get the best from their maize crop they must plant with the first rain and weed within seventeen days.' So said the maize specialist as we sat around the table at a major national research station.

'If they are to get optimum groundnut yields then farmers must plant with the first rains and weed within seventeen days,' said the groundnut breeder.

'If farmers are to get good yields of tobacco they must transplant with the first rains and weed within two weeks,' was the contribution of the tobacco specialist.

Now it was my turn. 'As it is impossible for the farmer to carry out these ideal instructions then which crop will suffer least from delayed planting and weeding?'

'You do not understand Mr Carr, it is essential that all these crops be planted with the first rains and weeded on time.' We went round in circles for a bit longer but I realized that I was making no headway at all. Each was focussing on the ideal for their crop and just was not prepared to face up to the fact that their recommendations were totally impractical, and that the reason that they were not followed had nothing to do with farmer ignorance but with the constraints on family labour which determined what people could actually do. The research that was needed was into how to spread the labour load at the busiest time of the year rather then into how to obtain the best yields under theoretically ideal circumstances. These scientists had all been trained in Western institutions and were all too often out of touch, and of sympathy, with the desperately poor smallholders whom they were meant to be serving. It was this attitude that was at the root of a number of failed World Bank funded projects aimed at improving on the quality of agricultural research in Africa.

The other group of failures that I had to deal with were investments aimed at improving the quality of advisory services to farmers, commonly known as extension. The problem here was that it was not usually a lack of money which was at the root of the failure of the civil service to provide appropriate help to farmers. It takes many years to build up a civil service which is made up of conscientious workers dedicated to the welfare of their fellow citizens and free of nepotism and corruption. A reading of Samuel Pepys' diaries will more than fully illustrate how far England had to go in this direction when that gentleman was Secretary to the Navy. Many of Africa's civil services are of very recent origin, and while they include many fine and dedicated people, the concept of conscientious, honest and unselfish work for the benefit of those who have paid for the service through their taxes has certainly not permeated the whole organization. A further problem with the agricultural staff was that their training often accentuated the superiority of a more Western approach to farming as compared to the untidy, mixed crop plots of the majority of local smallholders. They come out of college with a sense of bringing light into dark places by telling 'backward and ignorant peasants' what they ought to be doing. Very few are taught to learn from local farmers and then see if anything of what they learned in college can be of any use in the actual situation in which farmers find themselves. Given these fundamental weaknesses it is not surprising that simply lending money to improve the quality of the extension service seldom had the desired result, and I had to report on a number of failures. Many of these problems were confined to Africa and it was sometimes with a little envy that I listened to the stories of success from friends working on World Bank loans for agriculture in China, Turkey, Poland or Brazil where farmers had been exposed to new methods for much longer and where the organizations serving the industry were much more strongly established.

'And if you vote for me I will make sure that you never have to repay your loans to the Agricultural Bank!' The shouted words in Kiswahili rang out across the Kenyan crowd and raised a great cheer. At the edge of the crowd stood the general manager of the said bank and a Tanzanian staff member of the World Bank, which had made a loan to fund the institution. Following on reports of political interference in the working of the agricultural bank he had come to look into the veracity of the reports. In Nairobi he had been assured that, although there had been problems in the past, the government had stamped out any political meddling. Now, as a fluent Swahili speaker, he was hearing a rather different story. He returned to Nairobi and had to record that the reports of political interference were still all too true. Credit for small farmers has been the basis of progress and development elsewhere in the world and yet in Africa there are far more experiences of failure than of success, and once again I had to report on dashed hopes from investments made in this field. Apart from the political interference mentioned above there is the fundamental problem of mismanagement of overall government spending, leading to impossibly high interest rates. This is the case in Malawi today where loans to small farmers carry interest rates of up to 65%, which make them completely unattractive to the majority of farmers. If you combine this with artificially depressed prices to farmers from government marketing boards it is not difficult to see why agricultural banks have had little success in meeting the needs of the poor in much of Africa.

I have given space to these failures because it is those that drove the World Bank from its enviable position of offering loans for successful civil works to one which has become mired in attempting to influence government policies in a range of African countries. In desperation the organization has adopted a strategy which attempts to rectify the policies which it sees as undermining development. So if government over-expenditure is pushing up interest rates and killing credit schemes, then let's control government expenditure. If a marketing board is ripping off farmers let's find another way of purchasing the crop, irrespective of the fact that the profits of the marketing board are finding their way into the pockets of cabinet ministers who are therefore going to make sure that any alternative approach is made to fail. If it is political interference, corruption or nepotism which is the cause of the failure of the projects for which we are making loans, then let us tackle those constraints. So the World Bank in Africa has moved a long way from the institution which I joined 26 years ago when its whole focus was on project work, and I could concentrate on the problems of getting tools into the hands of Ugandan farmers or fertilizer on to the farms of women in Lesotho. Those were straightforward activities, and even with the problem projects involving research and extension I was able to concentrate on technical issues and not have to get involved in the infinitely more complex work of deciding what are the right political and economic policies for somebody else's country. I greatly appreciate the opportunities that the World Bank gave me to use my experience for the benefit of small scale farmers in Africa, but I am glad that I reached retirement age before I became too involved in the political and policy struggles into which the institution has been drawn in recent years, and I sympathize with those who now have to deal with them and incur so much adverse criticism of their efforts.

CHAPTER 24

# Into Retirement

'WHY ARE ALL the shops in these villages closed at ten o'clock in the morning?' I asked our guide cum interpreter as Anne and I travelled round the Malawian countryside for the first time.

'Because it is late January,' came the rather surprising reply.

'Is there a law preventing people from opening their shops at this time of the year?' I asked with some incredulity.

'Oh no. It's just that people use any of the little money that they have to buy food in the market because they have finished all the maize that they grew themselves. Now they have no cash to buy salt or soap or sugar or cloth so there is no point at all in the shopkeepers wasting their time and opening their shops. When the new maize ripens in April then the shops will open again.'

Anne, with World Bank permission, had joined me on a month long mission to Malawi on which I planned to travel the length of the country interviewing small scale farmers to ascertain whether the information that I had been given in the capital city on my first visit tallied with what I could see for myself on the ground. It was a journey which was to have a profound impact on the later years of our lives. Each day we drove ten or fifteen miles off a main road and then just walked along rural paths speaking to the farmers weeding their fields. Never in all the countries in which we had worked or visited in Africa had we seen such poverty. People eating once a day or once every two days. Virtually everyone looking thin with children dressed in rags and obviously under-nourished. People, as always, welcoming us warmly and making light of their troubles which they faced with the cheerfulness and courage which is the hallmark of rural Africa, but who nonetheless were amongst the most deprived that we had met.

On our return to the capital, Lilongwe, we were approached by several influential people who, having heard that I was to retire in eighteen months time, asked if we would consider settling in Malawi. Our immediate response was negative. We had already made plans to return to live at Nyakashaka in Uganda and had told our friends there that we would be coming to help to get smallholder tea growing back to a healthy and rapidly expanding condition. In addition we did not speak a local language in Malawi and reckoned that we were getting rather old to embark on yet another major learning exercise, we had no friends or contacts and did not know the country. After we returned to Washington the memories of the desperately poor families whom we had met, and the intransigent agricultural problems which they faced, would not go away. We realized that by comparison with Malawi our friends at Nyakashaka and their neighbours were well off. Should we disappoint the tea growers in Western Uganda or forget about the poverty in Malawi? We wrestled with the problem for some weeks and finally felt that we should provide a test to help us with our decision. On my next visit to Malawi I was again approached with a request to go and help there. 'Yes, we would consider coming to settle here, but only if we are granted permanent residence' (this gives the holder the right to vote, own land and reside in the country permanently without qualification).

'But Mr Carr, you were not born in Malawi and you are not married to a Malawian, how can we give you permanent residence?'

'I really do not mind how, but you are asking me to abandon my plans to settle in a country where I have friends, land and influence, to come and settle in your country about which I know very little. I am not prepared to change my plans and come here on some temporary permit which could be revoked at any time.' I must admit that I rather hoped that would be the end of our problem. I was wrong. A few weeks later an application form for permanent residence arrived in Washington. It asked 'Was I born in Malawi?' No. 'Was I married to a Malawian?' No. 'For how long had I live in Malawi?' Never. That should settle it I thought, but again I was wrong and six weeks later our permanent resident passes arrived in Washington. We had to inform our Ugandan friends that we would not be joining them, and prepare ourselves to settle in a new country and start on some hard thinking as to how we could help its small scale farmers.

My friends in the wealthier countries of the West find it hard to accept the conditions under which billions of people live in the same world as themselves. They cannot imagine living on less than a dollar a day as do a substantial part of the world's population. The dollar a day is the World Bank's benchmark to define poverty, but in Malawi, as in many other countries, a dollar a day puts one into the wealthier segment of society. The poverty definition in Malawi is those people with a total income from all sources of less than 30 US cents per day, and 65% of the population fall into that category. Dinner for two with a bottle of wine in a London restaurant costs the equivalent of most Malawians' total income for the year. Tiny farms, and no money to buy the improved seed and fertilizer which could increase their production, mean that families suffer severe food shortages for several months each year. This results in a quarter of the babies born dying before they are five years old. In Europe the figure is less than one in a hundred. And yet I am still reluctant to use the word poverty in relation to my neighbours' conditions because so often the word is equated with misery, and misery is certainly not a feature of most Malawians' lives. Poor in assets, yes. Hungry for months each year, yes. Facing the tragedy of losing their children, yes. But rich in courage, in fortitude, in cheerfulness in the face of hardship, and above all, in laughter. Was there anything that we could do to help these courageous people to ease some of the burdens which they have to carry? I would like to accentuate that in the following descriptions of our activities my role has largely been to produce ideas. It is the rural people of this country who have made some of these ideas actually work.

'Good morning Mr Burley, I see that some of your plans are beginning to take off.' I could barely believe it. Here was I, a passionate demander of non-smoking rooms and sections of public places, who had refused to help anybody grow tobacco during all my years in Africa, now being widely called Mr Burley Tobacco, the name of the kind of tobacco for which Malawi is famous. What had happened? It had not taken many visits to Malawi to realize that a country with only four to five months of rain per year and situated a couple of thousand kilometres from its main port was going to find it very difficult to identify any high value crop other than tobacco as the main source of cash for its farmers. Fifteen years and many studies later the situation has not changed, and nobody has been able to identify an alternative. What I found however was that small scale farmers were forbidden by law to grow the only crop which could put some money into the family purse. The previous ruler, Dr Banda, had seen that making a licence to grow burley tobacco a reward for loyalty would ensure a cadre of committed followers. Licences were issued to a small group of his inner circle, who then used thousands of share-croppers to actually grow the crop. These were among the poorest people in the country, whilst the owners of the licences became wealthy. I made my first target the repeal of this law, using the leverage of a World Bank loan to achieve my objective. It was a bitter battle, which made me highly unpopular with people whose licence to print money was under threat. The Bank gave its full support and after a couple of years of hostility the battle was won, the law was repealed and within a few years over three hundred thousand small scale farmers were growing the crop. Only those people who treated their share croppers fairly and well were able to continue with the old system. Numerous surveys have been carried out on the impact of burley growing on family welfare and have all shown that the money earned goes into buying fertilizer for their food crops and for actually buying food when home production runs out.

'Why don't you plant hybrid maize seed which would give you much higher yields?' I asked a farmer on one of my early visits.

'Because I grow maize for eating not for selling,' came the reply.

'Can't you eat hybrid maize, does it not taste good?'

'It's not the taste that is the problem, but you cannot turn it into flour at home. When you start pounding it with a pestle and mortar it all breaks into pieces and the hard outer coat gets all mixed up with the flour. Our traditional maize is different. When you pound it the outer coat comes off and we can separate it from the flour. Only rich people use hybrid maize and they sell it to the mills who have machines which can make it into good flour.' Here was a challenge. Poorer farmers not able to make use of improved seed which could increase their production. An approach to senior staff in the Ministry of Agriculture produced the reply that they had bred a high yielding maize and farm families would just have to get used to eating coarse flour (something that their own families would never have tolerated!). Pointing out that years of pushing their varieties had not resulted in families changing their eating habits simply resulted in comments on backwardness and conservatism. Visiting experts sympathized with my claim that we needed a hybrid with similar properties to the local maize, but said that it would take up to fifteen years to breed. I was not convinced, went to the International Maize Breeding Centre in Mexico and was told that they had material on hand which would produce a suitable hybrid for the Malawian smallholders within a year. By happy coincidence a young maize breeder had just returned to Malawi from his overseas training and needed little encouragement to start working with the new material supplied by the international centre through their local office. Released within a year the new hybrid was an instant success and so now any family able to afford seed can use a higher yielding variety and still produce the quality of flour that they want.

But there was a bigger challenge that had to be faced. With little more than an acre of farm, with no money to buy fertilizer, no animals to

produce manure, a shortage of labour, raw materials and water with which
to make the ten tons of compost per year that they would need to maintain
the productivity of their farms, there are hundreds of thousands of families
whose soil fertility and crop output is declining year after year. They well
know what is happening but do not know how to stop it. A hundred years
ago the population of this country was one sixteenth of what it is today and
farmers could allow land to lie fallow for many years to restore its fertility.
Now that option has gone and they are a loss as to how they can survive.
What could I do to help?

'You are not going to mention fertilizer because seventy percent of
farmers in this country cannot afford it. You are not going to work through
farmers' clubs because poor people never belong to them.'

'But if we are not going to preach fertilizer and not going to meet
farmers in their clubs what can we possibly do?' came the reply from the
ten new staff that I had recruited from the Ministry of Agriculture to
experiment with a new approach to helping the small farmers of Malawi.

'You are going to talk about ways of increasing fertility which need very
little money and you are going to work with the church women's groups
which exist across the country to which hundreds of thousands of women
belong. Let's start with stopping soil from washing away by helping people
to make their ridges on the contour.'

'We will need dumpy levels for that,' interrupted one of my new staff.

'No you won't. You will teach farmers how to do it with three pieces of
stick, some string and a stone. Come on, we have been in this classroom
long enough, let's go outside and I will teach you how to do it.'

So the week continued, lines of a particular grass planted on the contour
to stop erosion on very steep land. A tree that loses its leaves in the wet
season so you can plant crops underneath it, while its deep roots bring up
plant food to the surface. A small local shrub that enriches the soil and can
be planted in between the maize, and a variety of soya bean which both
enriches the soil and provides an ideal weaning food for babies, the lessons
went on.

'But how are we going to gain control over the farmers and make them
do what we want? In the Ministry we controlled credit so if they did not
obey us they got no credit. How can we make women in a church group
follow our advice?'

'How does a company force women to use their brand of soap?' I asked.
'Well they have their salesmen who go round advertising it and talking to
people in the markets to try and get them to buy their make,' came the reply.

'And that's what you are going to have to start doing. You are not going to force anybody to take up these new ideas. When you go to a women's group you will go as a guest and behave as a guest.' They were dubious but saw that if they were to work with me they would have to give it a try.

My old friends in Christian Aid had put up the money for this experiment and I now posted my new staff up an 800 kilometre line which covered a wide range of farm types and different tribal backgrounds. This involved me in a great deal of driving, as I visited each of them every month, but it also gave me the encouragement of watching these men and women from an autocratic system suddenly realize that there was a quite different way of dealing with farmers which really worked. 'How can you possibly sell 2,000 packets of soya bean seed in two weeks?' I asked a particularly enthusiastic worker.

'There are 400 women who meet at one church at five in the morning each day to pray before they go to the fields. There is another where there are 300, and several smaller groups. They are all expecting to get the seed and have saved money to buy it. Please don't let me down and make sure that I get the 2,000 packs on time. You know sir, I meet more farmers at one of these church groups than I used to see at my five farmers' clubs in the old days'.

Ridges went on to the contour, grass strips were planted, soya bean acreage increased rapidly and farmers started to experiment with planting trees and shrubs in their gardens. At the end of three years we were able to convince much larger players to adopt a similar approach and the American government and the European Union embarked upon widespread programmes to promote the ideas that I had pioneered and I was able to ease up on my punishing travel schedule. The EU and US are still expanding their programmes, but all of us who really care about the welfare of poor people are disappointed with the results. What is the matter?

After 14 years of implementing this approach I had hoped to see trees on half the farms in the country, grass lines on steep hills wherever I drove and farms nicely contoured to save soil and conserve water. Instead of that we have about 80,000 farmers who have adopted this approach, which is only four percent of the farming population. Do they not adopt because they are backward and ignorant? Of course not. The problem is that the benefits are just not quick enough nor immediately impressive enough to catch the imagination of the majority of farmers. Soil conservation benefits your children rather than yourself. Fertility enhancing trees last for a hundred and fifty years, but it is seven years before one starts to see their impact.

Planting shrubs in between maize can increase yields by 60% after three years but they only give a 20% increase in the first year so many farmers do not persist with them. There are striking examples of individual success, the EU is going to greatly intensify its efforts over the coming five years but the change is just not happening fast enough to relieve the desperate needs of large numbers of small farmers. And so three years ago I embarked on another tactic to meet the immediate needs of families while we wait for the more painstaking work on long term solutions to take effect. From being 'Mr No Fertilizer' I am quickly becoming 'Mr Fertilizer'.

I am not going to embark on a detailed defence of the value of fertilizer for the sake of those who disapprove of its use, although I appreciate some of their concerns. Suffice to say that much of the world is only fed today because farmers are able to use fertilizer to replace the nutrients lost from their soils. Neither India nor China, with their limited land area in relation to their population, could possibly feed their people without the use of millions of tons of fertilizer every year. Malawian farmers with their small plots of land are equally aware of its value as, in every village in the country, they see the huge increase in the productivity of the farms of the more prosperous members of the community who can afford fertilizer. Unlike my 'organic' methods of raising yields fertilizer has an immediate and vivid impact which makes virtually every farmer want to use it. But most have just have one problem, they cannot afford to buy it. Offering credit is certainly not the answer, as poor families would have to sell their basic food in order to repay their loans in the absence of any cash crop. What could they sell in order to buy their way into more abundant food from their farms? They mostly have just one asset, and that is their labour. With our long dry season there are more than six months a year when people cannot work on their farms, and yet for most people there is little other work available. How about using that spare labour to build up the facilities in their village and pay them with vouchers for fertilizer and seed?

A survey of farmers showed that this would be very popular. One after another the interviewees begged not to be paid in cash, which would soon evaporate, but with inputs for their farms. I took my idea to the head of the US development agency, managed to convince him that it could really benefit poor families, and he offered enough money to employ 30,000 people as an experiment. They built 250 kilometres of good rural roads and earned themselves enough fertilizer and improved seed to make a real difference to their household food supply. Nothing succeeds like success and some judicious lobbying in the House of Commons produced enough money to employ a hundred thousand people. This in turn caught the interest of the World Bank who are planning to fund another 80,000 people. Now I am turning my attention to using that labour for developing small scale irrigation and re-afforestation. I produced the idea but it is the enthusiasm of thousands of poor rural families which has made the idea work in practice. We also make sure that the recipients don't forget about the other messages of soil conservation and improvement.

'Bwana, you have no idea what a difference you have made to our lives. I used to have to keep my little boy tied to me because of his fits. He had them almost every day and I was so frightened that he might fall into the cooking fire. Now, with your medicine, he goes to school every day like all the other children. We thank God for that medicine every day.' I was out in a remote rural area with the nurse from the Sue Ryder Foundation running her clinic for epileptics when the woman came and clasped my knees and poured out her thanks. I was distinctly embarrassed at being apportioned so much praise for an activity in which many other people play a far more important role than mine. Lady Ryder, well known for her work in Europe, had decided that she wanted to extend her activities to Africa. Malawi, as a poor country, was brought to her attention and so she established work there. She had no experience of this part of the world, was not well served by the original staff that were recruited, and her experiment was soon in serious trouble. I was approached and asked if I would be prepared to take responsibility for it. Looking at its objectives it seemed worth a try and I have allocated a good deal of my time to the Foundation for the past seven years. Now with excellent Malawian staff, a good Board which I chair, and 300 unpaid volunteers in the villages, we have an organization which serves several thousand epileptics and asthmatics, scattered through hundreds of villages. We also offer physiotherapy to a range of young people with disabilities of various kinds. Africa is not all doom and gloom and initiatives like this are making a difference to thousands of people on the continent every day.

It never ceases to surprise me how quickly one can change expectations when moving from one society to another. Staying at a house in England I would be amazed to find a half a dozen people sitting on the doorstep when I got up in the morning. And yet at our home in Malawi the opposite is the case and I would consider it a most unusual day if the dawn found nobody waiting for me to appear. Some days it is just one, on others there are half a dozen. It may be a woman bringing a gift of garden produce to thank us for paying the cost of treatment which rid her of a horrific ulcer on her leg which was ruining her life. It could be a child, whose school fees we have paid, proudly bearing a good school report. But mostly it is people in need of help with the kind of problems faced by ordinary people in villages across the country. There are the elderly who have lost all their children to AIDS and are now destitute. There are the grandmothers who have suddenly been left with a group of grandchildren because their daughters and sons-in-law have all died and they do not know how they are going to feed them. There are fourteen year olds who are now family heads with four siblings to feed and they have completely run out of food. There are the parents who have collected most of the money needed to send a child to secondary school but would I please make up the balance. There is the teenager from a hundred kilometres away sent to stay with a relative who works in Zomba so as to ease the food situation at home, who arrives to find that the relative has moved to a far away district. There she is in the midst of complete strangers without a penny in her pocket to pay the fare to return home. Some kind soul points her in my direction. Offering help in these circumstances has become a part of every day's happenings in my retirement and it keeps the reality of the society in which we have chosen to live firmly in focus. There are those who would condemn such help as 'bandaid' or sticking plaster charity. It is a criticism which I have always found hard to follow. For that blister on the heel, that cut on the ball of the thumb there are few more helpful medical aids than a piece of plaster, and I have been grateful for its comfort times without number. If I am able to offer similar relief to those blistered and wounded by events beyond their control I will not be deterred by those who decry such personal assistance as being too superficial to be of real help.

When we return to visit Nyakashaka with its nectar-like air and its glorious views; when we are back in a situation in which we can converse in the local language with complete fluency; when we see the transformation that can be worked in a more fertile country like Uganda, there is a trace of nostalgia for what my retirement might have been. Deep down however there are really no serious regrets for having filled in that fateful application form for permanent residence in Malawi.

CHAPTER 25

# Anne's Turn

'ONE OF THE young men in our Hispanic congregation has lost his forearm in an accident. Because he is an 'illegal' he has no access to insurance or free medical help and so cannot obtain a prosthesis. He is now out of work and his family is suffering. If any of you feel that you could help him to obtain an artificial limb then he could get back to work once more.' We were in church in the suburb of Washington where we had a house while I flew off to different parts of Africa every few weeks on behalf of the World Bank. Anne and I looked at each other, nodded and after the service offered to pay for the prosthesis. That was the start of a major new activity for Anne. As we considered the plight of that young man we thought of all the people in Africa whose lives must be blighted because of the lack of orthopaedic care and wondered how we could use our limited resources to be of help. We did not have to wonder for long because a few weeks later Anne received a large financial windfall from her family's firm. Here was the start of an answer to our problem. Anne obtained the help of a few close friends as trustees and, using her family name, founded the Grant Charitable Trust which was to become one of her major activities over the next fifteen years until increasing age and declining health forced her to close it at the end of 2002.

The Trust was established with two basic aims. Firstly to assist disadvantaged children in the six countries of East and Central Africa and secondly to channel that help through people and organizations which were not currently able to tap the resources of major donors. We had thought that much of the giving would be for orthopaedic work, but we were quite wrong. Although by far the largest single donation went towards building a new orthopaedic hospital for children in Kenya, we soon found that the phrase 'disadvantaged children' brought a wide spectrum of needs to our door and, out of the more than a hundred projects which the Trust supported, less than ten percent were connected to what Anne had thought would be her main concern. What the Trust did was to involve us both in tens of thousands of miles of travel and, above all brought us into contact with some wonderful people of a range of nationalities whose dedication and concern was an inspiration to us and our trustees. It is almost invidious to pick out examples of these people but it would need a book to do justice to them all. I just hope that by introducing a few it will help to highlight the fact that behind all the bleak news that comes out of Africa there are not only millions of brave and cheerful people but points of bright light which unfortunately the media seldom allow to shine through the darkness.

'Are you sure that you can manage, Nightingale?' I asked as my seriously disabled companion virtually rolled through ditches and down muddy alleys of shanty slums on the edges of Kampala in Uganda.

'I come down here every week, you don't have to worry about me. We are nearly at the first family that I want you to meet.' Nightingale Kalinda was a highly qualified Ugandan nurse whose own disability had given her a profound concern for other disadvantaged people, particularly in the slums.

'Don't try to greet her, she will bite you,' said a worried mother as I stretched out my hand to the attractive looking eleven-year-old girl tied by a rope to her mother's wrist. 'She had a severe bout of cerebral malaria last year and it damaged her brain,' explained Nightingale. 'She has to be tied to her mother all day and yet there are four other children to be fed and looked after. Can you imagine what a problem the poor woman faces? I want to select bright young women from these slums, and send them off for special training at Mengo Hospital here in Kampala on how to help children like this. Then I would rent small houses in these locations and provide day care centres for these children. That would provide some professional help for them and, just as importantly, would give their mothers a few hours freedom each day to care for the rest of their families.' We visited another half a dozen equally distressing cases and then I asked Nightingale to prepare a budget for the training, the salaries, rents and any other expenses. She did it in no time and Anne had no problem in getting the trustees to agree to making a suitable grant. We supported this work for several years until its success attracted local funding. During that time I had more forays into the slums with Nightingale and had the great pleasure of meeting the girl who had been expected to bite me, now greeting me happily and actually helping her mother to care for her siblings, even though she would never be the same bright child who had been such a source of joy to her family before she got that crippling bout of malaria.

'This really must be the wrong address,' said Anne to the taxi driver as we drew up before a modest sized house in a poor area of Nairobi in Kenya.

'Well this is the address that you gave me,' responded the driver.

'Just hang on, don't go away while I check.'

At that moment the door opened and a group of young people came out and started singing a song of welcome. It obviously was the right address and I paid off the taxi driver.

'But how on earth can he squeeze over a hundred children into this house?' whispered Anne as a tall Ugandan came past the choir to greet us. Ernest Mbugua had got the name of the Trust from a friend and applied for help with caring for a hundred and ten street children. We had come to see what he was doing and were now seriously doubting the figure with which he had provided us. Behind the house in a small garden were gathered a large group of children and a quick glance showed that there could easily be over a hundred boys and girls from eight to sixteen years old. The following hour provided us with one of the most exuberant displays of music and drama that we had enjoyed for a long time. The morale of the children was quite amazing and Ernest was obviously a very charismatic leader. But where on earth did they sleep and eat? The welcoming concert over we moved into the house. In the first 'dormitory' cheap iron beds were welded one on top of the other four tiers high with a one foot gap between each set of 'bunks'. In this one bedroom 48 boys were sleeping under conditions which would have horrified any health inspector but, as the boys themselves told us, it was a great deal more comfortable and secure than the shop steps or empty culverts in which many had been sleeping before Ernest had found them. And the eating? Food was cooked in three lots of forty units by the older children and then eaten on knees wherever room could be found to sit. Certainly not conforming to any institutional standards but a lot better than rummaging in dustbins. We discovered that Ernest was a Ugandan refugee whose own hardships had made him concerned for the street children and he had managed to beg enough money to rent the house. Hotels were providing food and the beds had come from an institution that had been closed down. Ernest was obviously a highly successful 'beggar' but he was desperate to get some regular, dependable funding which would leave him freer to spend more time with the children. Once again the trustees agreed to a grant and within a couple of years his good work reached the ears of other donors and we transferred our efforts elsewhere, while the memory of the verve and morale of the street children brought warmth to our lives for many days.

'What an extraordinary name this man has, Pookie Evans, and the whole set-up sounds a bit odd, but I trust the person who recommended him to us.' We were driving down to Mazabuka in Zambia and Anne was looking through the notes on the three different people we were meant to meet in that area who had applied for grants. It turned out that Pookie did not just have a peculiar name but was a most unusual person. He had been a large scale commercial farmer who had a profound religious experience which led him to sell his farm and use the entire proceeds to build and run a hospital in a poor rural area at which all treatment would be free. His wife was a doctor and provided the core of the medical services. Pookie supervised the building and maintenance, drove the ambulance and did some fund-raising. They lived extremely simply but were finding it difficult to ensure a guaranteed supply of drugs for the hospital. Could Anne help? We duly went round the small, simple hospital and were amazed at how much they had achieved with their limited resources. The crowded wards and out-patients left no doubt that this dedicated couple were providing a much needed and appreciated service. Once again the trustees agreed to Anne's request that we support this remarkable initiative and we did so until a happy incident brought them another source of help. They picked up a couple of young Dutch hitchhikers one evening and when they found that they had nowhere to sleep offered them hospitality. The young people stayed for several days at the hospital, went back to Holland and started a charity to support Pookie and his wife on a long-term basis.

'I do not think that they need seven years to prepare for the primary school leaving examination, with good teaching we are getting there in five and our children are winning prizes and getting excellent results.' The speaker was a sixty-five year old German nun, Sister Gloria Dei, who was running one of the most unusual schools in the slums of Ndola in Zambia. Her efforts had been brought to our notice by the wife of the British High Commissioner who had come across her just as she was establishing her 'shipping container school' for orphans and destitute children. The nun had been concerned at the lack of education for poor children who could not afford school fees, but she had no funds for building a school. She had bullied a piece of land out of the local council and then wheedled eight 40-foot shipping containers from local companies and got them to move them to her site. Windows were cut in the sides and grass put on top to keep them cool and she had her seven classrooms and a school office and store. With no desks, blackboards or books she still had some more work to do, and it was at this point that her efforts were brought to Anne's notice, and on the basis of what we had been told the trustees made a grant to equip the school. Within a couple of weeks of the money being transferred we had the most comprehensive set of reports and receipts that we had ever received and realized that we were not just dealing with a dedicated nun but a highly efficient administrator. From desks we moved to funding for a good meal for all the children every day, for equipment for vocational training, for more furnishing for another four containers and so on. Visiting the school was an inspiration and also demonstrated what excellent classrooms containers make with a line of desks down each side and the teacher walking up and down the central aisle in close contact with all the children. The school has gone from strength to strength and has now attracted funding from other donors. We for our part are truly privileged to have known this remarkable woman whose energy and dedication have been such a blessing to so many poor children and provided yet another of those bright lights of which so few people outside Africa ever hear.

Lydya Kamya was a very different woman. A middle aged widow of deep Christian conviction she lived in a rural area of Uganda and had a household which, like Topsy, just went on growing as one desperate orphan girl after another came to her door for refuge. I forget how she got hold of Anne's name, but through the post came a hand-written request for the money to buy two hundred and fifty day-old chicks and the cost of the food to rear them. These poultry would then supply the money with which she could feed her growing family. I happened to be going to Uganda on other business so I found my way out to her village and met with Lydya and her 'family'. I was impressed by her concern for the girls, the sum involved was small and she was given the necessary funds.

'Dear Mr Carr, I am very sorry indeed to have to report that three of the chicks which you bought for me died before they reached adulthood. I do not know what went wrong.' So read her letter some weeks later. I could hardly believe my eyes. Ninety percent survival from day old chick to adult hen is good going in an African village setting, ninety nine percent was extraordinary and yet such was her concern that the poor woman was upset. I wrote and congratulated her on her achievement and our next visit found the hens being cosseted and duly making a major contribution to the costs of feeding her girls. One thing led to another. The girls needed to acquire skills and so did other orphan girls in the village, would we buy sewing machines and a second-hand typewriter? Now there were so many of them that her house was not nearly big enough, would we help to build a small hall for teaching, a girl's club and community meetings? On every occasion the requests were for such modest sums that we could not believe that they could fulfil their intended purpose, but every visit found the activities in full swing. Finally the remarkable impact of this woman came to the notice of others in Uganda who provided ongoing support, the details of which are regularly passed on to us in Lydya's generous letters.

I am tempted to go on, because there were so many remarkable people who came to the Trust's door, but I will just include one more project which carries a somewhat different lesson.

'Stephen I do not usually listen to other people's private conversations but I could not help hearing what you just read to Anne and I cannot really believe my ears'. The speaker was the senior producer of an American television network who was visiting us in Malawi. The letter was from the doctor in charge of Kisiizi mission hospital in Uganda. We had given a couple of capital grants to the hospital but on our last visit the doctor had an alternative proposal.

'Do you think that your definition of "disadvantaged children" includes those in the womb?'

'Tell us more,' said Anne.

'We get no funding from government so have to charge for our services. Our fee for a normal birth is ten dollars, but for a Caesarean it is fifty. A lot of women cannot afford the fifty and if they suspect that there may be something not quite right they do not come to the hospital at all. The results are often bad for mother and baby. I would like to announce that whatever treatment is required the charge for having a baby here is ten dollars and I would then charge you for any additional costs.' This seemed to make good sense to us, the trustees agreed and we were now sitting at home with the bill for the first twelve months. 'I have carried out 320 Caesarean sections over the past year and so, at forty dollars difference each, would you please let the hospital have 12,800 dollars.' Anne explained the arrangement to our friend.

'Who does the operations?'

'A highly qualified British surgeon.'

'And you are telling me that he can do that for fifty dollars. I suppose you realize that the money you are paying to save the lives of 320 women would barely have covered the anaesthetist's bill for one woman in Washington.'

We had not really thought about it but it did bring home yet again the disparity between the two halves of our world to-day and made us realize how fortunate Anne was to run a Trust for Africa where modest sums of money could help so many people. Caesarean sections in a remote hospital in rural Uganda may seem a long way from a suburban church in Washington, but it was the plight of that young Hispanic man that started Anne on this major task which brought us into contact with all those brave people who refuse to allow the darkness to win the day on the African continent.

# CHAPTER 26

# Why Should Anybody Laugh?

I N AN EARLIER chapter I promised that I would comment on why hard working and sensible farm families in Africa should be so poor. Now I have to fulfil that promise and tread the narrow line between presenting a dull academic paper and so shallow an interpretation that it offers no real help in understanding why most Africans remain so poor. For a continent with 46 countries it is all too easy to make sweeping generalizations, which certainly do not apply to every situation. There are, however, features which are common to all too many countries, and I will focus on these. I will start with those factors which are generally agreed play a major role in holding back many of Africa's people. I will then look more closely at the problems facing my farming friends.

There is widespread agreement that there are three factors which play a major role in the woes of the continent. These are war, corruption and bad government. I will deal with these in turn but also try to set them in a broader historical context. One quarter of the countries of Africa are currently experiencing a war situation of one kind or another which is taking a terrible toll of human life, absorbing a large part of their national budgets and stifling any improvement in the quality of life for millions of people. Distressing pictures appear on television and stories of barbarity surface in the newspapers from time to time which shock the 'civilized' world. Let's pause a moment before the criticism gets too strong. Over the past thousand years the people of the two small islands which make up the United Kingdom have seen wars between aristocratic families (read 'warlords' in Africa to-day), a major war between the middle classes and the aristocracy, wars between England and Scotland and centuries of violence and unrest in Ireland. All of this to try and get the population of four small countries with very similar ethnic and social roots to live together in unity. Compare this with an African country which has had forty years to try and build a nation out of forty different peoples without a common language and with widely differing ethnic and cultural backgrounds who have been thrown together by a circle drawn on a map in Europe at the end of the nineteenth century. The wars are having a devastating impact. They reveal the worst side of human behaviour. They are causing deplorable suffering for millions of civilians, but on the basis of European history they are entirely predictable and few Europeans are in a position to sit in self-righteous judgement. Helpful intervention where possible rather than criticism should surely be the reasonable response.

Unfortunately the impact of wars spreads beyond the countries where the fighting is taking place. Today, as millions of refugees move around Africa, a further quarter of the continent's nations are affected by conflicts in neighbouring countries. Tiny, poor Malawi hosted a million refugees from neighbouring Mozambique for over a decade, providing land, hospitality and food. As a proportion of the total population this is the equivalent of Britain having taken in six and a half million refugees from the former Yugoslavia for ten years. Given the problems that were raised by a few thousand, it is difficult to see how a wealthy country like the United Kingdom could have matched the performance of Malawi, but this generosity came at a cost which will take a long time to make good. All over the continent services to local people are stretched by the influx of those fleeing from war and so putting a brake on their development.

Few can be unaware of the universality of corruption as we read of the damage done by Maxwell in England, ENRON in America or Parmalat in Italy. Why then is corruption more damaging in Africa? Mainly because of the small size of the component countries' economies. The theft of 5 million dollars from government coffers in the United States represents the annual income of about 1,500 people and a infinitesimal proportion of the national budget. A similar loss in Malawi represents the annual income of 80,000 people, and an easily measurable amount of the national budget. But it is not just theft that slows down the improvement in the quality of services available to poorer people. Bribery results in the purchase of the wrong equipment for the two or three major hospitals in a whole country, in the building of clinics and schools of such poor quality that they actually collapse or quickly fall into disrepair, the construction of crucial main roads which all too quickly turn into ribbons of potholes which raises the cost of transport to all those who need to use them. A few years ago the issue of corruption was being swept under the carpet by international institutions dealing with Africa as being peripheral to the major issues of development. To-day that is no longer the case as it has become all too obvious how pervasive and pernicious its influence is in denying millions of ordinary people the opportunity of breaking out of poverty.

Thirdly there is bad governance, which is all too common a feature of the continent. Its most damaging and widespread feature is the adoption of policies which concentrate wealth in the hands of a ruling elite at the expense of the great mass of the population. Huge disparities of income are a typical feature of many African countries today. This was also the case in nineteenth century Britain, but there is a crucial difference between that situation and what we now see in Africa. In Britain much of the wealth was invested in enterprises which engendered widespread industrial employment and the creation of a broader prosperity. In Africa far too much of the money drawn from the mass of ordinary people finishes up in Swiss bank accounts or in the conspicuous consumption of imported goods, which bring no benefits at all to the national economy. It can be infuriating to watch this development but criticism from the West is hardly in place. An eighty to one ratio between the incomes of the top ten percent of an African population and the poorer segment may seem outrageous when the figure for Europe is about seven to one. But then one has to remember that the ratio between an average British income and that of a rural Malawian is over two hundred fold. If the African elite draw on the work and resources of the majority of their country to win their comfort then so does Britain run its health service by stripping poor countries of their desperately limited cadres of doctors and nurses. British families benefit from low prices for primary agricultural produce from poor countries at a devastating cost to small farmers across the world. European fishing fleets decimate fish stocks in the coastal waters of poor countries and thereby ruin the livelihoods of small scale local fishermen. Above all Western consumerism has provided ruling African elites with an example that they have been all too ready to copy. It is not long ago that prestige in Africa was earned on the basis of generosity. A wealthy man was respected, not because he owned a large house but because he fed a large number of people every day and was available to help any poor person who sought his help in time of trouble. Under Western influence that tradition has been replaced by the mansion and the Mercedes. It is a crippling development which denies millions of ordinary, hard working people any hope of improving on their own situation. There is little sign of change on the horizon, either of better quality of government in Africa or in a lessening of the consumerism which fuels the gross inequalities in the world to-day.

What about AIDS? A scourge indeed, with terrible consequences for millions of families, but with infection rates varying between one and twenty-five percent between regions, and with it being so recent a phenomenon, it is less easy to fit it into a broad brush review of the factors which keep African countries poor. Unfortunately it looks as if it will not be so far in the future when its continental impact will be much easier to estimate.

So to some of the specific factors which keep my farming neighbours both poor and hungry. There is the basic fact that farmers anywhere in the world who have access to less than two acres of land and use that to grow low value grains and root crops for food are bound to have limited incomes from their holdings. The people who cultivate small plots on the sides of the mountains in Madeira were little better off than African smallholders in the middle of the last century. Today their farms resemble those of my neighbours but, thanks to massive subsidies from the EU, their homes, cars and television sets are a far cry from a Malawian village. Small scale Japanese farmers are able to enjoy a middle class life style because the urban population is prepared to pay them many times the world price for their crops in order that they shall enjoy a reasonable standard of living. African farmers have no access to subsidies nor to a large wealthy urban population which is prepared to underwrite a modest level of prosperity for their rural compatriots. The balance between the two classes of population are of course very different. In Europe and Japan less than five percent of the population is involved in farming. In Malawi it is over eighty-five percent and it is therefore difficult for the urban minority to have any significant impact on supplementing the small income derived from a two-acre food farm. But what about those African farmers who grow crops for export, coffee, tea, cocoa or cotton? All of these have seen a dramatic decline in the price that they are paid. In terms of purchasing power a coffee grower in Uganda today receives one tenth of the value for his crop that his father did fifty years ago, and the situation with other crops is not very different. Cash crops help families to meet some of their basic needs, but on the scale that most African farmers can produce them they certainly no longer offer a path to modest prosperity.

'But Stephen, Chinese farmers feed themselves on much less land than your Malawian neighbours and they have been doing so for thousands of years, why are African farmers in many countries no longer able to adequately feed their families?' This is a question that I have to field quite frequently and the answer lies in the 'thousands of years' that the Chinese have been feeding their country from limited areas of land. African farmers have also been feeding themselves adequately for millennia with one of the most economical farming systems known to man. They used fire to prepare the land for planting. That same fire provided ash as a highly effective fertilizer and also killed off all the weed seeds and so eliminated one of the most time-consuming tasks in many farmers' calendars. Soil quality was maintained by nature during long fallows of up to thirty years. So, with a minimum of work, farmers were not only able to feed themselves more than adequately but they maintained the continent's environment unspoilt for millennia. Why then does it not work today? Because a dramatic change has taken place in Africa which has never before been known in the history of the human race. Populations have risen fivefold in half a century and that one factor has brought to an end an age-old farming system which is totally dependent upon there being very few people in any one area so as to allow most of the land to be resting. Suddenly African farmers are having to use the same piece of land year after year and most of them have no long term experience of such a situation. Chinese farmers were able to make the transition from one farming system to another over many centuries. Each generation had to do a little bit more work than the one before to keep the soil fertile and maintain productivity. Each generation added a tiny bit of knowledge to develop a system over millennia which served the country well but which ultimately demanded an enormous investment of human labour for which the Chinese became famous. To-day Chinese farmers have replaced the millions of man days per year required to make the compost, which was at the heart of their system, with millions of tons of inorganic fertilizer with which they have not only saved labour but dramatically increased their productivity. If African farmers are unable to copy the Chinese use of fertilizer then why do they not copy their use of compost? My neighbours have made great changes over the past century. They have accepted that they now have to prepare a seed bed themselves instead of relying on fire to do the job for them. They have been forced into the even more arduous task of hand weeding their crops. They have not been prepared to allocate six months work per year to make enough compost to maintain the fertility of their land. It was one thing for a Chinese farmer to have to do a couple more days of work per year than his father in order to keep up the production of the family farm. It is quite a different matter to have to do six months extra work per year. A Chinese peasant's memory would have to go back millennia to remember a time when nature restored soil fertility without any human labour. Most Africans only have to think back to their grandparents. The change in circumstances has been so fast that the majority of farmers have not found a way to keep up the productivity of their land. This has not resulted in the spread of deserts across great swathes of the continent, nor scenes of rural devastation like the dust bowls of America. What it has meant is a slow decline in food production per head of population, with an increasing incidence of under-nutrition and a more frequent occurrence of localized seasons of severe hunger. As I have indicated earlier in this book this situation can be dealt with in the short term with increased access to fertiliser, which is how the rest of the world is fed. In the longer term there has to be far more intensive work to develop methods of improving soil fertility which are acceptable to African farmers and are suited to their environment.

Here then we have millions of rural Africans who have to put up with poor public services, gross inequalities, incomes of less than a dollar a day, declining farm production, periods of real food shortages and no significant sign of any improvement in the foreseeable future. And how do they react? With a resilient cheerfulness and positive outlook which, outside of actual war zones, refuses to be cowed into misery by the conditions which they face. It is little wonder that for fifty years I have been surprised by their laughter.

# Chronological Summary

| Personal | Political |
|---|---|
| 1939-45 Argentina | |
| 1945-48 English farm work | |
| 1948-51 Wye College | |
| 1951-52 CMS training | |
| 1952-54 Nigeria | |
| 1954 May Married | |
| 1954-56 VTTC Yei, Sudan | 1955 Mutiny and start of 18 year civil war |
| 1957-62 Undukori Sudan | 1956 Sudan becomes independent |
| 1962-66 Nyakashaka Uganda | 1962 Uganda becomes independent |
| 1967-70 Wambabya Uganda | 1969 Amin comes to power in Uganda |
| 1970-73 Karengyere Uganda | 1972 Peace treaty signed for South Sudan |
| 1973-76 Min. of Ag. South Sudan | |
| 1977-78 Prime Minister's office Tanzania | |
| 1978-84 World Bank Nairobi covering Eastern Africa | 1979 Amin overthrown in Uganda |
| 1984-86 W.B. Washington/ West Africa | |
| 1987-89 W.B. Washington/ All of Sub-Saharan Africa | |
| 1989-Present Malawi | 1994 End of Banda's rule in Malawi |

# Index of Names